BEST
Bulbs
for
Temperate
Climates

BEST
Bulbs
for
Temperate Climates

JACK HOBBS &
TERRY HATCH

TIMBER PRESS
Portland, Oregon

ACKNOWLEDGEMENTS

Bulbs are such a large and diverse group that the assistance of many experts was sought by the authors. Our thanks and gratitude go to all those people who helped so generously, and without whom this work could not have been so complete.

Jim Forrest, Tauranga, shared his extensive knowledge of many rare and unusual bulbs for countless hours. His extensive collection was also much photographed. Eric Walton, scientist, Hort. Research, Ruakura, provided expert advice on many specialist genera. He also undertook to proofread much of the manuscript, and his comments and advice proved invaluable. Joy Amos, Associate of Honour, R.N.Z.I.H., also checked much of the manuscript, especially the introductory section. Her wisdom and advice were much appreciated.

Significant contributions were made also by the following:
Lindsay Hatch, Joy Nurseries; Jean Veal, Associate of Honour, R.N.Z.I.H.; Dr Keith Hammett, plant breeder and scientist; Tony Palmer, Grounds Superintendent, Auckland University; Jenny Palmer, Kellydale Nursery, Oratia; Beverley McConnell, Ayrlies, Whitford; Bill Dijk, Daffodil Acre, Tauranga; Ian Duncalf, Parva Plants, Tauranga; Chris Gill, Manager Parks and Gardens, Hamilton City Council; Alex Gardiner, Senior Foreman, Auckland Regional Botanic Gardens; Brian Buchanan, Superintendent, Auckland Regional Botanic Gardens; Roger Price, Education Officer, Auckland Regional Botanic Gardens; Cressie Garland. Te Toro, Manukau Peninsula; Sandra Vandermast, fern propagator, Whenuapai; Barbara Parris, botanist, Auckland; the late Jim Shoemark, New Plymouth.

Special thanks must go to our wives for their patience, support and the countless hours they gave so willingly. Pam Hatch bravely typed Terry's handwritten script, inserting the appropriate punctuation and transforming his great knowledge into legible form. Sandra Hobbs typed the entire final manuscript, and then patiently made the daunting number of corrections and amendments which followed without complaint. To all who helped in so many ways, we extend our gratitude.

Most of the photographs in the book were taken by Jack Hobbs. Others who contributed photographs were: Terry Hatch, pp. 55, 59 (above), 67, 68, 98 (above), 132 (above), 150, 151, 155 (below), 163, 165; Chris Gill, pp. 46, 97; Jim Forrest, pp. 49, 71 (left); Parva Plants, p. 115 (above).

First published in North America in 1994
by Timber Press, Inc.
The Haseltine Building
133 S.W. Second Ave., Suite 450
Portland, Oregon 97204-3527, U.S.A.

ISBN 0-88192-293-5

Front cover (clockwise from top left): *Tecophilaea cyanocrocus, Sprekelia formosissima, Scadoxus puniceus, Fritillaria imperialis, Ornithogalum dubium, Ipheion sellowianum.*

Back cover: double tulip.

CONTENTS

Freesia 'Super Emerald' is brightly coloured and easily grown. It is suitable for gardens or containers and provides a plentiful supply of cut flowers.

INTRODUCTION

The world of bulbs contains countless treasures that are truly outstanding but little known in cultivation. This book aims to bring these to the attention of gardeners and bulb enthusiasts around the world. It includes many species from the Southern Hemisphere, particularly South Africa and South America. Many of the bulbs described thrive in regions with warm climates; in cooler climates some will require protection and possibly additional heating if they are to be grown successfully.

DEFINING BULBS

The correct term for all plants which produce fleshy underground storage organs is geophyte. This term includes true bulbs, corms, tubers and rhizomes. In this book, as is common practice, they are referred to collectively as bulbs.

The purpose of such organs is to store nutrients and moisture, enabling the plant to survive during a period of drought or extreme cold. Most bulbs have a growing period that coincides with favourable conditions in their natural habitat, followed by a dormant period that coincides with the unfavourable season. Most should be kept dry when dormant and moist when growing. Species that will tolerate moisture when dormant are generally the best for naturalising in areas where rainfall occurs throughout the year.

A true bulb consists of a stem, and leaves that have been modified to store food. The stem is in the form of a basal plate from which roots are produced and on which the modified fleshy leaves grow. Bulbs are of two types, defined according to the arrangement of their leaves. In tunicated bulbs the outer leaves form a tunic around the bulb, with the outermost leaves often dry and brownish. Examples of this type include tulips and daffodils. The second type is scaly bulbs, in which the leaves are very succulent and overlap rather than being wrapped around each other. Lilium bulbs are an example of this type.

Leaves and flower-stems emerge from buds on the top of the basal plates and grow up between the leaves. Offsets, often called daughter bulbs, usually develop around the basal plates and eventually replace the parent bulb when it dies. The longevity of different bulbs varies; tulip bulbs die each year after flowering, while daffodil bulbs can live for more than two years. Bulbs which grow from nodes on creeping underground stems can be the most invasive, examples including some species of *Oxalis*.

7

A corm is a modified swollen stem which is adapted for food storage. Usually these are rounded, with a flat top and a slightly concave base. Shoots emerge from buds located on top of the corm, and roots grow from the base. Corms are solid when cut through, unlike the layers of modified leaves found when a true bulb is dissected. New corms are produced on top of the old corms, growing at the base of the shoots. Often large quantities of cormels (small young corms) are produced at the base of the parent corms. Example of corm-producing plants are *Gladiolus, Watsonia* and *Crocus.*

Tubers are also modified stems but differ from corms in that they do not develop from the base of the new season's stems. They are usually fleshy and rounded, with scaly leaves. New shoots are produced from buds known as eyes. Tuberous begonias and potatoes are examples of tubers. Dahlias produces tuberous roots which have their buds located at the base of where the old stems grew.

Rhizomes are underground stems which produce new shoots, with leaves on top and roots at the base. Many irises have rhizomes, although some are true bulbs. Only bulbous irises are included here, the others being more appropriate in books on perennials. In fact, most species which produce rhizomes are excluded from this book as they are generally associated more with herbaceous perennials. Some deciduous genera such as *Bulbinella* have been included, whereas *Agapanthus* has been excluded.

BULBS IN NATURE

Bulbs, as with any group of plants, are most successful if the conditions where they are being grown closely resemble those in their natural habitat. Parts of the world where bulbs originate that are often suitable for growing in warmer climates include:

South Africa, especially the winter-rainfall Cape Province.
South America, especially coastal Chile.
Australia, especially the western and southern regions.
California, especially coastal areas.
Mediterranean regions, extending into central Asia.

Most of the bulbs which can be successfully grown in warm climates are winter growers that originate from regions with Mediterranean-type climates, with mild wet winters and warm dry summers. The botanically rich Cape Province of South Africa is the most significant bulb-producing region with a climate of this type. It is regarded as one of the six floral kingdoms of the world and provides an abundance of horticultural treasures. Other regions with Mediterranean-type climates which are important sources of bulbs include areas around the Mediterranean, parts of California and South America, and western and southern Australia. Examples of genera from these regions include *Freesia, Ixia, Tecophilaea, Ipheion, Wurmbea* and some *Calochortus.*

Bulbs which originate in regions with warm wet summers and dry, often cool winters grow during summer and become dormant in winter. Examples of regions with this type of climate include parts of South Africa, parts of Chile and Argentina, and the Himalayas. When they are grown in regions with wet winters, bulbs will often rot when dormant if the soil becomes waterlogged. In well-drained soils many of these species will naturalise easily. Because they grow during summer, they are often prone to the numerous pests and diseases which are prevalent at this time of the year. Examples of bulbs from these regions include *Crocosmia*, *Eucomis* and *Galtonia*.

Bulbs which are often unsuccessful in mild regions are those which in their natural habitat become dormant to survive a period of extreme cold. These often grow and flower poorly if not exposed to sufficient winter chilling.

Bulbs perform best when their growing conditions resemble those in their natural habitat. *Cyclamen hederifolium* is at home in the litter beneath deciduous trees.

Sparaxis are among the easiest spring-flowering bulbs to
naturalise in regions with mild climates. They thrive in gardens
or at the base of large trees.

Popular examples in this category include *Galanthus* (snowdrops), *Crocus* and
some *Narcissus*. Parts of the world with native bulb species which experience
severely cold winters include Siberia, northern China, northern Japan, northern
Europe, parts of central Asia and eastern North America. Species from these
regions are seldom successful in warm climates.

SOUTH AFRICAN BULBS

With so many outstanding bulbs native to South Africa, it is appropriate to
include a separate section about them. Their growing period and requirements
vary according to whether they originate from the summer-rainfall or winter-
rainfall regions, and these two groups are dealt with separately.

The species which naturally grow in winter-rainfall regions of South Africa
become dormant in summer to survive drought, and most need to be kept
dry during this period. Examples include *Babiana, Lachenalia* and some *Gladiolus*.
When grown in regions with wet summers, many species will tolerate high
rainfall levels at this time if they are planted into well-drained soil or containers;
it is often beneficial to surround each bulb with sand. Bulbs which are very
prone to rotting when dormant can be lifted when their growth dies back in
early summer and stored until replanting in late summer or autumn. Water
should be withheld during dormancy but applied at the start of the growing
season.

Growth commences in late summer or autumn, and this is the time for
planting bulbs and sowing seeds. Flowering periods vary according to species,
ranging from autumn until summer. Those which flower during winter and

Scadoxus puniceus is a distinctive South African species which
flowers in autumn before the foliage appears.

Crocosmias are ideal subjects for summer flower gardens.
Crocosmia 'Solfatare' combines nicely with bulbs and perennials
in this sunny garden.

early spring, such as *Babiana pygmaea* and *Romulea sabulosa*, are often best grown in containers so that they can be protected from heavy rainfall which might otherwise damage their blooms.

Winter-growing bulbs must be kept moist throughout their growing period. Once flowering is finished, they must still be allowed to grow until their foliage dries off. This often entails tolerating a period when the plant looks unsightly. Not much can be done about this in the garden, but plants in pots can be shifted out of sight once flowering is over. Allowing the foliage to die off naturally ensures the bulbs are fully nourished when dormancy commences, and produces better growth and maximum flowering the following season. These bulbs are generally best left undisturbed in the soil for several years.

Some winter-rainfall species produce their flowers in late summer or autumn before the leaves have emerged. Examples include nerines, *Amaryllis belladonna, Haemanthus coccineus, Cybistetes longifolia, Boophane guttata* and *Brunsvigia josephinae*. It is important to plant the bulbs before their flowers are produced or they will be spoiled. It is advisable to plant about a month before flowering, although the bulbs can be planted earlier provided they are kept dry.

South African bulbs also occur naturally in regions with hot wet summers and dry cool winters. These grow during summer and sprout with the onset of rains in spring, which is the correct time for planting bulbs. The plants become dormant to survive drought during winter. When grown in regions with wet winters, they must be lifted unless growing in very free-draining soil. Examples of summer-rainfall bulbs which can be naturalised include *Crocosmia, Galtonia* and *Eucomis*.

A few bulbous plants from South Africa are evergreen. These occur naturally in regions where rainfall is spread throughout the year, particularly some coastal districts. Evergreen bulbs generally prefer partial shade and deep rich soil, and should be kept moist throughout the year. Examples include *Dierama* and *Wachendorfia thyrsiflora*.

Some bulbs from the winter-rainfall regions are almost evergreen, dying down briefly in mid-summer before regrowing about one month later. These must be divided and replanted during their brief dormant period.

A NOTE ON TAXONOMY

Plant names undergo constant revision by botanists, and sometimes the resultant changes can be difficult to accept. The large family Liliaceae, for example, has recently been revised and split into several smaller families. Although this revision is yet to be universally agreed upon, the changes have been incorporated in this book. Some well-known genera remain in Liliaceae, notably *Lilium* and *Tulipa*. The following new families which have been separated from Liliaceae are represented here: Alliaceae, Alstroemeriaceae, Asphodelaceae, Colchicaceae, Hyacinthaceae, and Tecophilaeaceae.

This book is intended for gardeners and collectors rather than for botanists. Every attempt has been made to ensure that names and descriptions are accurate. Synonyms which are still in common usage are included in the index to assist

Habranthus robustus is ideal for rock gardens. Its flowers appear over a long period in summer, emerging a few days after rain.

with the search for certain species. Most emphasis is placed on the growing and enjoyment of bulbs, and only bulbs which are considered to be worthy garden subjects have been included. As with any plant group, the world of bulbs contains unattractive members which may appeal to collectors and the botanically curious, but which do not warrant general cultivation. These have been omitted.

Each species is described, along with the natural habitat, if known. Full cultural guidelines are given, and suitable uses in the garden are suggested. Some species that are rare in cultivation are included in the hope that they will become better known. Much of the information has not previously been documented.

All the bulbs described have been grown by the authors or by their colleagues, and the information is based on actual experience. Not all of the species are generally available as bulbs or plants, but many of these can be raised readily from seed which is offered by various growers and suppliers. The authors have spent most of their plant-growing careers in regions with warm climates. Most of this time, collectively about fifty years, has been near Auckland in New Zealand. Here the relatively mild climate has allowed them to grow and enjoy a vast range of bulbs. The intention is to share the knowledge and experiences they have gained, and to celebrate those jewels of nature, bulbs.

CULTIVATION

It is essential that bulbs be located in a suitable position if they are to grow and flower well. The requirements of different species vary considerably, some, for example, requiring full sun and others shade; their individual requirements are detailed in the alphabetical section of this book.

Careful consideration should be given to the placement of bulbs which look untidy at a certain stage. Sometimes these can be located behind other plants, which will grow and conceal them at the appropriate time. Freesias, if located behind deciduous daylilies, will disappear from view when their foliage looks unsightly in late spring.

The most suitable position for bulbs differs from one climatic region to another. Often bulbs which can be naturalised in regions with mild winters require protection where winters are severe. A species which enjoys full sun in one locality may need partial shade in another. Usually a good understanding of a species' requirements can be reached if the growing conditions in its natural habitat are known.

Many bulbs, such as *Oxalis* and *Ixia,* open their flowers only when it is sunny. Obviously these should not be grown in shady positions.

PREPARING THE SOIL

Soil should be thoroughly prepared before planting. Good drainage is essential for most bulbs, and heavy soils can be improved by incorporating gritty material such as pumice sand or gravel. Raising the beds with good-quality topsoil will also improve drainage and result in vigorous growth. Most bulbs dislike too much compost or other organic matter, although it does benefit some such as lilies and dahlias. Before planting commences, the soil should be worked until it is fine and friable; it must not be lumpy and full of clods.

PLANTING DEPTH

Planting bulbs at the correct depth is very important. Most should not be planted too deeply — a general rule is that the depth of soil above the bulb should be twice the length of the bulb. However, the planting depth should be varied according to the soil type, deeper in sandy soils and shallower in heavy soils. If annuals are to be planted above, it is advisable to plant the bulbs slightly deeper. Many bulbs, if planted at an incorrect level, will gradually move themselves to their desired depth.

Some bulbs, such as *Brunsvigia* and *Amaryllis,* should be planted on top of the soil. Others, such as *Eucomis,* should be planted with their necks at or just below soil level. Soft bulbs, such as *Lachenalia,* should be planted just below the soil. Some small bulbs, such as *Babiana,* should be planted very deeply.

A common method of planting small bulbs is to remove topsoil from the planting site to the depth at which the bulbs should be planted. The bulbs are then spread out evenly at the desired spacing and covered by the topsoil. Larger bulbs are usually planted individually, using a trowel. The soil should be lightly firmed but not compacted too heavily.

MULCHING

Many bulbs respond well to mulching, which keeps the soil cool, ensures the surface does not crust and suppresses weeds. Inorganic mulching materials such as gravel are best for most bulbs. Gravel is free from pests and diseases, and does not easily blow around or wash away. It also clearly defines an area where bulbs have been planted, minimising the risk of digging them up or planting on top of them when they are dormant. A fine grade of gravel is best. Road metal which contains particles up to 7 mm in diameter is ideal, and it is relatively inexpensive. Species which enjoy soils high in humus can be mulched with organic matter. Granulated bark is an ideal material for this.

Ixia hybrids are tall brightly coloured bulbs suitable for a sunny well-drained position. Here they combine strikingly with cinerarias.

Nerines require a sunny well-drained position such as this gravel
bed. Succulents like this *Sempervivum* enjoy similar conditions.

The appropriate depth of a mulch depends on the vigour and size of the species. Tall bulbs, such as lilies, enjoy a deep mulching of about 8 cm. For dwarf bulbs, such as lachenalias, the mulch should be spread thinly, no more than 2 cm deep.

FERTILISING BULBS

The appropriate time to fertilise bulbs is just as they start into growth — winter-growing bulbs should be fertilised in autumn and summer-growing bulbs in spring. Inorganic fertilisers are best for most species, and pelleted formulations which release their nutrients slowly throughout the growing period are ideal. Osmocote and Nitrophoska are popular brands which offer a variety of formulations. These vary in the quantities of different nutrients they contain and in the period over which their nutrients are released. Those which release their nutrients over an eight- to nine-month period are usually best.

The fertiliser chosen should not contain too much nitrogen, which can produce excessive leaf growth, suppress flowering and increase disease susceptibility. Potash (potassium), however, is extremely beneficial to most bulbs, improving their flowering, promoting good bulb development and increasing resistance to some diseases. Sources of potash include synthetic formulations such as sulphate of potash, and wood ash. Potash can sometimes be supplied by burning off the old foliage when it has completely dried. Nerines can be burned in late summer, shortly before their flowering commences. Not only will this promote better flowering, but pests and diseases such as pepper pot fungus (*Fusarium* sp.) are suppressed.

SUPPORTING TALL BULBS

Many tall bulbs require staking or other support during their growing season. They are usually most susceptible to wind damage when laden with flowers, especially when they become rain sodden. It is advisable to put stakes into position when plants are small, ensuring the plants will grow erect from the start. Many bulbs are extremely vigorous once they start into growth, and if left too long they can be difficult to support. It is important to place the stakes carefully so that they do not damage the bulbs. A good staking system should be inconspicuous by the time the plants come into flower.

The stakes used must be strong enough to support the particular plant. Bamboo canes are often adequate, although they may snap if used for very tall plants, especially in windy situations. Solid timber stakes or even metal rods are sometimes necessary.

A method of support often used for dahlias involves placing three or four stakes around the tuber. These should be positioned in late spring at planting time, or just as the first shoots emerge. The stakes should lean slightly outwards so that they are further apart at the top than at their base. Twine is then looped around the stakes at intervals about 35 cm apart. If any shoots grow outside the twine, these can be tied in later. The height of the top layer of twine should be about two-thirds the height of the plant.

Gloriosa superba 'Rothschildiana' is a spectacular climbing bulb which can be supported with stakes or by planting under shrubs.

Netting can be stretched horizontally to support taller bulbs. This is particularly effective when they are being grown in large groups, as with these sandersonias.

Horizontal netting is a good method of supporting dahlias, sandersonias, lilies and other tall bulbs when mass planted. Plastic netting used for the commercial production of cut flowers such as carnations is ideal for this purpose. Various grades are available, and those with about a 15 cm gauze are ideal for dahlias. A frame to support the netting can be made simply using 50 x 50 cm tanalised stakes. These should protrude out of the ground to about half the height of the plants. Soft wire, such as electric-fence wire, can then be secured to the top of the stakes and the plastic netting attached to the wire with kitchen ties (twisties). Many tall bulbs, such as some *Gladiolus,* require only their flowering stems to be supported. This can be achieved using a single cane for each stem. Purpose-built metal hoops provide support to several stems. A range of these supports is available, varying in height and in the size of their hoop.

Some bulbs require their floppy foliage to be supported to keep it away from other plants and paths. Commercial hoops can also be used for this purpose, or they can be simply tied together with string.

Growing plants close together provides them with mutual support, and this is often sufficient in sheltered gardens. Some bulbs, such as *Gloriosa,* can be grown up through shrubs such as proteas to provide them with support.

CARE WHEN GROWING

Most bulbs require little attention during their growing season. Slugs and snails should be watched for, especially when the new shoots are emerging. Do not allow small sun-loving bulbs to become overgrown by neighbouring plants.

Spiloxene alba is a dwarf autumn-flowering bulb which naturalises easily and is ideal for growing among rocks.

19

Unless seed is required, spent blooms should be removed. This can improve flowering and prevents the plants from wasting their reserves in seed production. One of the main objectives during the growing period is to encourage healthy vigorous leaf growth. This will promote maximum production of healthy bulbs and will result in optimum flower production the following season. Foliage must always be allowed to die down naturally, even if this means enduring an untidy period. It is important that the nutrients contained within the foliage are fully transferred to the bulbs so that they are well nourished when commencing their dormancy. Premature removal of foliage can result in poor bulb development, and flowering may be reduced or may not occur at all the following season. Some bulbs, such as tulips and daffodils, can be lifted as their foliage starts to turn brown. The foliage should not be removed but allowed to dry off completely in storage.

Daffodils planted in grass present a problem in spring when the grass begins growing vigorously but the daffodils have not yet died back. Once their foliage has turned brown, they can be cut back without affecting them too much. It is advisable to use a dwarf strain of grass in combination with daffodils. Dwarf perennial ryegrass is a good choice, especially in regions with warm climates.

STORAGE

Some bulbs can be stored dry when they are dormant, whereas others resent this treatment. The soil should be dry when the bulbs are lifted. Wet bulbs are more susceptible to fungal infections, and if necessary they should be placed in a sunny position to dry before storage. Remove as much soil as possible from the bulbs before storing them in a well-ventilated position. Suitable storage trays can be made using a netting base. This allows good air circulation right around the stored bulbs and reduces the likelihood of fungal infections. The netting must be sufficiently small to prevent the bulbs falling through. Chicken netting with a 12 mm gauze suits medium and large bulbs such as tulips and hyacinths; small gauze is necessary for tiny bulbs.

The bulbs should be spread out evenly on the netting, preferably in a single layer. They should not be piled too thickly as this can result in rotting. Racks can be built to accommodate several storage trays. It is important that the trays are not too close together as air movement will be restricted. Many bulbs can be stored in netting bags or sacks suspended in an airy place. Damaged bulbs and those showing signs of fungal infection or pest infestation should not be stored. It is common practice to dust bulbs with fungicide prior to storage. It is advisable to check the bulbs regularly when stored to ensure they are remaining healthy.

Plants with soft fleshy storage organs, such as lilies, zantedeschias and dahlias, should not be allowed to dry out completely when they are dormant. If stored, they should be kept slightly moist to prevent shrivelling. They are often stored in sawdust, but coarse sand is an even better material for this purpose. When stored, they should be protected from excessive rainfall and frosts.

BULBS IN THE GARDEN

Bulbs provide colour and interest in a wide variety of situations. Some can be naturalised, providing years of enjoyment with little or no attention. Others perform best if regularly lifted and stored.

The contribution made by bulb foliage is often overlooked. Bulbs with sword-like leaves contribute significantly to the overall texture of a garden, contrasting effectively with the bold or lacy foliage of many perennials. The foliage and flowers of watsonias combine strikingly with the delicate silver of *Artemisia* 'Powis Castle' or the boldness of bergenias. Watsonias can also be mixed with *Agapanthus* to cover a bank or difficult steep area, providing months of colour with very little maintenance. Such combinations are also weed suppressing, leaving more time for the garden's more pleasant tasks.

Many summer-flowering bulbs are suitable for cottage gardens and perennial borders. *Dahlia* species and cultivars will provide an abundance of colour from summer until autumn. *Crocosmia* cultivars contribute striking foliage and bright flowers to summer displays; 'Lucifer' and 'Star of the East' are both useful for this purpose.

Lachenalia aloides 'Pearsonii' is vigorous and naturalises easily. The warmly coloured flowers make their welcome appearance in spring.

Lilies are also great companions for perennials and shrubs, and species such as *Lilium formosanum* contribute both height and late-season colour to the garden. Some *Alstroemeria* cultivars are also good subjects for perennial borders, the long-flowering hybrid 'Walter Fleming' being outstanding.

Galtonia species are ideal mixed with perennials in well-drained sites, providing valuable vertical accent among plants of contrasting habit. *G. candicans* produces stately racemes of pure ivory-white bells. *G. princeps* and *G. viridiflora* have blooms in an attractive greenish shade. All grow easily and multiply rapidly when in suitable conditions.

Bulbs which grow in winter can be interplanted with perennials which become dormant at this time. The ideal perennials for this purpose are those

Galtonia candicans provides valuable vertical accent in the garden
when it bursts into flower in summer.

which die down completely in winter, *Coreopsis verticillata* being a good example. Other suitable perennials include deciduous daylilies (*Hemerocallis*), especially miniatures such as 'Stella d'Oro', 'Golden Chimes' and 'Corky'. When these become dormant in early winter, bulbs such as dwarf *Gladiolus* will gladly take their place. This type of plant association results in a constantly changing garden, with colour and interest provided throughout the year.

Many small bulbs are ideal for rock gardens and for edging. Some *Lachenalia* species naturalise readily in well-drained sunny gardens. *L. aloides* var. *aurea* is one of the most vigorous and reliable, its warm golden yellow blooms a most welcome sight from winter until spring. Bulbs with grassy foliage, such as *Romulea rosea,* are pretty alongside *Ajuga* 'Jungle Beauty', provided they are protected from its advances.

Colchicum speciosum brightens the rock garden in autumn with its pink or white cups, and it can be effectively planted in groups with late-flowering perennials. One of the best bulbs for naturalising in gardens to provide autumn colour is *Moraea polystachya.* It thrives in full sun or partial shade, and provides an abundance of mauve-blue flowers for a long period. *Sternbergia lutea* is another autumn-flowering bulb which deserves greater popularity. It naturalises easily, and the golden cup-shaped blooms are most welcome when little else is blooming.

Anomatheca laxa is a dwarf bulb which naturalises easily, especially in a well-drained position in partial shade. A succession of small blooms appear from early summer, and once established, it multiplies freely. *Rhodohypoxis* planted in large groups in a rock garden make a stunning display throughout summer. Full sun and good drainage are necessary.

Dwarf winter-growing *Gladiolus* make wonderful garden plants in sunny positions. In well-drained soil the bulbs can be left in the ground when dormant in summer. 'The Bride' is an old-fashioned cultivar which has recently become popular again, its pure white blooms coinciding with the flowering of old-fashioned roses. Also tough and reliable is *G. carneus,* which naturalises easily and flowers abundantly in spring.

Bulbinella species are ideal for naturalising in large groups, providing welcome winter and spring colour, and attractive foliage. They become completely dormant in summer and can be planted over with annuals. Freesias are extremely popular for massed garden display. Few sights are more colourful or warming than a group of these bright bulbs at their peak in spring. Unfortunately, the foliage looks rather untidy after flowering but must be allowed to die naturally if a good display is to result the following season. 'Super Emerald' is considered to be the best seed-raised strain available. 'Burtonii' is a wonderfully fragrant cultivar which produces an abundance of white blooms from early spring.

In hot dry sunny positions, *Sparaxis* and *Ixia* will naturalise readily. They are especially effective when planted in large groups and often do well at the base of a hedge. Another bulb which thrives in a dry position is *Amaryllis belladonna.* It is under-utilised in modern gardens but is often prominent in older gardens or where houses or cottages once stood. Clumps established decades ago and neglected since will still make a wonderful display in autumn when little else is in flower. It will tolerate severe competition, thriving at the base of trees such as *Eucalyptus.*

Brunsvigia do well in very hot dry positions on the sunny side of trees. Spectacular flowers on tall stems are triggered by moisture in late summer. Another species which grows naturally in very dry conditions is *Scilla natalensis.* Its large papery bulbs and tall spikes of blue flowers look very effective among large rocks and boulders.

Scilla peruviana can be easily naturalised in large clumps and tolerates sun or partial shade. The bulbs spread quite slowly, and it is advisable occasionally to divide them and spread them about. The usual form has blue flowers, but white and lilac forms are also sometimes available.

Eucomis thrive in full sun, or in partial shade beneath trees in fallen leaf litter. They are particularly effective in large drifts, eventually forming vigorous weed-suppressing colonies. Hybrids are most commonly grown, producing pineapple-like flowers in summer in shades of green, cream, pink, white and maroon.

Vigorous bulbs which thrive in cool partially shaded positions can be naturalised beneath trees. *Crinum* are very effective beneath large evergreen trees, especially when planted in large clumps. Good companions for them include *Geranium maderense, G. palmatum* and *Helleborus argutifolius,* providing a succession of flowering times and attractive foliage.

Scadoxus can be grown in heavy shade beneath trees, giving an unexpected splash of colour and handsome foliage where few plants thrive. A clump of ferns growing nearby will considerably enhance a patch of these striking bulbs. Beneath deciduous trees such as maples and flowering cherries, groups of *Synnotia* or *Zephyranthes* will give a prolonged display. They flourish when planted into a mulch of fine gravel or sand and associate well with thymes.

Few sights are more pleasing than a large drift of daffodils beneath a cherry tree in full blossom. Clumps of winter-flowering daffodils will enliven a bed of hellebores. Miniature daffodils are particularly pleasing when used in clumps among rocks and other small plants. 'Hawera', 'Jumblie', 'Tête à Tête' and forms of *Narcissus bulbocodium* are some of the most reliable garden subjects.

Several *Albuca* species are suitable for naturalising in well-drained positions, especially beneath trees. *A. canadensis* is particularly desirable, its pendulous yellow flowers with green stripes carried on erect stems for a long period in spring and summer.

Cyclamen species will carpet the floor beneath trees with handsome foliage and delightful small flowers. Large plantings are most effective, and well-drained soil is required. Another good subject for shaded situations is *Crocus serotinus* ssp. *salzmannii,* which produces lilac flowers as the leaves emerge in autumn.

Tuberous begonias (*Begonia* x *tuberhybrida*) are ideal for colouring a shady spot in summer. 'Nonstop' is the best strain available for massed garden display. In well-drained soil where frosts are not severe, the tubers can be left in the ground when dormant during winter.

Dierama pulcherrimum favours moist soil, and the long arching stems of bell-shaped flowers are particularly effective near water. *Onixotis triquetra* also favours a moist position. The diminutive *Spiloxene alba* thrives in damp soils, producing

Daffodils are popular subjects for naturalising in grass. Here *Narcissus* 'Carlton' makes a golden spring carpet beneath *Prunus* 'Pink Cloud'.

Many *Narcissus* mix well with perennials. Here *N. pseudonarcissus* makes a striking combination with *Helleborus orientalis* in early spring.

a dense mass of starry white flowers in autumn and early winter. Other bulbs suitable for moist soils include *Schizostylis coccinea*, *Zephyranthes flavissima* and *Ranunculus cortusifolius*.

A few bulbs can be naturalised in paddocks without being grazed by livestock, usually because animals can sense that they are poisonous. Cattle won't touch *Amaryllis* or daffodils, although sheep occasionally nibble the leaves without apparently being harmed. Pigs eat virtually all bulbs except snowflakes (*Leucojum aestivum*) and daffodils. Snowflakes appear to be the only bulb never to be eaten, and they provide welcome colour among pasture for many months. Planting bulbs along fencelines or on steep banks will reduce the likelihood of their being trampled.

The bulbs mentioned are all good vigorous garden subjects which do not generally become invasive. Some bulbs have become serious weeds in certain places, and these should not be grown in those localities. Troublesome species include *Watsonia meriana* 'Bulbillifera', *Allium triquetrum* (onion weed), some *Oxalis* species, and *Crocosmia* x *crocosmiiflora*. Most of these do not withstand grazing and often occur alongside roads without becoming established in neighbouring paddocks. Goats can be used to control some weedy bulbs on roadsides.

FERNS WITH BULBS

The luxuriant lacy foliage of ferns complements perfectly the erect foliage and glorious flowers of bulbs. When growing ferns and bulbs together, it is important that the subjects chosen succeed in similar conditions, with the bulbs tolerating partial shade and some moisture throughout the year. Spanish bluebells (*Hyacinthoides hispanica*) are most effective when planted in large drifts among ferns beneath trees. Other good garden bulbs which tolerate shade for part of the day include some *Allium*, *Amaryllis belladonna*, *Arisaema*, *Begonia*, *Cardiocrinum*, *Colchicum*, *Crinum*, some *Crocus*, *Cyclamen*, *Cyrtanthus*, *Erythronium*, *Eucomis*, *Hippeastrum*, *Hyacinthus*, *Ipheion uniflorum*, *Leucojum*, *Ranunculus*, *Narcissus*, *Scadoxus*, *Scilla*, *Tigridia*, *Urginea*, *Veltheimia* and *Wachendorfia*.

There are various situations in which bulbs can be combined with ferns. Evergreen trees provide a quite different environment to deciduous trees, and different subjects should be chosen. Evergreen trees extend the range of frost-tender ferns and bulbs which can be grown, whereas deciduous trees are ideal for underplanting with winter-growing bulbs and ferns which tolerate high light in winter.

The most suitable ferns for mixing with bulbs are those which tolerate average garden conditions and do not need to be kept so moist that the bulbs are likely to rot. Ferns will use most of the soil moisture, benefitting bulbs which prefer dry conditions. Most of the following ferns prefer partial shade at midday but will tolerate direct morning and late afternoon sun.

Aspleniums thrive beneath trees in quite dry conditions. Species recommended for use with bulbs include *A. bulbiferum* (hen and chicken fern) and *A. oblongifolium* (shining spleenwort). An outstanding hybrid between these two New Zealand natives is known as 'Maori Princess'. *A. aethiopicum* and the similar but smaller *A. lividum* are also suitable.

Maidenhairs make delightful bulb companions with their delicate lacy foliage. *Adiantum hispidulum,* the rosy maidenhair, has pinkish new fronds which become dark green. It forms large clumps about 40 cm tall and requires less moisture than most ferns. *A. aethiopicum* is a spreading species about 20 cm tall. It tolerates very dry conditions and full sun. *A. raddianum* (delta maidenhair)

Ferns and bulbs make delightful companions in a cool position, as *Ranunculus* 'Tecolote' demonstrates here.

forms slowly spreading clumps about 45 cm tall. It resembles *A. capillus-veneris*, which is an even tougher species.

Most *Doodia* species have attractive raspy foliage and pinkish new fronds. *D. media*, *D. mollis* and *D. aspera* mix especially well with bulbs and cope well with dry conditions. *Cyrtomium falcatum*, the Japanese holly fern, tolerates the extremely dry conditions beneath trees particularly well. *Dryopteris erythrosora* produces a flush of bright pink new fronds in spring and grows about 30 cm tall. In winter the fronds fall to the ground and begin rotting, and they can be cut away once the rootstock is smothered with bulb foliage.

The common ladder fern (*Nephrolepis cordifolia*) is too rampant for use with bulbs, but an unnamed species native to New Zealand is an ideal companion. It forms clumps about 40 cm tall which spread slowly, and its leaves (pinnae) are smaller than those of the common ladder fern.

Sun ferns (*Cheilanthes*) tolerate more sun than most ferns. *C. humilis* is a small New Zealand native about 10 cm tall and is ideal in rock gardens with small bulbs. *C. lendigera* is an attractive species from Mexico and the southern United States.

Ferns which grow naturally on dry banks tolerate more sun and drier conditions than most. *Blechnum capense* reaches about 90 cm tall and looks rather like a small palm. *B. minus* is similar but more upright and usually only about 40 cm tall. Both these species have bright pink new fronds, which combine attractively with spring-flowering bulbs such as *Ixia*.

Paesia scaberula is a New Zealand native known by several common names, including lace fern. It tolerates dry sunny conditions well but can be invasive and should be controlled by annual division. The beautiful fresh green new fronds look splendid alongside vigorous spring-flowering bulbs such as watsonias. *Pellaea falcata* (sickle fern) has dark glossy green fronds and also mixes well with bulbs.

Polystichum species are undemanding subjects in slightly acid moist soils. *P. braunii* and *P. vestitum* can be used with bulbs. A recently introduced unnamed species from the Chatham Islands is proving to be outstanding and is now becoming available.

Bulbs can also be combined with ferns which become completely dormant in winter. The ferns provide luxuriant foliage from spring until autumn when they start dying back. The bulbs commence growth in autumn and die back when the ferns re-emerge, and so the cycle continues.

Ferns which become completely dormant include *Athyrium nipponicum* 'Pictum', with greyish silver and green fronds. It forms a slowly spreading clump and is most handsome in heavier shade, where it can be combined with *Crinum* and *Scadoxus*. *A. filix-femina*, the lady fern, has bright green ruffled fronds which are sometimes heavily crested.

Dryopteris filix-mas (male fern), *D. affinis* (golden shield fern), *D. intermedia* (fancy fern) and *D. dilitata* become completely dormant, even in frost-free gardens.

Onoclea sensibilis (sensitive fern) becomes dormant in winter and is ideal for mixing with *Leucojum aestivum* in deep shade.

BULBS IN CONTAINERS

Versatility is the great advantage of growing bulbs in containers. The plants can be paraded in a prominent position when in flower and placed elsewhere at other times of the year. Dying foliage, often so unsightly in the garden, need not be on view. When growing, the plants can easily be located in a suitable situation: those which like it cool can be located under trees or in a shadehouse; heat lovers can be grown against a wall which faces the sun.

Many difficult bulbs species can only be successfully grown in containers. Using a sterile growing medium reduces the incidence of soil-borne diseases. Provided a well-drained sandy mix is used, a range of choice but difficult species can be grown and enjoyed. Bulbs which are especially choice, expensive, rare or newly introduced are best planted in containers at first. The experience of growing and observing them will assist in deciding where and how to grow them in the garden. It will also build up stocks for planting later.

Perhaps the greatest advantage of growing bulbs in containers is the control it allows over the moisture they receive. Growing bulbs beneath protective covering, such as a greenhouse or bulb frame, provides total control over the moisture they receive. Watering can commence at the onset of the growing period and cease or become infrequent when the leaves begin to die back. This allows many species to be grown which would never survive in a normal garden situation.

The moisture received by plants growing outside in containers can also be controlled, although to a lesser degree. Small pots can be tipped on their sides when their growing season ends, ensuring the bulbs remain dry when dormant. Another method is to cover the pots with plastic or a similar material. Several different microclimates exist in most gardens and around houses, and these can be used to meet the requirements of certain species.

Light and temperature levels are also easily controlled with container-grown bulbs. Most bulbs prefer warm sunny positions when in growth, but a cool position in some shade is suitable for most when dormant and can often be found under a hedge or bench.

The nature of the potting medium used is vital when growing bulbs in containers. The main requirement is good drainage, and the mix should contain a high proportion of gritty material such as coarse sand. Organic matter and topsoil are best excluded from potting mix for general bulb use, although some species will tolerate their inclusion. It is often a good idea to surround the

29

bulbs with pure sand rather than putting them straight into the potting mix, as follows. The container is first filled to just below the desired planting depth with potting mix, a thin layer of sand is then spread on top of the potting mix, and the bulbs are placed evenly over this. The container can then be filled with sand. This reduces the incidence of bulb rot, and if the bulbs are subsequently lifted, they emerge clean. The roots of the bulbs will grow into the potting mix below, obtaining the nutrients required for healthy growth.

The best fertilisers for container-grown pots are slow-release formulations. These should contain a high proportion of potassium and relatively little nitrogen. Fertiliser should be applied to the surface of the mix just as growth commences.

Container size will vary according to the size and vigour of the plants being grown and how many bulbs are being planted. The appropriate depth of containers also varies. Large deep containers are best for plants which grow deeply in the soil and for those which prefer a cool deep root run, for example tulips.

Many species with small bulbs are ideal for growing in wide shallow troughs and containers. This suits heat lovers, such as many *Oxalis*, as the mix heats up much more quickly in shallow containers than in deeper ones. However, shallow containers dry out relatively rapidly and must be watered frequently.

Many vigorous bulbs make a great spectacle when mass planted into large tubs or terracotta pots. Tulips are very effective when deeply planted in containers of this type, with annuals planted above. Suitable annuals include

Oxalis thriving in shallow containers: *O. luteola* (yellow), *O. glabra* (pink), *O. purpurea* 'Alba' (white) and *O. massoniana* (orange).

Tulips are spectacular when mass planted in large containers. The brilliant red flowers of 'Oxford' make a stunning spring display.

alyssum (*Lobularia maritima*), Cape jewels (*Nemesia*) and pansies (*Viola* x *wittrockiana*). If these are all planted in late autumn, they will flower simultaneously in spring and make a wonderful display.

Many bulbs can be very effectively displayed in hanging baskets. Wire baskets of various size are available. These should be lined with sphagnum moss or coconut fibre and then filled with potting mix. The containers can then be turned upside down on a board and bulbs pushed through the lining material. When the bulbs are well grown and buds have developed, the container can be turned the right way up. This method is suitable for *Lachenalia* and *Cyrtanthus*.

The majority of bulbs can be grown in containers, and the potential for creating visually exciting combinations is endless. Generally, the directions for growing bulbs given in the alphabetical section of this book apply to both garden and container growing.

PROPAGATION

Propagation of bulbs can be by either sexual or vegetative means. Sexual propagation is by seed, and it is the best method for building up large numbers of many species. Seedlings may resemble the parent from which they are harvested, but they can also differ. Hybrid seed, the result of two or more species crossing, can produce considerable variation.

Plants propagated vegetatively invariably resemble their parent, and selected cultivars must be raised this way to remain true to type. Vegetative methods include cuttings of stems, foliage and bulbs, separation of offsets, and micro-propagation.

VEGETATIVE PROPAGATION

Vegetative methods should be used only with strong healthy plants which are true to type and free from pests and diseases. Plants infected with virus, in particular, must be avoided.

SEPARATION. The simplest and most common method of increasing bulbs is by separating bulbils or offsets from mature bulbs. Some bulbs, such as *Gladiolus, Sparaxis* and *Freesia,* produce numerous offsets and can be multiplied rapidly in this manner. The bulbs should be lifted when dormant and the offsets separated. Some species should be replanted immediately; others are best stored until just before the next growing season.

STEM CUTTINGS. Some species can be grown from cuttings of new shoots taken early in the growing season. These can be treated as normal cuttings, with the lower third of the stem stripped of leaves and inserted into a tray of sand. As the cuttings are very soft, humid conditions must be maintained until roots have developed. Dahlias are commonly grown in this manner, and will flower and produce good-sized tubers in their first season.

LEAF CUTTINGS. A few genera, notably *Lachenalia,* can be propagated by leaf cuttings. Healthy mature leaves are removed and used whole or cut into segments about 3 cm long. These should be inserted to half their depth, correct way up, into trays of clean sand. The trays should be placed in a shaded position and kept moist but never over-watered. Bulbs will develop from the leaves in a few weeks, and some will even form roots. The foliage can be allowed to die off in summer and the small bulbs potted into a well-drained mix the following autumn. Rooting hormone used on the leaf segments can suppress bulb production.

TWIN SCALING. Also called bulb cuttage, this is a simple and inexpensive method of producing large numbers of bulbs. It is suitable only for true bulbs, although a few such as tulips do not respond well to this technique. It cannot be used for corms or tubers. Examples of bulbs which can be propagated by twin scaling include *Nerine, Galanthus, Narcissus, Lycoris, Brunsvigia* and *Amaryllis*. The best time for this is early in the dormant period. Outer leaves should be removed from the bulbs and they should be thoroughly cleaned by dipping them into a solution of household bleach diluted with 10 parts of water.

The roots and upper third of the bulbs should be cut off, taking care not to remove too much of the basal plate. The bulbs can then be cut into segments, each segment containing as much basal plate as possible. These segments should then be cut again between every second leaf scale, producing small sections which contain two leaf scales and a small portion of the basal plate. Often 30–50 such sections can be obtained from a single bulb.

These sections should then be placed in clean plastic bags, together with a medium such as vermiculite or clean moist sand. A small amount of fungicide can be added to this material, which should be slightly moist but never wringing wet. The bags should be kept in a shaded position, neither cold nor too hot, until roots develop, usually in about six weeks. The developing bulbs should be planted into pots or trays before the roots get too long.

Twin scaling. The bulb is cleaned and the roots and top cut off (above). It is then cut into segments and the scales separated, each with part of the basal plate attached. These will sprout (below, right) if placed in a moist medium.

MICRO-PROPAGATION. Also known as tissue culture or meristem culture, this is a highly specialised technique that involves the removal of growing tips, which are cultured in vials containing agar until large enough to be handled. This allow huge numbers of plants to be produced from a single specimen.

SEED PROPAGATION

Seed is a relatively simple method of increasing many species, although hybrids may result where different species are grown together. Another advantage of bulbs raised from seed is that they are free from virus disease.

The best time to sow most bulb species is at, or shortly before, the time when they normally come into growth. Therefore seeds of winter-growing species should be sown in late summer or autumn, and summer-growing bulbs in spring. Seed of some species should be sown as soon as harvested.

It is best to allow bulb seedlings to grow throughout their first season without disturbance. This can be achieved by sowing thinly so that the seedlings do not compete too much. The pots or trays must be deep enough to allow sufficient root development so that transplanting is unnecessary. When the seedlings become dormant, they can then be transplanted.

A well-drained sandy seed-sowing mix suits most bulbs. It should not contain too much fertiliser. A good method is to partially fill a container with well-drained potting mix, cover this with a layer of sand, and sow the seeds on top. If required, a further thin layer of sand can be spread over the seeds.

Seeds vary greatly in their shape and size. Bulbs with soft seeds include *Nerine, Crinum* and *Amaryllis*. These are usually viable for only a short period and should be sown as soon as possible. Most require light to germinate and are best sown on the surface of a well-drained mix; if covered, they often rot. Seed of some species begin growing roots before they fall from the parent plant. Fleshy seeds contain an abundant food supply and quickly produce small bulbs, often becoming dormant shortly after.

Soft seeds can also be papery, for example *Hippeastrum* and *Cyrtanthus*. These are also viable for only a short period, usually up to about six months. Large seeds of this type are best planted on their edge by gently pressing them into the seed-sowing mix. Smaller seeds can be scattered on the surface of the mix and lightly covered with fine sand when germination has commenced.

The majority of bulbs have hard seeds, often with impervious seed coats, which require time to break down before germinating. Examples include *Ixia, Dierama, Gloriosa* and *Lachenalia*. These seeds generally remain viable for a long time and can be in the soil for many years before suitable conditions stimulate germination. They should be sown in trays of well-drained sandy mix then covered with a layer of sand or similar material to a depth of about 1 cm. The trays can then be placed outside or in a greenhouse. Usually seeds germinate at about the same time that bulbs of the same species come into growth.

Seed which is extremely hard to germinate can be gathered before fully ripe and, if sown immediately, will often germinate promptly. Examples include *Scilla natalensis* and some *Romulea* species.

PESTS
AND DISEASES

A large number of pest and disease problems can occur on bulbs. Usually these are the result of unsuitable growing conditions, and the best method of control is to correct the physical factors which are allowing the problems to occur. The commonest cause of most problems is poor drainage, which can be rectified relatively easily.

Poor air circulation is a major cause of disease as flowers and leaves remain wet for too long, allowing fungal spores to germinate. Good air circulation results in more rapid drying and less incidence of disease. Bulbs grown in sunny, well-ventilated positions are generally disease-free.

Insect pests can be expected to occur occasionally on most plants, and bulbs are no exception. A wide range of insecticides is now available, many of which provide excellent control without being highly toxic to the user. Plants infected with serious diseases such as virus and fusarium should be destroyed to prevent the disease spreading.

The following are descriptions of the main pest and disease problems encountered when growing bulbs. Although the list is fairly long, it must be remembered that the bulb world is a large one and attracts a number of predators and parasites. It is again stressed that with good cultural practices, most of these ailments can be prevented.

PESTS

MITES. These are close relatives of spiders and can debilitate many bulb crops by sucking the sap from their leaves, often resulting in the foliage turning yellowish and the plants lacking vigour. Although mites are tiny and often invisible to the naked eye, they can build up to such enormous numbers that the damage they cause can be devastating.

Mites prefer warm dry sheltered conditions and are most prevalent during summer. They are especially troublesome in greenhouses, which provide an ideal environment for their rapid reproduction. Because the mites themselves are so difficult to see, it is necessary to watch for symptoms such as yellowing and distortion of foliage. The most obvious sign of their presence is a very fine webbing over the foliage. This is most noticeable on the underside of leaves, especially along any prominent veins.

Because mites are most prevalent during summer, they are seldom a problem on winter-growing bulbs, except in greenhouses. They mainly attack summer-growing bulbs such as galtonias.

Different species of mite attack different hosts. Cyclamen mites attack cyclamen, especially when grown indoors, causing poor growth and distorted flowers and leaves. Red spider mites attack a range of different species. Bulb mites attack many genera, including *Narcissus, Gladiolus* and *Lilium*. They attack the bulbs, causing them to grow poorly, and in severe infestations to become soft and rotten. The plants can look stunted and unhealthy, and the flowers may be distorted. Severely damaged bulbs should be lifted and burned. Lesser infestations can be controlled by dipping the bulbs in a miticidal solution.

Because mites are not insects, many insecticides give poor control of these pests; miticides are much more effective. It is important to commence a spray programme early in the growing season as mites are very difficult to eradicate once they have built up to large numbers. Several repeat sprays at weekly intervals may be required before adequate control is achieved.

An interesting recent innovation is the development of mite predators. These are available to commercial growers and will often provide adequate control and eliminate the need for spraying.

THRIPS. These extract nutrients from their host plants by rasping the foliage, causing the sap to flow out, which they then consume. They are extremely debilitating to the plants they attack, turning the foliage streaky silver or brown, and making the flowers and buds distorted.

Thrips enjoy warm sheltered conditions and multiply rapidly during summer, reaching a peak by late summer. For this reason they are most troublesome on summer-growing bulbs such as gladiolus and dahlias.

Many alternative host plants can harbour thrips, which then transfer to bulbous crops during their growing season. Weeds also act as alternative hosts, and good weed control is one method of lessening infestations.

Spraying is the only really effective method of eradicating thrips. Synthetic pyrethroids and acephate are generally effective, but several applications at seven- to ten-day intervals may be necessary before control is achieved. Plants with waxy foliage, such as gladiolus, may require the addition of a wetting agent to the spray mixture. Young thrips are much easier to kill than adults, and commencing a spray programme in early summer before numbers have built up will give most effective control.

MEALY BUGS. These insects get their name from the white mealy substance which covers their bodies. They are usually found on roots and on young leaves, especially inside the sheaths at the base of the leaves. They suck the sap from plants, causing them to become weakened and distorted, and are mainly a problem on evergreen bulbs, although they attack a wide range of different types.

Insecticides are available which will kill mealy bugs. Control is often difficult because the insects occur in positions where it is difficult to contact them with sprays. If plants in containers are infested, it is best to immerse the entire container into a bucket of insecticidal solution. Mealy bugs on plants growing in the ground can be eradicated by drenching them with insecticide poured from a watering can.

APHIDS. Also known as green fly, these are common pests. They mainly attack new soft growth and flowers, and their numbers can build up at an alarming rate from spring onwards. They have a needle-like protuberance called a stylet, which they insert into plants and through which they suck out sap. This weakens the plants and results in them becoming distorted and stunted. They can also spread virus diseases when they move from one plant to another. In the garden their numerous natural predators, such as birds and ladybirds, keep their numbers under some control.

Often a black fungal infection called sooty mould can develop in association with aphid infestations. This fungus grows on the sweet sticky honeydew secreted by the aphids. If the aphids are eradicated, the fungus will cease to develop.

Several insecticides, such as synthetic pyrethroids, will provide satisfactory control. Often two or more applications seven to ten days apart may be necessary.

BLACK VINE WEEVILS. *Otiorhynchus sulcatus* are a serious pest of many bulbs such as cyclamen. The grubs live in the soil, and eat roots and sometimes bulbs. Adults eat holes in the leaves and stems of the plants. Severe attacks can kill entire plants.

The adult weevils are black and have a prominent snout. They hide during the day and feed at night, and are usually most prevalent during spring and summer. They lay eggs in the soil near their host plants, and the grubs hatch in a few weeks. They burrow into the soil and commence feeding on the bulbs and roots, causing wilting and collapse of plants.

The creamy coloured grubs are about 12 mm long, with a large brown head and tapering body. Eventually they make earthen cells in the soil, often beneath the plant, in which they pupate. When the adults emerge, mainly in spring, they commence feeding, chewing the edges of the leaves, flower-buds and stems, causing the flowers to become distorted. Weevil numbers can build up very quickly in suitable conditions, and if not checked, they can completely decimate cut-flower crops and potted bulbs.

Common dock is a favourite food of the black vine weevil, and a single plant left in the vicinity of a bulb crop can be a useful indicator of their activity. If rolls of paper are left adjacent to bulbs, many of the weevils will hide inside these. The paper can then be collected and burned. Dead foliage and plant litter should always be removed as it will harbour the pests.

Potted bulbs which are infested can have the soil washed from their roots, and they should be repotted in fresh clean mix. Pesticides such as synthetic pyrethroids will give some control of weevils. Drenching the soil with an insecticide solution or granules can give effective control.

BULB FLIES. This major pest attacks a wide range of bulbs. Two species are common problems: the narcissus bulb fly and the lesser bulb fly. The narcissus

Bulb fly attacks a wide range of species, the maggots causing considerable
damage when they burrow into the bulbs. Seriously
damaged bulbs such as these *Cyrtanthus* should be destroyed.

bulb fly is most active in late spring and summer, attacking a range of hosts
including *Narcissus, Amaryllis* and hyacinths. Adults lay eggs close to the potential
host. When the creamy white grubs hatch out they enter the bulbs and eat
out the centres. The bulbs become soft, and when they are cut open the maggots
can be seen. The adult flies are seldom noticed and are difficult to control.

Badly infested bulbs should be burned. Less serious infestations can be
controlled by soaking the bulbs in an insecticide solution. If the surface of
the soil is cultivated to a fine tilth, it will make access to the bulbs more difficult
for the grubs. This should be done after the plants die down in spring.

The lesser bulb fly causes damage similar to that caused by the narcissus
bulb fly. The maggots are usually greyish or greyish yellow and are very
wrinkled.

BULB EELWORMS. Eelworms (nematodes) are tiny pests which attack a wide
range of plants. Bulb eelworms attack many genera, including *Narcissus, Tulipa,
Gladiolus, Scilla* and *Iris*, invading the bulbs and causing them to become
blackened. They also attack flowers and foliage, making small swollen blisters
appear on the leaves, which become distorted and yellowish.

Affected bulbs often become soft and, if cut through, blackened rings can
be seen. Badly infested bulbs should be burned. Chemicals are available which
provide control, but these are too toxic to be considered for home garden use.

Other control measures include removing and burning old foliage. Weeds can be alternative hosts and should be eradicated. Bulbs should not be replanted in soil known to be infected for several years.

SLUGS AND SNAILS. These are a particular problem when new growth and flowers emerge in moist conditions. Baits should be applied before growth begins and replenished as necessary. Some bulbs with very succulent leaves, such as hippeastrums, are susceptible to severe damage throughout their growing season. Using sharp, gritty mulching material such as fine gravel will help deter slugs and snails.

DISEASES

GREY MOULD. *Botrytis* sp. can be a major problem in very humid conditions, especially if air circulation is poor. It can seriously damage greenhouse crops, particularly in winter. Soft growth and flowers are most susceptible, and the bulbs can also be infected. The first symptoms are small spots, which enlarge and eventually develop into a grey mould. Many bulbs are attacked, including tuberous begonias and tulips.

The most effective control is prevention. Increasing ventilation in glasshouses will lessen infection. Plants should not be watered late in the day, and their foliage and flowers should be kept dry whenever possible. Several sprays have been developed to control this disease, but resistance to these rapidly develops.

DOWNY MILDEW. This is most serious during cool wet weather. It can be recognised by the soft downy growth which develops on foliage, especially on the underside. Mancozeb is an effective fungicide for preventing infection. Susceptible bulbs include alliums.

POWDERY MILDEW. This is a very common disease during summer, particularly towards autumn. It attacks a wide range of bulbs, first causing small white spots to develop on the older leaves. Eventually the infection spreads until the entire foliage becomes covered with a fine white powder. Plants can become severely weakened. Several fungicides are available to prevent this disease. These should be applied at regular intervals throughout the susceptible period. Summer-growing bulbs, such as dahlias, are most severely affected.

PEPPER POT FUNGUS. *Fusarium* is a devastating disease which spreads quickly in warm moist conditions. It is most severe in summer when the weather is hot and wet. The large spores resemble pepper and, after germinating, invade dormant bulbs, causing them to rot. Large numbers of bulbs are rapidly infected, turning soft and mushy. Huge numbers of spores are then produced, and these are spread by water movement and on tools and implements.

Infected bulbs should be burned. Contaminated soil can be fumigated or disposed of. Heavy dressings of sulphate of potash (100 g per square metre) will suppress the disease. Susceptible bulbs should be grown in sandy soil or gravel. Organic fertilisers and humus will encourage the fungus to develop.

BACTERIAL SOFT ROTS. The major cause of soft rot in bulbs is a bacterial disease, *Erwinia carotovora*. Potential infection exists in most soils and occurs on susceptible host plants when conditions become suitable. Bulbs which are seriously affected include dahlias and calla lilies. Soft rots most commonly occur in wet poorly drained soils, especially when they are warm. Mulching keeps soils cooler and can reduce infection levels. Bulbs are particularly prone to soft rots when dormant, and should be completely dry, with soil removed, before they are placed in dry storage. Dipping the bulbs in a copper spray solution can also restrict this disease.

INK SPOT. This is a serious disease of bulbous irises and can destroy plants if it is not controlled. The first symptom of infection is usually premature dying of the foliage. The bulbs, if lifted, display black sooty patches, and eventually only dry husks will remain. Severely infected bulbs should be destroyed. Early stages of infection can be arrested by dipping the bulbs into a fungicidal solution. The bulbs should be stored dry before replanting late the following summer. Only healthy bulbs should be planted, and they should not be overcrowed. Copper sprays can be used to prevent infection.

DAMPING OFF. Diseases which cause damping off of seedlings are soil borne. They attack young seedlings, causing them to appear water soaked and finally to collapse and die. It is especially troublesome in moist humid conditions with poor air circulation.

The best control is prevention. Seed should always be sown into well-drained sterile mix which contains little nitrogen. It should not be sown too thickly as seedlings growing close together have little air circulating around them, and if disease does break out, it will quickly spread from plant to plant. Seedlings should be kept moist but not sodden. Seed can be dusted with a fungicide prior to sowing, and seedlings can be drenched with a fungicidal solution to arrest outbreaks.

VIRUS. Virus diseases can infect virtually all plants. Symptoms of viral infection are generally yellow streaking of foliage, distortion of flowers and leaves, and blotching and even abortion of the flowers. Nothing practical can generally be done to control viral disease, and infected plants should be removed and destroyed.

The main carriers of virus disease are insects such as aphids. Controlling these will reduce the risk of infection. Virus can also be spread on tools such as secateurs. Picking flowers without using cutting implements and trimming the stems later will prevent spread in this manner.

BULBS
FOR GARDENERS
AND COLLECTORS

ALBUCA
Hyacinthaceae

This genus of about 75 species is centred in South Africa, mainly in the Cape Province and Natal. Only a few are worth cultivating, and these are particularly suitable for warm climates. Most species have pale yellowish flowers striped with either green or red, and several are carried per stem. The flowers are long-lasting when picked, and some are pleasantly scented. Most species grow during winter and are dormant in summer, flowering mainly in spring. They require a sunny position in well-drained soil if they are to be naturalised successfully.

A. canadensis has flowers of pale yellow flushed green with a distinctive green stripe along each petal. They are pendulous whereas those of most species face upwards. It has a long flowering period, lasting from late spring until early summer, and the flowers are very good for

Albuca altissima

picking. The foliage is broad and greyish green, and the bulbs are edible. It is generally regarded as the outstanding species for cultivation.

A. nelsonii has upright white flowers, usually striped with green, carried on stems about 1.2 m tall in spring and early summer. It prefers a position in partial shade and thrives in average well-drained garden soil.

A. altissima also produces flowers of white and green at a similar time.

Albuca canadensis

ALLIUM
Alliaceae

About 700 species of *Allium,* flowering onions, occur worldwide, all those in cultivation being from the Northern Hemisphere. Although the individual flowers are small, they are carried in attractive clusters which are often quite large. Many make excellent garden subjects, preferring a sunny position but tolerating extremes of climate. They should be more widely grown, but many gardeners are put off by the pungent onion-like smell of some species and the invasive tendencies of others. Onion weed (*A. triquetrum*) is the worst weed in temperate climates. Although its pure white pendulous flowers striped with green are very pretty, it is far too invasive to be cultivated in many regions.

Edible species include onions (*A. cepa*), shallots (*A. fistulosum*), leeks (*A. porrum*), garlic (*A. schoenoprasum*) and chives (*A. tuberosum*); of these, only chives are useful ornamentals.

Taller species are suitable for general garden use while small species are useful in rock gardens. The large flower-heads of many are good for drying. The main flowering period of most species is from spring until summer.

Alliums prefer full sun and dislike overwatering, especially North American and central Asian species. Many require good drainage, especially some of the choicest species. A number of vigorous species are well suited to growing through mat-forming plants such as thymes and prostrate hypericums. This avoids bare ground and allows this area not to be watered during summer.

Most alliums germinate readily from fresh seed, with most species best sown in late autumn in temperate regions and in spring where winters are severe. Some North American species can take two to three years to germinate. Cold storage for two to three months prior to sowing will assist the germination of old seed.

Other methods of propagation are by removing offsets when dormant and by the division of clumps. Spring-flowering species are divided in summer, and summer-flowering species when dormant in winter/spring. Some species produce bulbils in their leaf axils; these can be collected and sown in a sandy mix.

Pests and diseases are less common on ornamental alliums than on those grown as vegetable crops. Occasional problems include onion fly, thrips (which distorts foliage), downy mildew and powdery mildew.

The following species have been separated into three groups according to their area of origin: North America, Europe and western Asia, and China and eastern Asia.

NORTH AMERICA

Most Californian species are brightly coloured, often in shades of red or pink. Species that are summer dormant can be difficult where summers are wet; they need good drainage and may require lifting in summer.

A. acuminatum has flowers that are a distinct blend of pink and mauve. They are bell-shaped and carried in loose heads on stems 20 cm or longer. It thrives almost anywhere in sun or partial shade and mixes well with perennials.

A. brandegei covers itself in small white flowers in late summer. Its evergreen foliage resembles that of chives It grows to about 15 cm tall and is suitable for pots and gardens.

A. campanulatum has cup-shaped flowers in loose umbels during summer. They are usually purplish, occasionally white, and are carried on stems up to 30 cm long.

A. cernuum is the wild onion of North America, where it grows in gravelly rocky places in mountains. The pendulous cup-shaped flowers are usually rose-pink or purplish, or occasionally white, and are followed by attractive seed-heads. Flowering is from spring until autumn, and the plants reach about 30 cm tall. Chive-like, lettuce-green leaves that are strongly scented emerge from the herbaceous rootstock. The bulbs are edible.

A. dichlamydeum has bell-shaped flowers in shades of pink to purple. Foliage appears in spring then withers away, and the purplish flowers emerge in early summer. These die away to reveal the attractive ivory-white bulbs. Plant height is about 30 cm. Plants should be grown in pots and baked during summer in a bulb frame for best results.

A. platycaule produces numerous deep pink flowers with paler tips in spring.

A. purdyi has pale pink flowers with darker mid-ribs in spring.

A. stellatum, the prairie onion, has pink flowers, and its foliage resembles a more upright version of *A. senescens*. Although it produces lots of seed, it does not usually self-sow. 'Album' has white flowers.

A. unifolium (syn. *A. murrayanum*) has flowers in an attractive shade of deep pink. It is similar to *A. acuminatum* and has much the same requirements, being easily grown in pots or gardens. It is dormant in summer and is one of the very best species.

EUROPE AND WESTERN ASIA

Tall central Asian species typically have globular inflorescences, and their foliage dies back when the flowers emerge. Most thrive in hot dry situations.

A. akaka grows on stony mountain slopes in Turkey and Russia. Numerous white to lilac pink flowers are carried in rounded heads on short stems. Usually only one or two broad glaucous leaves are produced.

A. carinatum is the keeled garlic, an outstanding small species ideally suited to the front of gardens. *A. carinatum* ssp. *pulchellum* is a dainty plant about 50 cm tall which resembles *A. flavum* but is different in colour. Flowers vary in colour from pink to purple, the best forms being a good pinkish purple. In these better forms the whole plant including the flower-stems has a purplish hue. The flowers are carried in 30 cm long flower-spikes and are sheathed in a membranous cloak-like cover through which the small bell-shaped flowers burst. This robust attractive species is ideal for pots and gardens. When established it will self-seed readily.

A. carinatum f. *album* has pure white flowers and is very handsome. It usually comes true from seed, although some variation may occur.

A. christophii (syn. *A. albopilosum*) grows on rocky slopes in central Asia. Numerous star-shaped silver-pink flowers are carried in distinctive large heads. These are good for picking and excellent dried. The foliage withers away by mid-spring when flowering commences. It is easy to grow in a hot dry position. Superior flowering occurs in areas with cold winters, although it will generally produce some flowers in warmer regions. It multiplies readily from seed.

A. flavum is the small yellow onion that grows naturally in dry rocky hills from France to Greece. Its flowers are a good rich lemon-yellow. They are variable in colour so selection of seed-raised plants is necessary to obtain the best forms. The small sweetly scented bells appear from late spring until summer. The few greyish leaves remain throughout the year. It is an excellent subject for pots and the front of gardens, and is easy in a sunny place, although it seeds freely and can overwhelm small plants.

A. flavum 'Minus' is a dwarf form with purple flowers which is ideal for rock gardens.

A. giganteum is found growing at low altitudes in Afghanistan and Iran. Numerous star-shaped flowers of purple, occasionally white, are carried in rounded heads. Flowering commences in late spring and continues until well into summer. It is easy in most climates, preferring a sunny well-drained position.

A. insubricum has pretty bell-shaped flowers of pink to purple-pink with papery white spathes. Its foliage is evergreen, and it closely resembles *A. narcissiflorum*, with which it is often confused.

Allium moly

A. moly is known variously as golden garlic and yellow onion. It grows naturally in shady rocky places in mountainous areas and is easily grown in well-drained positions. Numerous bright yellow star-shaped flowers are carried in flattened heads on stems of about 35 cm. It has no onion scent so is good for picking. The broad waxy green foliage dies in summer after flowering. It can be naturalised where there is lots of room but can be invasive in some situations, although it is not usually a problem where climates are wet. It is certainly one of the most desirable of the yellow-flowered species.

A. narcissiflorum grows in limestone screes in the alps of Europe. It is one of the most attractive species, easy in a well-drained position. Deep pink to purple bells appear on 35 cm stems in spring.

A. neapolitanum is sometimes called the daffodil garlic and is a native of grassy fields in the Mediterranean region. Its flowers are brilliant glistening white with green centres and dark anthers, carried in flattened heads early in the season. The foliage is dormant in summer. It is a good subject for naturalising, tolerating sun or shade without being too invasive. It prefers moist soil and spreads by seed and offsets. It is one of the very best subjects for pots and makes a good cut flower, although it is rather strong smelling when first picked. 'Grandiflorum' has larger flowers and is more vigorous.

A. obliquum grows from Europe to Asia, producing numerous greenish yellow cup-shaped flowers in dense heads on stems to 1 m long.

A. oreophilum is a dwarf species found in stony

slopes in central Asia. Numerous bell-shaped flowers of purplish red with darker mid-veins are carried in dense umbels on slender stems about 20 cm tall. This small clump-forming species is suitable for pots and rock gardens. It is easy in a sunny place and will perform best if baked in summer. It tends to suffer from some dieback in summer, which detracts from its appearance. 'Zwanenburg', with deep carmine flowers, is the best cultivar.

A. regelii grows in sandy deserts and rocky places in central Asia. Its flowers are pale pink to deep purple with darker central veins and are carried in unique candelabra-like inflorescences with up to six whorls of flowers on each 1 m stem. It is easily grown but must be kept dry in summer.

A. rosenbachianum has deep purple star-shaped flowers, occasionally white, on stems about 1 m long.

A. senescens is German garlic, a native of Europe and northern Asia. Bell-shaped blooms of rose-pink are carried in dense heads on stems up to 60 cm tall, although usually shorter. It is one of the last to flower, usually in late summer. The curly greyish foliage resembles that of chives. This robust easily grown species is a good one to start with and is useful for edging in gardens.

A. senescens var. *glaucum* has nice lilac-pink flowers and bluish foliage.

CHINA AND EASTERN ASIA

A. aflatunense produces large rounded flower-heads of starry lilac-purple blooms with dark central veins on stems up to 1.2 m tall. The bluish leaves are much shorter than the flowers. It is ideal for gardens and looks good in terracotta pots. 'Purple Sensation' is a good deep purple cultivar. Because the onion-like perfume is absent, it is particularly suitable for picking.

A. amabile is found in stony alpine meadows in southwest China. Its funnel-shaped flowers are delicate pink to magenta with darker spotting. It will grow in sun but, unlike most species, it also grows well in shade.

A. beesianum grows in stony high mountain meadows in western China. Pendant bell-shaped flowers of bright blue to lavender-blue are produced in summer. This easily grown species reaches up to 50 cm and is ideal for large rock gardens.

A. caeruleum is the blue garlic, one of the best garden species. Masses of star-shaped flowers of amethyst-blue with darker central veins are carried

Allium senescens

in tight rounded heads. The foliage has withered by the time flowering commences. It is an ideal subject for pots and gardens, provided drainage is good. It is certainly one of the loveliest summer-flowering species.

A. cyaneum has nodding bell-shaped flowers of intense violet-blue. Its foliage is rush-like, and it is an ideal rock garden plant.

A. cyathophorum is found growing on grassy slopes in China. Bell-shaped flowers of rosy purple appear in loose heads and on quite short stems in late summer. It is easy in well-drained soil and is ideal in rock gardens.

A. cyathophorum var. *farreri* has maroon bell-shaped flowers carried in loose heads. It is easily grown and a good garden subject.

A. macranthum produces pendulous bell-shaped flowers of deep purple, resembling a larger version of *A. cyaneum*.

A. sikkimense has bell-shaped blooms in shades of deep blue to purple. It also resembles *A. cyaneum* but is a paler blue.

A. victorialis is the alpine leek from Asia and parts of Europe. It has numerous starry flowers of white to yellow.

Nectaroscordum is a small genus closely related to *Allium* from eastern areas of the Mediterranean. They are easy, sometimes invasive plants that thrive in most soils. They flower during summer and prefer a dry period when flowering is finished.

Once clumps are established they should be left undisturbed. The most attractive species is *N. siculum*, one of the best of all the flowering onions. The bell-shaped flowers are carried in heads, each on a long stalk. When the flowers open they burst through a cobweb-like covering. Usually they are rose-pink becoming flushed with green inside their tip. The foliage sprouts in spring and dies off as the flowers emerge in summer so that only the blooms remain.

ALSTROEMERIA
Alstroemeriaceae

Most members of this genus have long-lasting showy flowers. They are wonderful for picking, each stem lasting two or three weeks in water, and many species are good garden or container subjects. Their habitats range from alpine to tropical, and their cultural requirements vary accordingly. Most species go dormant during the hottest months, and all require well-drained soil. A position in partial shade is ideal for most. Mulching provides a cool root run and helps prolong the flowering period. Once the soil temperature exceeds about 23°C, flowering is usually impaired.

A. pelegrina typically has soft pink flowers with a dark blush, 5–8 cm across and looking like large butterflies. They appear from late winter until summer, and both flowering and non-flowering stems are produced. The foliage is grey-green and somewhat succulent. This species is ideal for containers and large rock gardens. Although it is not tall, usually reaching 30–50 cm in height, it is a useful cut flower. Its major requirement is very good drainage. When grown under cover, the flowers double in size and more are produced per stem. Excessive nitrogen should be avoided or flowering will be suppressed by rampant foliage growth. Storage roots should not be allowed to dry out at any time and are best stored in moist sawdust until replanting occurs. The rhizomes generally contain several dormant buds and can be divided in early autumn if care is taken not to damage the storage roots. Seed can be sown into a sandy mix when ripe, usually germinating in early winter and requiring potting when young.

Nectaroscordum siculum

46

Alstroemeria 'Walter Fleming'

Few pests and diseases give problems apart from thrips, which can spoil the flowers, and occasionally slugs and snails. The roots will rot if kept too moist.

A. pelegrina 'Alba' is the much sought-after lily of the Incas. It was cultivated in early times and is pure white with soft green tips. It likes particularly good drainage.

A. hookeri has very dainty 3 cm wide butterfly-shaped flowers in pleasing shades of pink or soft pink and pale green. These appear in autumn on stems 10–40 cm tall. The green or grey-green non-flowering foliage and stems completely die off before the flower-stems emerge; these usually appear after rain. This small species is best in rock gardens, and many forms are available. Some have barely any stem while others grow fairly tall but can be weak with a tendency to fall over. Well-grown plants will carry numerous flowering stems at one time. Large quantities of viable seed are often set, germinating easily in a sandy mix.

'Walter Fleming' (syn. 'Orchid') is an outstanding cut flower and garden subject, as are many of the hybrids. Flowers of gold and white appear during spring and summer. Mulching to keep the roots cool will extend the summer flowering period. It reaches about 1 m tall and has green semi-succulent foliage. It has often been difficult to obtain, being exacting in the timing

of its propagation by division. This is best done a few days before regrowth starts in late summer following a dry resting period. The rhizomes should be divided carefully, with some storage roots attached to each segment, and placed in a well-drained mixture of sand and sawdust. If positioned in a shady area and kept fairly dry, they make numerous new growths in a matter of weeks. They can be potted when well rooted.

Numerous butterfly hybrids are now available, many with plant patents (PVR) on them and unavailable to home gardeners.

A. ligtu is an extremely variable species from Chile and Argentina with flowers in various shades of pink to reddish orange. The narrow petals are usually striped and spotted with maroon or gold, although a strain without markings has recently been developed. Plant height varies from 1 to 1.5 m, and the weak stems require some support. Many seed strains have been developed from this species, 'Dr. Salters' and 'Los Andes' being popular and producing a wide range of flower colours.

A. ligtu var. *pulchra* is a dainty variety which grows up to 80 cm tall. The petals are broader than those of the species. The flowers are cream flushed with pink, and they have gold and purplish markings at the tips.

A. magnifica is a rare species from central Chile.

Alstroemeria magnifica

The flowers are in various shades of pink with yellow and reddish purple markings, and appear mainly in spring.

A. aurea (syn. *A. aurantiaca*) is a showy species from Chile with flowers of yellow to orange. These are variably spotted and appear mainly in summer. It forms large clumps about 1 m tall and is ideal for mixing with perennials. It tolerates dappled light and dry conditions, and can be planted under trees. The flowers are good for picking. Self-sown seedlings frequently appear and can become a nuisance.

AMARYLLIS
Amaryllidaceae

Amaryllis contains just one species, *A. belladonna*, commonly known as naked lady because its flowers appear on long bare stems before the foliage emerges. It grows wild in rocky places in the Cape Province of South Africa and thrives in regions with warm climates. It is one of the easiest bulbs for naturalising in warm well-drained positions which become dry during the dormant period in summer. Baking of the bulbs in the hot summer sun produces maximum flowering. The large bulbs should be planted with their necks above ground and should be left undisturbed once established. They thrive under trees if sufficient light is received.

Flowering commences in late summer, the large sweetly scented trumpets appearing in clusters on long sturdy stems. The usual flower colour is pink but can be deep cerise or pure white. Strap-shaped leaves emerge in autumn once flowering is finished, disappearing again early the following summer.

Large fleshy fruits are produced soon after flowering. If they are sown immediately, the seed germinates readily. It takes several years before bulbs of flowering size are produced.

The more common method of increase is to separate offsets during dormancy in summer. Replant these immediately, ensuring the fleshy roots do not become dry.

Pests and diseases are seldom a major problem, although vine weevils can chew the buds and flowers. Fusarium can be a problem if the plants become too wet.

Several colour variants have been selected and named. 'Beacon' has cerise-coloured flowers. 'Hathor' has white flowers flushed with apricot in the throat which are carried on long stems. *A. belladonna* var. *blanda* has large pure white blooms.

Amaryllis belladonna seedling

Several double-flowered forms are becoming available, producing up to four large flowers per stem and two stems per bulb. Most of these are multi-coloured, pink and white or red and white being two of those offered.

The name *Amaryllis* is commonly, and incorrectly, applied to the large-flowered *Hippeastrum* hybrids which are derived from South American species. See *Hippeastrum* for information on this genus.

ANDROCYMBIUM
Colchicaceae

This is a small genus of about 10 species that occur naturally mainly around the Mediterranean and in northern and South Africa. The small tuber resembles a tulip bulb. The plants are small, usually only about 15 cm tall, and the leaves are up to 15 cm long and about 5 cm wide. Sets of two or more bracts are produced, which can be of various colours, usually white or in shades of rose-pink. In the middle of the bracts are the small flowers, which give rise to the common name of little men in a boat.

The tubers should be planted in autumn about 5 cm deep into very sandy soil. A position in full sun is best, although potted plants can be grown under glass. Do not over-water. Seeds sown in pots of sandy mix will take three to four years to reach flowering size.

Androcymbium ciliolatum

A. ciliolatum from South Africa produces two or three 15 cm long leaves. Clusters of white flowers appear among greenish white bracts in mid-winter. The leaves have finely fringed margins and lie on or close to the surface of the soil.

A. pulchrum resembles *A. ciliolatum* and grows naturally in the same part of South Africa. It produces reddish purple bracts and small pink flowers. If it is cold and damp plants can become infected with botrytis. Slugs and snails can also be a problem.

ANEMONE
Ranunculaceae

This large genus contains about 120 species, many of which do not produce underground storage organs and so are not considered here. Tuber producing species generally prefer well-drained soil in cool woodlands. The tubers should be planted in autumn, and most will flower the following spring. They can be lifted and divided when dormant in summer. Seed usually germinates readily when sown in a sand mix. Seedlings resent disturbance and should be handled carefully when transplanting.

A. coronaria thrives in regions with warm climates. Flower colour is variable and includes red, pink, blue, white and also bi-colours. The stems can be 15–45 cm tall, and the leaves are finely dissected. This species is the parent of many hybrids that are popular with gardeners and florists. 'St Bridgit' is the collective name given to forms with semi-double flowers; 'De Caen' is a group with single poppy-shaped blooms.

A. blanda, native to Greece, has small single flowers on short stems. These appear in spring and are usually blue, but pink and white forms are also available. Many cultivars are now offered, and these are becoming increasingly popular as pot plants. The bulbs are mass produced and inexpensive, and they are often discarded once flowering is over.

A. nemorosa is native to Europe, where it grows in woodlands and is known as the wood anemone. The flowers can be white or blue, with bright yellow anthers. It is a good subject for naturalising

in colonies beneath deciduous trees. It prefers well-drained soil and multiplies well in suitable conditions.

A. rivularis is a beautiful species which thrives in warm climates. It can be planted in full sun or partial shade in ordinary garden loam and will self-seed when happy. The flowers are white flushed with mauve outside, and they appear from spring until summer. Often they commence flowering again in autumn, only stopping during the hottest part of summer.

ANOMATHECA
Iridaceae

This genus consists of six species from South Africa, closely related to *Lapeirousia* and having similar requirements. Most are fairly easy in cultivation, all needing well-drained soil and a warm sunny position. They can become a pest to other plants in containers or rock gardens. The small corms resemble those of another close relative, *Freesia*.

A. laxa (syn. *A. cruenta*) is a good garden subject, preferring a partially shaded position. The form most commonly grown produces a succession of salmon-red flowers with darker markings on 15 cm stems in early summer. White, scarlet and blue-flowered forms are also occasionally available, the blue form being more difficult to grow. The large deep orange-red seeds also make an attractive display. Established plantings often self-sow and multiply freely. Seedlings flower about 12 months after sowing.

A. grandiflora flowers in spring and early summer. It produces large red flowers and resembles a large-flowered version of *A. laxa*. It prefers partial shade.

A. fistulosa grows naturally in rocky coastal places in the Cape Peninsula of South Africa. It also resembles *A. laxa* but is smaller and has white or creamy white flowers. The tiny blooms are slightly fragrant and are carried on separate stems in spring. It is easy to grow but requires massed planting to be effective.

Opposite, above: *Anemone nemorosa*

Opposite, below: *Anomatheca laxa*

A. viridis is an easily grown miniature species, unusual rather than beautiful. About four small pale green flowers with a sweet fragrance are carried on stems 7.5 cm above the ground which bend horizontally.

ARISAEMA
Araceae

Natives of Asia, North America and East Africa, these unusual plants have flowers that range from arum-like to the bizarre. The stems (strictly pseudo-stems) and leaf-stalks are often attractively mottled in shades of pink, brown and grey. Often the foliage is divided into several sections, resembling *Helleborus*.

These are plants for woodlands or other semi-shaded positions. They enjoy soil that is moist but not boggy, never becoming hot and dry, and grow well among small evergreen trees.

Seed should be sown while fresh, after first removing the red pulp. Sow into a sandy medium, cover with about 1 cm of mix and keep shaded. The first flowers usually appear after about three years.

The corms are often lifted and divided in very cold areas, but this is unnecessary in warm climates. When lifting, dig well out from the plants to avoid damage to the corms. Small cormels develop around the central bud on the top of old corms, and when separated these take two to three years to flower. If stored, the corms should be placed in a slightly damp medium such as spaghnum moss or peat.

More than 150 species exist, many very rare and even more extreme in the shape of their blooms. Some, in fact, change their sex according to the size of their corms. They take many years before commencing flowering, at first producing only male flowers before changing into females as they increase in size. If a heavy crop of fruit is produced, they can change back to males again. They appear to be pollinated by insects attracted by the often sweet scent. Pests and diseases are seldom a problem.

The sizes given for the following species are a guide only. Well-grown plants form larger corms and grow taller.

A. sikokianum is a native of Japan, with long-lasting brownish purple flowers (spathes) with green stripes and a prominent white drumstick-like spadix. The foliage is usually divided into three to five segments. The flowers are unusual, to say the least, and the bright green foliage and red fruits are most attractive. It is not surprising that this species is becoming increasingly popular, and even a small group will create considerable comment and admiration. It is best planted in woodland gardens or in pots in a shady place.

A. candidissimum is a native of western China, where it grows in moist shady situations. The attractive blooms are white or pink with green stripes.

A. griffithii grows in Himalayan forests at high altitudes. It produces extraordinary large hooded spathes in shades from green to purple, but it is hard to obtain.

A. triphyllum, known as Jack-in-the pulpit, has dark purple-chocolate flowers carried on short stems. It has very attractive divided foliage and

Arisaema triphyllum

makes a good ground-cover under trees. It is native to North America.

A. amurense is a small early-flowering species, about 20 cm tall, with green and white flowers. It resembles *A. triphyllum,* but its leaves are divided into five segments.

A. ringens is the most commonly grown species in New Zealand. Its flowers curl up so that only the purple-brown and white outsides can be seen. It reaches 20–30 cm tall and is easily grown.

A. fragrans is a small species, about 20 cm tall, which has the widest distribution of all. The flowers are dull pale yellow, and it sets large amounts of seed. It tolerates more sun than most species.

A. speciosum is an attractive species that carries brownish flowers with white stripes on stems 30–40 cm tall. The trifoliate leaves are mottled and have red edges.

A. tortuosum has pure green flowers with a long twisted vertical spadix. It is easily grown, reaching about 1 m tall, and sets seed readily.

A. consanguineum is variable in flower colour, a green form being most commonly grown.

Arisaema sikokianum

52

Forms with brownish or white stripes are attributed to this species but may belong elsewhere. It usually reaches about 80 cm tall, and the foliage is very attractive.

A. costatum is a recent introduction with dark reddish brown flowers with white stripes. The long spadix lies on the ground, and the trifoliate leaves have distinctive raised parellel veins. It grows about 45 cm tall.

A. ciliatum has reddish brown flowers with white stripes and reaches about 60 cm tall.

Several new species have recently been introduced from Asia and will soon extend the available range of these fascinating bulbs.

ARISARUM
Araceae

Arisarum are usually easily grown in partially shaded positions. They form effective ground covers beneath trees but can be too rampant when grown in good soil in average garden conditions. They form a dense mass of attractive foliage and have unusual flowers that are long-lasting when picked.

Propagation is usually by division of the tubers when dormant in summer.

A. proboscidium is known as mouse plant because of the unusual tail-like tips on the flowers (spathes). The distinctive hooded dark brown flowers are slightly obscured by the foliage, with usually only their long tails being conspicuous. The flowering period varies in different climates but tends to be long, often lasting from winter until spring. The dark green leaves are shaped like arrowheads and do not have markings.

A. vulgare has flowers shaped like small hooded cobras, brownish purple with white stripes, appearing in winter and spring. The blooms are carried above the foliage, which is shaped like arrowheads and usually has silver spots. The plants become dormant in summer.

ARUM
Araceae

Many *Arum* species were formerly grown for food, known as arrowroot. They were used only in times of famine, the tubers requiring drying or cooking to rid them of toxins.

Several species of these European and Asian natives are in cultivation. Typically they have soft

Arisarum vulgare

Arum italicum ssp. *italicum*

fleshy shoots and form medium to large clumps. Most are easily grown, preferring well-drained soil in sun or semi-shade. They perform particularly well among shrubs that have an open habit.

The tubers should be planted as soon as possible after lifting but can stay dormant for a long time in dry soil conditions. They thrive in ordinary well-drained loam but dislike heavy clay. Over-fertilising is also detrimental. Pests and diseases are seldom a problem.

Propagation is usually by chopping up the tubers, most chips and pieces producing growth. It is advisable to dust cut surfaces with fungicide to prevent rotting. They can then be placed into trays of sandy medium until they grow large enough to be planted out. Seed should be sown as soon as it is ripe, after first carefully removing any soft flesh.

A. palaestinum originates from Israel, Syria and Lebanon, usually growing among rocks, at the base of old rock walls, or at the edges of fields and olive groves. It ranges in height from 30 to 60 cm. The flowers are pale creamy olive on the outside and velvety purple within. Sweetly scented, they appear in late winter and spring. The most conspicuous flower-like portion is strictly a spathe. Inside this is a fleshy spike called a spadix, which has female flowers on its lower portion, male flowers at the tip, and non-fertile flowers in between. Large handsome arrow-shaped foliage appears from mid-winter until summer. It is dark green, about 20 cm long and 10 cm wide, and has pale purple stems. This is an excellent subject for general landscaping and garden use. It is also ideal for floral art.

A. dioscoridis from Turkey is closely related to *A. palaestinum.* Its spathes are purple with spots of darker or paler purple. A number of forms occur, most reaching 30–40 cm tall.

A. creticum from Crete has sweetly scented soft yellow flowers and grows 30–40 cm tall.

A. italicum is the rampant weed often seen in huge numbers in neglected parks and old gardens. It has a number of forms, some with very attractive silver markings on their leaves. Spring flowers are followed by heads of red fruit. It is still sometimes referred to by its old English names, cuckoo pint or lords and ladies.

A. italicum ssp. *italicum,* commonly known as 'Pictum', has attractive white markings on its handsome foliage. Shining red and orange fruit appear in summer after the foliage has withered away. The best position to grow this rampant species is at the base of deciduous trees, where the competition and dryness will restrict its spread.

BABIANA
Iridaceae

This is an African genus of about 60 species, mostly from the southwestern Cape Province. They are known as baboon flowers because the corms of several species (e.g. *B. hypogea, B. stricta* and *B. rubrocyanea*) are eaten by baboons and other animals. As a defence against these animals, the corms usually grow deeply in the soil. Even when planted shallowly, they will eventually pull themselves down to a greater depth.

Hybrids are most commonly grown, derived mainly from *B. stricta,* and many lovely species are neglected by gardeners. Lavender shades predominate, and some species are delightfully fragrant. All are deciduous, growing in either winter or summer. Usually the foliage is lance-shaped and slightly hairy.

Most species do well in regions with warm climates, generally thriving in sunny well-drained positions. The corms should be planted deeply, up to 15 cm below the soil, and are best left undisturbed for several years. When they become overcrowded they should be lifted and thinned out. Most are suitable subjects for gardens or deep containers, and many are good for picking.

B. pygmaea is a lovely species from the Cape Province, producing very large soft yellow blooms with darker centres in late winter and early spring. These can vary slightly, some being more cream coloured, and are carried on stalks about 6 cm long. The flowers are easily damaged by the rains which are usually prevalent at the time they appear. They are generally best when grown in pots, which can be placed in a sheltered position near a house or in a greenhouse at flowering time. The bulbs should be divided every few years when they become overcrowded, and they can be stored dry over summer. Seed should be sown in early autumn; it germinates freely and usually produces flowering plants in two years.

B. stricta is a tall showy species (to about 25 cm) from the Cape Province. It is easy in gardens and is a parent of most of the garden hybrids. It grows in winter and becomes dormant in summer, flowering in late spring and early summer. It has been separated into several varieties.

B. stricta var. *stricta* is variable, usually producing flowers in shades of blue and purplish blue with pale yellow markings. It has a slight scent.

B. stricta var. *regia* is similar but with a small dark red circle in the centre of each flower.

B. stricta var. *grandiflora* has larger flowers, ranging in colour from mauve-blue to pinkish mauve. Several cultivars of this species have been selected. 'Zwanenburg Glory' has blooms of dark violet with paler blotches inside and dark eyes; peak flowering is in late spring. 'White King' is a robust cultivar, its white flowers flushed faintly with blue. 'Purple Star' is showy and easily grown, with richly coloured dark cyclamen blooms with white-striped throats.

B. rubrocyanea is most attractive and an excellent garden subject. It originates from the western Cape Province, where it grows in heavy soils. Its large showy flowers are bright blue with red markings, which act as nectar guides for pollinators. It flowers in spring, commencing after *B. pygmaea* and several weeks before *B. stricta.* The strap-like foliage is slightly hairy and has prominent longitudinal veins. It emerges in autumn and disappears the following summer. This excellent garden subject tolerates a range of soils and prefers full sun. It also grows well in partial shade but does not produce as many flowers.

The following species, listed alphabetically, are also recommended.

B. ambigua produces heavily scented showy flowers of lavender-blue with white or yellow markings. They appear in early spring on 8 cm stalks. Remarkably large flowers are produced by such small corms, which multiply freely. It grows during winter, being dormant in summer, and is an easy subject for naturalising in the garden. It is similar to *B. mucronata* but is smaller and fragrant.

B. angustifolia (syn. *B. pulchra*) is a very attractive winter-growing species. It flowers in spring and is usually best in pots, although it can be tried

Babiana pygmaea

in gardens. Its flowers are the most deeply coloured of all, dark violet-blue with dark purplish or reddish markings.

B. blanda, not commonly grown, produces large pink flowers on stalks about 6 cm long.

B. disticha (syn. *B. plicata*) is sometimes called the blue babiana, producing fragrant flowers of pale blue to violet with a yellow throat. The foliage grows taller than the flowers, which is not a desirable characteristic.

B. dregei has bold flowers of rich violet-purple with a darker blotch at the base of each petal. It is a vigorous species with large upright spiny-tipped leaves that can be painful if touched.

B. ecklonii is very common in gardens, its lavender flowers marked with cream on the lower petals.

B. hypogea has nicely scented flowers which are clustered at the base of its hairy foliage. The flowers are lavender-blue with cream markings and purplish stripes.

B. mucronata var. *mucronata* commences flowering in early winter, producing mauve

blooms on 10 cm stalks. The leaves grow taller than the flowers and are covered with fine hairs. It is easily grown in a well-drained position.

B. nana is a dwarf species, producing highly scented lilac blooms with spotted cream eyes in spring. They are carried on 12 cm stalks and are surprisingly large in relation to the tiny corms. It multiplies prolifically.

B. odorata produces sweetly scented yellow flowers on 12 cm stalks. It somewhat resembles a freesia when the flowers are first opening.

B. patersoniae has purplish blue to pale blue flowers on 30 cm stalks.

B. pubescens, about 20 cm tall, begins flowering in early winter. Its flowers are rich violet-purple with creamy yellow blotches and they are lilac on the outside. The erect strap-like leaves are covered with fine hairs. It requires a sunny position in well-drained sandy soil.

B. secunda (syn. *B. reflexa*) is a vigorous tall species that produces lavender-blue flowers with white marking on the upper petals. These appear in early summer on 30 cm stalks.

B. tubulosa var. *tubulosa* is a tall species from coastal South Africa. Creamy white blooms with red markings appear on 30 cm stems in spring.

B. vanzyliae has large pale yellow flowers. It is easy to grow but difficult to obtain.

B. villosa var. *villosa* is an easily grown species from the Cape Province. Lovely velvety flowers shaped like small tulips are carried on stalks up to 20 cm long. Flower colour is dark red or purplish red with prominent dark anthers.

BEGONIA
Begoniaceae

Most *Begonia* species have fibrous roots but some develop tubers. Several tuberous species are native to South America, with others occurring in parts of China, Africa and elsewhere. Few are currently available.

Modern tuberous begonias (*B.* x *tuberhybrida*) were developed from South American species. They have long been grown by specialists for exhibition. Their flowers vary greatly in colour and form, and several strains now available make outstanding garden subjects. These can be used

Babiana pubescens

in bedding, and they are very effective when planted in large drifts in partially shaded positions.

Seed of tuberous begonias should be sown in early spring in a well-drained seed-sowing mix. The seed is extremely fine, resembling dust, and should not be covered. It requires warmth to germinate, and the trays should be placed in a heated greenhouse or on heated benches. Pelleted seed is now available, which makes sowing much easier.

Seedlings can be transplanted into trays or pots when they are large enough to handle, but they must be kept warm in a greenhouse until temperatures outside rise. If the plants are intended for garden use, they must be hardened very carefully before planting. The best time for shifting the seedlings out of the greenhouse is when the weather is warm and overcast, and likely to remain so for several days.

Planting into gardens or containers is usually done in early summer. Garden soil should be well prepared, with a generous quantity of compost or other organic matter worked in before planting. A dressing of blood and bone or general garden fertiliser should also be applied. When planted in full sun, the blooms of most varieties become bleached, especially in mid-summer. A position which receives some shade in the middle of the day is preferable. Plants should be set out about 25 cm apart and kept moist throughout their growing period. The first flowers appear in mid-summer, and the regular removal of spent blooms will ensure a long display.

Tuberous begonias make outstanding container subjects. One or more plants can be used in pots, but mass plantings in large containers are even more effective. Hanging baskets dripping with tuberous begonia blooms make a stunning sight.

Powdery mildew is the only common disease, and it often occurs during dry weather in late summer. It can be reduced by keeping the plants moist, and spraying occasionally with a preventive fungicide will provide complete control.

In late autumn the plants begin to die back, and the soil should be allowed to dry out at this time. In well-drained frost-free positions the dormant tubers can be left in the ground throughout winter. When the new shoots emerge the following spring they must be protected from slugs and snails. Pinching out the growing tips will encourage a compact habit. Tall plants may

Begonia x *tuberhybrida* 'Pin Up'

require staking to prevent them collapsing.

The tubers can be lifted and stored during winter and replanted when temperatures are warm enough from late spring.

The best strain for garden use is 'Nonstop'. Developed in Germany, it produces an abundance of medium-sized camellia-shaped blooms from mid-summer until autumn. The compact plants, about 25 cm tall, are basal branching and have less tendency to split or collapse than many strains. This strain tolerates more sun than any other, although in full sun the blooms can be blemished in mid-summer. 'Memory' resembles 'Nonstop' but has larger flowers. It is also outstanding for garden and container use. 'Clips' is a smaller-flowered strain that is more susceptible to weather damage. It is best used as a pot plant.

Some strains have been developed particularly for use in hanging baskets. 'Happy End' produces semi-double blooms on pendulous stems. 'Musical' is semi-pendulous and is suitable for gardens and hanging baskets. These pendulous strains have been developed mainly from *B. boliviensis*.

B. x *hiemalis* was developed by crossing *B.* x *tuberhybrida* with *B. socotrana*. This species is native to Socotra, an island off the northeast coast of Africa. The hybrids became known as the winter-flowering begonias.

Reiger begonias are a further development from

Begonia 'Nonstop'

B. x *hiemalis.* These were bred in Germany and have been widely available since the 1970s. They grow readily from cuttings, and huge numbers are produced as pot plants. Many new cultivars can be grown successfully in gardens. The flowers are generally smaller than those of tuberous begonias, and the green or bronze leaves are smaller and usually glossy. The flowers can be single or double and occur in a wide range of colours including pink, yellow, orange, red and white.

A recent introduction from Germany is 'Charisma', the first strain of reiger begonia that can be raised from seed in a similar manner to tuberous begonias. Two separate colours are available, 'Charisma Coral' and 'Charisma Orange'. These produce compact plants about 25 cm tall with small double blooms and glossy dark green leaves. Flowering is abundant throughout most of the year, and in warm climates the plants do not become dormant.

Few tuberous begonia species are generally available.

B. grandis ssp. *evansiana* from China appears in some seed catalogues. It is known as the hardy begonia, tolerating far cooler conditions than most. It has large handsome leaves with bristly hairs on the toothed margins. Clusters of pale pink flowers appear in summer. It grows in summer and becomes dormant in winter.

B. boliviensis from Bolivia has tall succulent arching stems about 1 m tall. Panicles of lovely scarlet-red flowers hang from the branches in summer. It will become more widely available in future and is an outstanding subject for large containers.

BESSERA
Alliaceae

These dainty bulbs from Mexico have grassy leaves and flowering stems of about 50 cm or taller carrying numerous flowers shaped like small parachutes, 4 cm wide and ranging in colour from bright red to pink or purple. Some may also have white stripes. The bulbs can be stored dry over winter and planted 10 cm deep into sandy soil in spring. They produce small bulblets, but seed when available is the best means of increase. It should be sown in pots of sandy mix, slightly covered and kept shaded until germination commences, which can take several months. Seedlings will flower in three to four years. No pests apart from slugs and snails have been found so far.

B. elegans is the only species available at present. It flowers during summer and is good for rock gardens and containers. A range of colour variants occurs, mainly in shades from scarlet to purple with various green or white markings.

BLANDFORDIA
Blandfordiaceae

This is a small genus of slow-growing bulbs from Tasmania and eastern Australia, reaching about 40 cm tall with tufts of long-lasting rush-like foliage. In their natural habitats they grow in a range of soil types from heavy clays to stony hillsides, often in areas which become flooded after heavy rains.

Commonly called Christmas bells in the Southern Hemisphere, they produce up to 15 bell-shaped flowers per stem from summer until early autumn, with occasional flowers at other times. Some flower after fires in nature. Flower colour is yellow, reddish orange or red with a yellow lip. After flowering, long thin seed-pods develop and soon ripen.

In cultivation they grow best in well-drained soils which remain moist for most of the year— sand can be added if necessary. Mulching suppresses weeds and keeps the soil cool. Bulbs can be difficult to establish, often taking three to seven years to reach flowering size. Once established they produce glorious waxy bells, usually in mid-summer, for 50 years or more. The flowers are very long-lasting in the vase but split easily if packed without care. Because they take so long to develop large free-flowering clumps, they have not become an important commercial cut-flower crop. They are, however, very good garden plants for those who like something rather special.

B. grandiflora, *B. nobilis* and *B. punicea* are most commonly encountered. They are fairly similar in the shape and colour of their flowers, but they

Bessera elegans

vary so much in size and appearance according to the conditions under which they are growing that they can be difficult to distinguish.

B. grandiflora has the largest flowers of the Christmas bells. It produces up to 12 campanula-like blooms of rose-red to scarlet with yellow tips on stems about 40 cm tall. It grows naturally in New South Wales and Queensland.

Blandfordia grandiflora

B. nobilis has the brightest flowers, and its bells are more tubular in shape. Yellow blooms with red tips are carried on 30 cm stems.

B. punicea from Tasmania tolerates the coolest conditions but requires good drainage. It is a larger species with strong grassy foliage and tall stems. Flower colour can be red, orange or yellow and many shades in between.

B. cunninghamii is known as mountain Christmas bells, producing five or more yellow bells with red tips on 30 cm tall stems. It originates from New South Wales and tolerates cooler temperatures than most species.

Propagation is by careful division or by sowing the furry seeds into a sandy mix in pots or trays. They will germinate over a period of three months and grow very slowly, and should be allowed to grow undisturbed for one or two seasons as the grass-like seedlings often die if shifted earlier. Transplanting is best done in mid-autumn into individual pots of sandy mix containing little fertiliser. They can be planted outside in full sun or partial shade when large enough.

In humid climates plants often succumb to phytophthora infections. Sometimes pests eat flowers and seed-heads, and birds often split the flowers in search of nectar.

BOMAREA
Alstroemeriaceae

Most of the *Bomarea* species in cultivation are climbers, although non-climbing species are also grown. They are very closely related to *Alstroemeria* and also originate in South America.

The climbing types are vigorous plants producing numerous flowers per season. The showy flowers are usually reddish orange but sometimes pink, and they are carried in terminal umbels on the flowering stems; non-flowering stems are also produced. The climbers require strong support as eventually most grow very large.

Non-climbing species can make good ground-covers for shady situations. Some are evergreen. The flowers are usually bright orange-yellow and small, and are followed by orange berries.

The rhizomes produce edible tuber-like storage roots. Their major requirement is well-drained sandy soil.

Increase is by division or seeds. Plants should be divided in early autumn and replanted as soon as possible afterwards. Seeds germinate in 6–12 weeks or sometimes longer. They should be grown in pots of sandy mix and repotted when they send up their second young stem.

Slugs and snails are their major pests, being especially damaging to new growth.

B. multiflora is a climber from Venezuela and Columbia, eventually reaching about 3 m tall. Its bell-shaped flowers are reddish orange outside and orange-yellow with brown spots inside. They appear in pendant clusters of up to 40 during spring and summer. Although their stems are short, they make good long-lasting cut flowers. The oblong, pointed dark green foliage is about 8 cm long. It is an ideal species for covering a fence or an old tree stump.

B. salsilla from Chile is a climber of moderate vigour which reaches about 2 m. It produces open bell-shaped flowers of violet and green.

B. sp. from Ecuador forms a ground-cover about 30–50 cm across. Stiff stems are covered in glossy dark green foliage, which is good for picking. Orange flowers about 2 cm across appear in small umbels and are followed by orange fruits. It can be grown in sun or semi-shade.

BOOPHANE
Amaryllidaceae

These interesting bulbs from South Africa and Angola grow slowly and eventually become very large. Blue-grey or grey-green strap-shaped leaves grow into an attractive fan after the flowers have finished in autumn. They need very well-drained soil or sandy gritty potting mix. The bulbs should be planted two-thirds deep in large pots or into a prepared bed. As they resent being shifted, it is best to remove some of the old compost every few years, while the plants are dormant, and replace it with fresh mix. A few grains of slow-release fertiliser plus extra sulphate of potash will

Opposite, above: *Bomarea salsilla*
Opposite, below: *Boophane disticha*

help speed up flowering, which can take many years. Keep the plants dry in summer.

B. disticha, or poison eye, has 30–40 cm flowering stems with heads of many pink flowers carried on long stalks. The flowers have a very sweet fragrance and can sometimes cause headaches or sore eyes. When the seeds have ripened, the large head will break off from the stem. In nature this will roll around and distribute the seeds. The dried heads are ideal for large dried arrangements. The foliage is about 35 cm long, wavy and blue-grey.

B. guttata produces up to a hundred small flowers in each head. They are greenish purple, and the green leaves have downward-pointing hairs on their edges.

B. haemanthoides, rare in cultivation, has cream and red flowers. Fresh seed should be sown on the surface of well-drained mix in pots, which should be kept in semi-shade for the first season.

BRODIAEA
Alliaceae

This genus of about 30 species, mainly native to North America, has undergone considerable revision by botanists over the years, and many species previously placed under *Brodiaea* are now regarded as belonging to other genera such as *Triteleia, Dichelostemma* and *Ipheion.*

Most species are natives of California, where they typically grow in dry stony clay soils. The flowers are carried in onion-like heads, and the grass-like foliage generally dies off at flowering time.

Planting in clumps is usually most effective, and several species are suitable for container growing. Most prefer well-drained moisture-retentive soils or heavyish potting mix with soil added; clay soils are unsuitable in high-rainfall areas unless coarse sand or other gritty material is incorporated to improve drainage. Moisture is required in winter but should be reduced in summer, especially late summer. Plants must never become waterlogged.

B. californica grows naturally in northern California in well-drained soils. It is the tallest species, producing heads of pendulous flowers on stems 60 cm or more in height. The large flowers range in colour from lustrous pink to violet-blue with violet stamens, and they appear in early summer. A warm sunny position is ideal, the plants naturalising and self-sowing in suitable conditions.

B. elegans is also widely available. It is commonly called harvest brodiaea and grows naturally in grasslands and open woods in California and Oregon. Clusters of cup-shaped stars appear in summer on stems 10–50 cm long. The glistening wax-like flowers are typically in shades of lilac with violet tips. Although only a few are produced at any one time, they continue to appear for a long period. The leaves die off at flowering time. It produces small bulbils which can easily be lost and is generally most satisfactory when grown in pots.

Few other species are available. *B. terrestris* is listed in some catalogues and is quite distinctive. Large clusters of mauve-pink flowers with darker streaks appear just above soil-level in mid-summer.

Dichelostemma ida-maia (syn. *Brodiaea coccinea*) is closely related to *Brodiaea* and has similar requirements. It is known as the firecracker flower, producing scarlet flowers with green tips in late spring and summer. Several flowers are carried on stems about 45 cm tall, and they are good for picking. The foliage is grass-like. It is easily grown in well-drained soil, tolerating very dry conditions. Seed germinates readily, and the first flowers usually appear after three years.

Dichelostemma ida-maia

BRUNSVIGIA
Amaryllidaceae

This striking genus from Southern Africa is closely related to *Amaryllis* and *Nerine*. Usually the bulbs are very large, up to 20 cm across, and they take many years to reach flowering size. They resent being shifted and flower best when growing in a tight clump where they get a good baking during summer. They grow in a variety of soils in their habitats, but all have a long resting period during the summer drought. In cultivation they should have well-drained soil and full sun in a position which remains relatively dry during summer. Containers can be kept in a warm sunny position and dried off during summer.

Sulphate of potash helps produce good buds and benefits foliage growth, which in turns helps the bulbs increase in size and weight.

If necessary, bulbs can be stored dry but will require an extra year to flower.

Large bulbs produce offsets, which can be removed and grown on. Twin scaling will produce a number of small bulblets, which will take four to six years to flower. The pea-sized seeds sown on the surface of a sandy mix will germinate in a few days and take about seven to nine years to flower.

Thrips sometimes spoil the flowers, and viruses can be the cause of lack of flowering.

B. minor produces clusters of 20–40 bright pink flowers on 15–25 cm tall stems. They appear for several weeks in late summer, about the same time as nerines. After a dry summer period, the application of water results in rapid growth of the flower-stems. If pollinated, the large heads eventually break free from the bulb and in the wild roll away, scattering seeds from the papery pods. The bulbs are usually 4–7 cm across.

B. josephinae is the candelabra lily, producing in late summer spectacular heads of 15 or more bright rose-pink flowers. These are long-lasting and are carried on stems up to 1.5 m tall. The huge bulbs prefer growing on top of the ground. Strap-like green foliage reaches about 60 cm long during winter and disappears over summer. This is an ideal subject for dry areas and containers. There is some doubt that the plant commonly grown is the true species. Some authorities believe it to

Brunsvigia josephinae

be a hybrid, possibly with *Amaryllis belladonna*.

B. josephinae often does not flower, which can be the result of various factors. The bulbs must be very large before they will flower, and they require a very well-drained position which remains dry for a long period during summer. Many plants have virus, evidenced by yellow streaking in the foliage, which suppresses flowering.

B. litoralis produces 15–25 rusty red flowers per 1 m stem after watering in late summer. This is a fairly rare species, similar to *B. josephinae* but with bulbs half the size. It usually flowers more reliably. Generally two clones are necessary for seed to be set.

Hybridisation between *Brunsvigia*, *Amaryllis* and *Nerine* is relatively easy, although flowering of seedlings takes many years.

BULBINELLA
Asphodelaceae

This is a genus of 22 species, 16 originating from the winter-rainfall Cape Province of South Africa; the other six are natives of New Zealand. Only three species are commonly grown, all South African. These grow during winter, flower in late winter and spring, and become dormant in summer. Their succulent rhizomatous rootstocks

Bulbinella nutans var. *nutans*

store food and moisture, enabling them to survive summer drought in their natural habitat. They somewhat resemble kniphofias, with erect racemes of starry flowers, usually in shades of orange, yellow or white. Their long narrow foliage may be erect or drooping and is also very attractive.

They are excellent subjects for naturalising in sunny well-drained positions and are well suited to regions with warm climates, where they should be more widely used. They flower best when undisturbed. Division when plants are dormant in late summer is the usual method of increase, but it damages the roots and the plants take some time to recover. Segments should be replanted as soon as possible and not allowed to dry out.

Seed should be sown into deep trays of sandy mix in autumn. Transplanting into individual pots should take place the following summer when plants are dormant. The first flowers can be expected three years after sowing. Self-sown seedlings often emerge in the garden around established clumps.

B. nutans var. *nutans* produces numerous golden yellow flowers in striking racemes, those at the base opening first. Flowering usually continues for about 10 weeks from late winter and is most prolific if adequate moisture is received during winter. The flowers are carried on stalks about 1 m tall and are good for picking. Planted in large drifts, it makes a dramatic sight when in full bloom. The dense clumps of narrow grassy foliage are also most handsome. This variety is most commonly, and incorrectly, offered as *B. floribunda* (yellow form).

B. nutans var. *turfosicola* produces cream-coloured flowers later in the season. It is more difficult to cultivate.

B. latifolia var. *latifolia* also produces bright golden yellow flowers carried in racemes which are slightly longer and wider than those of *B. nutans*. It can be distinguished by its broader foliage, and it is slightly taller at about 1.2 m.

B. latifolia var. *doleritica* produces bright orange flowers on 1.2 m stems in late winter and spring, and also has broad foliage. It has previously been known incorrectly as *B. floribunda* (orange form.)

B. cauda-felis is called cat's tail on account of the shape of its racemes and its unusual cat-like smell. The buds are apricot-pink and the fluffy flowers creamy white when open. They appear on stems up to 80 cm long from late winter until early summer, carried above clumps of grassy foliage. This very attractive species deserves to be more widely grown. It thrives in a well-drained position, preferably containing plenty of humus. It is especially suitable for warm climates, although it can die out during prolonged wet weather. It makes a good long-lasting cut flower, although if too many are used in an arrangement the scent can be unpleasant.

CALOCHORTUS
Calochortaceae

This genus of lovely North American bulbs deserves to be more widely grown. There is considerable diversity among the species, and most have exacting requirements for successful cultivation. Many are high-altitude plants which are under snow during winter and come into growth in spring; others are found growing naturally near sea-level. It is important to know the natural habitat of a particular species so that its cultural requirements may be determined. Generally, winter-growing species are easier to cultivate than those which grow during summer.

Winter-growing species must be kept dry from when flowering finishes until growth restarts the following spring. As with other plant species from winter-rainfall areas, the key is to neglect them when dormant and provide ample moisture and good drainage when they are growing. Most thrive where summer rainfall is low and benefit from a mulch of gravel or coarse sand.

Calochortus fall into three main groups. Exceptions include high-altitude desert species such as *C. kennedyi*.

EUCALOCHORTUS The cat's ear (hairs inside flowers) or star tulip group.

CYCLOBOTHRA Summer-flowering Mexican species such as *C. madrensis*, *C. purpureus*, *C. gesbrechtti* and *C. barbatus*.

MARIPOSA Globe lilies, large upward-facing flowers and usually small leaves. *C. venustus* and *C. luteus* are two of the easiest mariposa lilies to start with, before moving on to other species when successful. Those with pendulous flowers are termed fairy lanterns, e.g. *C. amabilis*.

Propagation of winter-growing species is usually from seed sown in autumn. Most germinate freely but dislike high humidity so should be sown thinly. Grow on for as long as possible to develop large bulbs. Summer-growing Mexican species should be sown in spring. No specialist treatment is required. The bulbs are best lifted in winter and stored in sand.

Many species are erratic flowerers but prolific seeders. The seed-pods are often attractive but

Calochortus amabilis

Calochortus uniflorus

should be removed to prevent drain on the small bulbs.

C. uniflorus (syn. *C. lilacinus*) is the pink star tulip from western USA. An extremely variable species, it is also one of the easiest to grow in gardens. It produces hairless upward-facing blooms in shades of soft pink to pale lavender and is one of the earliest to flower in winter. It reaches about 30 cm tall and likes a sunny well-drained position and lots of water when flowering. It multiplies rapidly from bulb offsets and also forms bulbils in the leaf axils.

C. tolmiei has small open hairy white flowers, often tinted with blue or lavender and covered inside with long silky hairs. Blue anthers contrast attractively. This is one of the earliest and most desirable of the winter-flowering cat's ear group. As with most hairy plants, it resents excessive moisture and humidity. It can be tried in a rock garden in dry rocky soil in a cool position protected from midday heat, but it is generally most successful when grown in pots.

C. coeruleus is another cat's ear, found growing naturally in California in stony ground in mountain forests. Its cream flowers tinged with blue are covered in hairs. Suitable for pots or rock gardens, it is really a plant for the specialist.

C. amabilis is Diogenes' lantern, from cool rocky coastal ranges in northwest California. Its globular blooms are golden yellow, the outer petals forming a triangle and the inner petals folding over each other. It is certainly one of the best of the fairy lanterns for use in pots and gardens. It also makes an excellent cut flower, lasting well in water. In hot areas it prefers a position which is shaded at midday.

C. pulchellus is a similar-looking species with softer golden yellow flowers. These are globular and hairy inside. It is one of the easiest species to grow, preferring very good drainage and either sun or partial shade.

C. amoenus is the another fairy lantern, and cultivation should be as for *C. amabilis*. Its open blooms are rose-red, and it reaches about 45 cm tall.

C. albus is a native of central California, usually found at low altitude in the shade of rocky forests. Many forms are available from different habitats. Numerous beautiful globe-shaped blooms are carried on 15–60 cm long stalks. These are usually cream, sometimes pinkish. It usually flowers better in cultivation than in the wild, preferring a well-drained, partially shaded position.

C. albus var. *rubellus* has red flowers and is relatively easy to grow. Seed germinates readily.

C. kennedyi is a showy but difficult mariposa lily from the deserts of California and Arizona. Flower colour is variable, usually scarlet but occasionally orange or yellow. A tall species, it is probably best grown in a cactus house.

C. venustus, sometimes called the mariposa tulip, is a diverse and beautiful species. It is regarded by many as the most spectacular of all the species. The range of flower colours includes shades of pink, red, cerise, scarlet, gold, cream, lavender and bronze with various markings. Often several colours blend together in the large flowers. Generally it is most successful when grown in pots, but it is worth trying in well-drained sandy soil. It should be kept dry in winter then watered well until flowering.

C. luteus is known variously as gold nuggets and yellow mariposa. It is similar to *C. venustus* and has similar requirements, but its flowers are always clear bright yellow. It produces numerous blooms for a long period on 30–60 cm stems and it is one of the easiest garden subjects, preferring a sunny position.

Summer-flowering members of the cyclobothra group include the following:

C. barbatus is a variable species, up to 50 cm tall,

from the mountains of Mexico and southern California. Its pendulous flowers are usually golden yellow with reddish brown spots inside the petals. Although the flowers are small, they are extremely bright and appear for several months. Usually two blooms are carried per 15–30 cm stem. Numerous bulbils form in the leaf axils so it multiplies readily. The bulbs should be lifted in winter and kept dry.

C. gesbrechtii is found in the mountains of Mexico and Guatemala. Its beautiful small flowers are such a deep reddish brown they appear almost black. They resemble *C. barbatus* and are also usually carried two per stem. Bulbils are produced in the leaf axils.

C. madrensii has small creamy white flowers with yellow eyes. These are cup-shaped and face upwards. It can be difficult and is best grown in pots.

C. purpureus is also extremely difficult but very pretty, with gold and brown blooms—well worth trying.

CALOSTEMMA
Amaryllidaceae

This small Australian genus produces sprays of smallish flowers which resemble those of some species of *Narcissus*. The flowers appear quickly after rain in mid- to late summer, and the foliage emerges after the flowers have faded. They require well-drained sandy soil and very little fertiliser; a position in full sun is ideal. The flowers are useful for picking. The large long bulbs pull themselves down deeply into the soil with strong contractile roots. Bulb fly can destroy the bulbs, as can very wet soils.

Seeds mature and fall within about a week or so of pollination. Roots often form on the seeds while they are still attached to the stem. They germinate on the surface of the soil and produce small bulbs before becoming dormant in early spring. They take about three years to reach flowering size. Seed is the usual method of propagation as even mature bulbs do not appear to produce offsets.

C. purpureum produces 20 or more purple blooms on stems up to 40 cm tall. The flowers are shaped like those of *Narcissus fernandesii* and appear in mid- to late summer. The green foliage is about 2 cm wide and 30–50 cm long. It requires full sun and well-drained sandy soil. If grown in containers, the mix should be gritty and free-draining. In their natural habitat plants can cover several acres of sandy semi-desert.

The bulbs are oblong and up to 10 cm long, and they can be stored dry. They should be planted just below the surface of the soil and will pull themselves to a greater depth.

Although no cultivars or hybrids of this species are currently grown, plants vary in the wild, and larger-flowered forms would be worth selecting.

C. scott-sellickiana (syn. *C. album*) produces white flowers in summer which look like small *Eucharis* blooms. The green foliage grows about 35 cm long. This species is extremely rare in cultivation. It is best grown in pots, requiring very well-drained sandy mix.

C. luteum carries golden blooms, often spotted red at the base of the petals, on stems about 35 cm tall. Some very nice forms with larger flowers occur in the wild and would be valuable introductions. The foliage usually grows 30–50

Calostemma luteum

cm tall. It requires a well-drained position in a sunny garden, or free-draining mix when grown in containers. Its requirements are similar to those of *C. purpureum*, which it resembles except in its flower colour.

CAMASSIA
Hyacinthaceae

This is a genus of six species from the Americas with erect narrow spikes which provide striking vertical accent in the garden. They also naturalise well in grass, being most effective if planted in large groups. Once established they are best left

Camassia leichtlinii ssp. *typica*

undisturbed. They tolerate more moisture than most bulbs and can be grown in full sun or partial shade. The bulbs bury themselves increasingly deeper with time and need lifting occasionally and replanting nearer the surface if they are to continue flowering.

C. leichtlinii ssp. *leichtlinii* is one of the tallest species, originating from mountain meadows in Oregon. The form usually grown has flowers in an unusual shade of soft electric-blue carried on 1.3 m stems in early summer. It prefers a rich moist soil and germinates easily from seed sown as soon as it is ripe.

C. leichtlinii ssp. *typica* has creamy white flowers and is usually offered as 'Alba'. Forms with double white flowers are occasionally obtainable but are not as attractive.

C. quamash (syn. *C. esculenta*) grows naturally in marshy meadows in western USA and was eaten by the North American Indians. Graceful spikes of strong electric-blue appear in late spring and early summer on stems of about 50 cm. It is easily grown in rich moist soil and is a good subject for naturalising in cottage gardens.

C. cusikii produces spikes of soft blue carried on erect stems up to 90 cm tall in summer.

CARDIOCRINUM
Liliaceae

C. giganteum is the best species, one of the most spectacular of all bulbs when in full bloom. It is essentially a woodland plant, preferring cool moist conditions and growing poorly in windy situations. It seldom flowers well in regions with warm temperatures throughout the year. Soil should be deep and rich with a high humus content, and plants should be kept moist.

Huge waxy white bell-shaped flowers, highly fragrant, appear in clusters on strong stems, which can exceed 3 m in height. The plants die after flowering but produce copious seeds. The flowering bulbs also produce offsets which can be separated from the parent plants when they die in autumn. These can be replanted and will take several years to flower.

Snails are the major pest, especially when the plants are young.

CHASMANTHE
Iridaceae

This is a small genus of three species from the Cape Province of South Africa, all winter-growing and becoming dormant in summer. They produce an abundance of long-tubed flowers during late winter and spring. They naturalise readily where climates are warm, and some can become rather weedy. Once established, they should be left undisturbed as lifting can reduce flowering the following season. They grow happily in full sun or partial shade.

C. floribunda var. *floribunda* produces an abundance of reddish orange flowers on 1.2 m tall stems during late winter and spring. It is most effective in large drifts, providing colour and striking lance-shaped foliage during the winter months. It also flowers well under trees. Increase is usually by separating offsets when dormant in

Chasmanthe aethiopica

summer. Seed should be sown when ripe, and some plants may flower in their second season.

C. floribunda var. *duckittii* is identical except that its flowers are an attractive shade of primrose-yellow.

C. aethiopica is the most widely distributed species in the wild. Its flowers are dark reddish orange, and they appear on stems up to 70 cm tall in early winter. It can be distinguished from *C. floribunda* var. *floribunda* by its smaller size and its flowers, which are smaller and deeper in colour.

CHIONODOXA
Hyacinthaceae

These are small bulbs from Crete and Asia Minor, commonly known as glory of the snow. They flower in spring on 10–20 cm tall stems and are very like scillas. The bulbs should be planted 5 cm deep in autumn into gritty soil containing

Cardiocrinum giganteum

some humus in a sunny position. They make very good rock garden plants and grow well in pots, looking best when mass planted. They can be stored dry and appear to be pest-free.

C. forbesii (syn. *C. siehei*) is the correct name for the plant commonly grown as *C. luciliae*, which is a separate species. This is the plant most often seen in gardens. It has a number of flowers, usually 5–12, on a 10–20 cm tall stem. These are in a glorious shade of blue, varying in size and in the amount of white in their eye. There are several other forms in soft blue, pink and white, and many named selections are available. 'Blue Giant' has sky-blue petal tips and white centres. 'Pink Giant' has very pale pink flowers with a white eye. Other cultivars include 'Alba' (pure white), 'Naburn Blue' (dark blue with a white centre) and 'Rosea'. They all form numerous seed-pods full of black seeds. If sown into trays or beds of sandy mix, these will germinate in winter and quickly grow to flowering size.

C. sardensis from Turkey produces numerous gentian-blue starry flowers with a hint of a white eye. These appear in spring on stems up to 12 cm tall. The glossy green leaves are about 10 cm long.

It is fairly rare in cultivation and can be grown in pots or rock gardens. Bulbs should be planted in autumn and kept cool until growth emerges in late winter, then given full sun.

CHLIDANTHUS
Amaryllidaceae

This South American genus contains only one species, *C. fragrans*. It derives its common name of sea daffodil from its golden yellow blooms, which vaguely resemble daffodils without trumpets, and its narrow daffodil-like foliage. The lemon-scented flowers appear in summer, with a few carried on each 40 cm tall stem. Flowering is not usually abundant but can be increased with an annual dressing of sulphate of potash. Some selections flower more freely than others. This is an easily grown species in the right conditions.

Bulbs should be planted when dormant during winter into well-drained soil, just below the surface, and the soil firmed. The bulbs tend to

Chionodoxa forbesii

70

Chlidanthus fragrans

divide and multiply freely rather than growing large enough to flower. Increase is usually by separating the bulbs when they are dormant.

Bulb fly is the major pest, and virus infections sometimes occur.

COLCHICUM
Colchicaceae

This genus, commonly called autumn crocus, contains numerous species with flowers that resemble crocuses but are not closely related. Generally the flowers are large and cup-shaped and the corms quite enormous. Most species flower during late summer and autumn, providing welcome colour when little else is flowering. They are among the few autumn-flowering bulbs that are sufficiently vigorous to thrive in normal garden situations. They prefer rich well-drained soil and partial shade, and can be naturalised in grass.

C. speciosum is one of the best for gardens, producing goblet-shaped flowers in late summer and autumn. These are usually in shades of purplish pink with a paler throat, occasionally white, and they are delightfully fragrant. The foliage is large and very attractive. It naturalises readily in well-drained soil and is very effective when planted in large groups. Increase is usually by lifting and dividing the bulbs when they are dormant, otherwise the bulbs are best left undisturbed, eventually forming large clumps which flower freely every year.

C. speciosum 'Album' has large pure white flowers.

C. speciosum is the parent of numerous large-flowered hybrids. 'The Giant' is one of the largest, freely producing purplish flowers with white centres. 'Waterlily' has large double flowers shaped like waterlilies.

C. autumnale is native to meadows in much of Europe. It is one of the earliest species to flower, producing a succession of soft lilac flowers from late summer. The leaves emerge once flowering is finished.

Colchicum speciosum

C. agrippinum is regarded as being probably of hybrid origin. Its tiny starry flowers are pale violet with darker mosaic patterning. These reach about 10 cm above ground in autumn. It prefers a sunny position and can form large clumps.

C. bornmuelleri is native to Turkey, producing pinkish purple flowers with brownish anthers in autumn.

C. bowlesianum is native to Greece and has large flowers of rose-lilac mottled with white. It is a parent of many hybrids.

C. byzantinum is a free-flowering species with blooms of lilac or mauve with white centres. Long stigmas are tipped with crimson. It is regarded by some as a form of *C. autumnale* and by others as possibly a hybrid. It is robust and easily grown, with large pleated foliage about 30 cm long.

C. luteum is the only species with yellow flowers, sometimes tinged with lilac. It is a native of Afghanistan and northern India, where it grows on mountain slopes near the snow-line. It is not easy to cultivate, requiring gritty well-drained soil. It is generally best grown in a bulb frame to protect the flowers from botrytis.

CRINUM
Amaryllidaceae

This large genus has about 130 species, which are widely distributed throughout tropical and temperate regions of the world. Only a few species are generally available, and these are mainly natives of South Africa or Australia. Most are summer growers. They are becoming increasingly popular with gardeners and collectors, and are the focus of much breeding work. Typically the species produce large beautiful flowers, extremely large bulbs and strong bold foliage. Because they occur naturally in a diversity of habitats, ranging from arid deserts to tropical swamps, it is difficult to generalise about their requirements. The majority grow well in association with evergreen trees, their bold stems and foliage providing an interesting focal point.

The bulbs grow and multiply fairly slowly, and small offsets take about three years to reach flowering size. Offsets can be removed at any time

Crinum x *powellii* 'Alba'

but receive least setback if separated in late spring. The bulbs are best replanted as soon as possible after dividing. They can be stored for several weeks if kept moist and cool. Twin scaling is another method of propagation occasionally used.

Seeds of different species vary considerably in size and in the time before the first flowers appear. Seed should be sown as soon as it ripens, on the surface of a well-drained mix; when covered, the seed often rots. Sometimes roots form on seeds while they are still attached to the plant, and these can be removed and planted like small bulbs.

C. moorei is the most commonly grown species, thriving in shade beneath mature trees. Large bell-shaped flowers of pale pink appear in summer, up to 10 scented blooms carried on stems about 1.2 m tall. The large bold almost evergreen leaves are about 1 m long but look rather untidy after flowering. The foliage can be damaged by frost. It is a very easy plant to grow, flowering reliably despite neglect. The clumps can be divided in spring, and the large rounded seeds germinate freely when ripe. The first flowers usually appear three years after sowing and can vary in colour.

C. moorei var. *minor* is a dwarf form which becomes dormant in very dry summers.

C. moorei var. *schmidtii* is a white-flowered form.

C. x *powellii* is a cross between *C. moorei* and *C. bulbispermum*, and is intermediate between its two parents in many of its characteristics. Its trumpet-shaped flowers are pink or white and are carried on stems about 1.5 m tall. It flowers in summer and sometimes blooms twice per season. The mid-green foliage is upright. It is a good landscaping plant and very widely grown, thriving in shade in either wet or dry soils and forming very large clumps. The foliage may die off for a time in early winter but can be evergreen if the soil is moist. The clumps can be divided at any time of the year. Seed is not set by this hybrid. Trimming back the foliage assists recovery after division. 'Alba' produces a profusion of white flowers, and 'Rosea' has deep pink blooms. A form with variegated leaves is also available.

C. bulbispermum (syn. *C. longiflorum*) is a hardy South African species of variable flower colour, usually white and often flushed with pink. Each petal has a broad reddish stripe running along the centre. It is an ideal medium-sized plant for a well drained sunny garden and provides a useful supply of cut flowers. The large flaring trumpet-shaped

Crinum 'Mrs James Hendry'

flowers appear in late spring and combine nicely with the greyish 1.2 m stems which arise from the base of the foliage. The distinctive arching strap-like leaves are very handsome and die down in winter. The first flowers usually appear three years after sowing.

C. asiaticum var. *sinicum* (syn. *C. pedunculatum*) is a frost-tender native of eastern parts of Australia and some Pacific Islands. It prefers moist soils and produces large handsome leaves more than 1 m long in striking rosettes. The scented starry white flowers have very narrow petals, and usually about 25 are carried on stems about 1.3 m tall. It eventually forms very large clumps, which flower for a long period in summer. Seeds can lie on the soil surface for over 12 months and produce bulbs without roots growing into the soil. The bulbs grow quickly when potted but take between four and seven years to flower.

'Ellen Bosanquet' is a choice hybrid between *C. moorei* and *C. zeylanicum*. It produces large bell-shaped flowers of dark rose-red on stems 40–60 cm tall. Flowers appear in summer, and healthy established clumps can produce a succession of flowering stems. The soft semi-erect foliage is evergreen and susceptible to frost damage. It is usually between 60 cm and 1 m in length, and it is easily kept tidy. Vine weevils occasionally chew the edges of the leaves and flower-buds. This is a very good garden subject and can be used in containers. Associating it with plants with grey or silver foliage sets the dark flowers off particularly well. *Artemisia* 'Powis Castle' and *Nepeta* 'Six Hills Giant' are good companions.

C. 'Mrs James Hendry' is an attractive hybrid

x *Crinodonna*

bred in the United States in 1912. It carries large fragrant white trumpets flushed with pale pink on stems about 1 m tall.

Hybrids between *Crinum* and *Amaryllis belladonna* are known as x *Crinodonna*. They have large attractive trumpets and long arching leaves.

CROCOSMIA
Iridaceae

This genus containing nine species, commonly known as montbretia, is centred in the eastern summer-rainfall region of South Africa. Most are summer growing and dormant in winter, although some can be evergreen. They are among the few summer-flowering bulbs suitable for mixing with the wide range of perennials which flower at this time. They are heavy feeders, responding well to the addition of manure to the soil, and they can be grown in full sun or partial shade.

C. x *crocosmiiflora* is a hybrid between *C. aurea* and *C. pottsii*, developed in France in the nineteenth century. It is extremely vigorous and has become a serious weed in many regions with warm climates, naturalising near streams and along roadsides. Numerous colours have been developed, mainly in orange-scarlet shades.

C. aurea var. *aurea* is less invasive and more attractive than *C.* x *crocosmiiflora* and should be more widely grown. Large star-shaped flowers of bright golden yellow appear in late summer, giving it the common name of falling stars. The flowers are carried on stems about 90 cm tall. It prefers a warm moist position in partial shade.

C. pottsii produces bright flowers in shades of orange or orange-yellow on stems up to 1.2 m tall. It grows and flowers in summer, and is easy in moisture-retentive soils.

C. masonorum produces flowers of brilliant scarlet-orange which are carried horizontally in spikes up to 75 cm tall. It thrives in moist well-drained situations and in some places has become a weed of roadsides. Grazing with goats is a good method of control.

Several named hybrids are available, and the following are ideal for cottage gardens and general garden use: 'Lucifer' has flowers of vibrant scarlet and comes true from seed. It is early flowering and has distinctive sword-like leaves. 'Spitfire' has orange blooms. 'Star of the East' has yellowish orange blooms and is very striking. 'Solfatare' is yellow with bronze foliage. 'Vulcan' produces an abundance of bright scarlet flowers.

CROCUS
Iridaceae

This is a large genus of mainly spring-flowering species which generally do best in regions with cold winters. There are also many species which flower in the autumn, and these are often more suitable for districts with warm climates. Most require good drainage, and heavy soils should have material such as coarse sand added before planting. Most species prefer full sun.

AUTUMN-FLOWERING SPECIES

C. serotinus ssp. *salzmannii* (syn. ·*C. salzmannii*) grows naturally on stony slopes in Spain and North Africa. Lilac-coloured flowers appear with the leaves in autumn. It is very adaptable and can be naturalised, thriving beneath deciduous trees. It is particularly reliable in warm districts, although unfortunately it is not fragrant.

Opposite, above: *Crocosmia* 'Vulcan'
Opposite below: *Crocosmia* 'Star of the East'

C. serotinus ssp. *clusii* is preferred by many crocus-lovers, producing fragrant blooms in shades of lilac with darker veining. These appear before the leaves in autumn.

C. serotinus ssp. *serotinus* is similar to the above but has leaves at flowering time.

C. banaticus (syn. *C. byzantinus*) is one of the few available species which prefer shady positions. Its flowers vary in colour from lilac to purple and are most attractive.

C. boryi has creamy white goblet-shaped flowers which are sometimes veined purple.

C. cancellatus grows on stony hillsides in Greece and Turkey. Its masses of small pale blue flowers are heavily veined with purple.

C. caspius is native to the shores of the Caspian Sea. Its flowers are soft greyish mauve or white with yellow anthers.

C. goulimyi has goblet-shaped flowers of white or soft lilac and multiplies readily.

C. hadriaticus has white flowers marked with purple outside.

C. kotschyanus ssp. *kotschyanus* is one of the best autumn-flowering species. The large blooms are lilac or mauve with a yellow throat and an orange band inside the petals. It can be grown in pots and multiplies freely when naturalised. 'Albus' is a lovely white-flowered form.

Several subspecies have been described. *C. kotschyanus* ssp. *leucopharynx* is commonly grown and particularly recommended. It produces blooms of deep mauve with white throats but without orange bands.

C. laevigatus has lilac-mauve blooms with yellow throats.

C. longiflorus has fragrant flowers of unusual colouring. The petals are pale violet outside and bluish inside with darker veins.

C. medius resembles *C. serotinus* ssp. *salzmannii*, producing rounded blooms of rich lilac-purple with darker veining.

C. niveus produces blooms in a stunning combination of pure white with golden throats and scarlet stigmas. It is one of the best species for pots or in a well-drained position in the garden.

C. nudiflorus has very large bright purple flowers. It tolerates damper soil than most and can be naturalised in grass, multiplying freely.

C. pulchellus has soft lavender blooms with dark veining and white anthers. It is suitable for naturalising in full sun or partial shade. 'Zephyr' has pearl-grey blooms which are white inside.

C. speciosus produces quite large flowers of mauve with darker veining which appear almost before the leaves emerge in autumn. It is one of the best and easiest of the autumn-flowering species, ideal for a rock garden. 'Oxonian' has bigger bolder flowers than is typical, in a good shade of blue.

SPRING-FLOWERING SPECIES

Crocus species which flower in spring can be depended upon to flower abundantly in regions with cold climates, but in warmer districts they do not generally flower as reliably. Large-flowered hybrids in particular often do not flower after their first season.

C. chrysanthus produces rounded flowers in a range of colours, usually in shades of golden yellow and often striped. It grows best in well-drained stony ground in full sun and is one of the better species for warm districts.

Numerous hybrids, particularly with *C. biflorus*, are available. These do well in dry sunny positions, especially where summers are dry. They generally have large flowers, often in unusual colour combinations with various markings. 'Cream Beauty' has lovely cream flowers with brownish markings outside at the base. 'Advance' has creamy yellow blooms flushed with mauve. 'Saturnus' is yellow with purplish markings. 'Snow Bunting' is creamy yellow with yellow centres.

C. biflorus is a variable species which has now been divided into 14 subspecies. Typically its blooms are in shades of lilac or blue. It thrives in dry stony ground. 'Fairy' is a pure white cultivar tinged with greyish shadings outside.

The following spring-flowering species are listed alphabetically.

C. angustifolius has bright blooms with brownish markings outside. It is known as cloth of gold and requires a sunny position.

C. corsicus has pale lilac flowers heavily flushed with purple, and unusual markings. It is very late flowering.

C. dalmaticus is a variable species with blooms in shades of lilac to lavender with yellow throats, which are usually veined.

C. flavus has rich orange-yellow flowers without markings. It is deservedly popular.

Crocus serotinus ssp. *salzmannii*

C. fleischeri grows naturally on dry rocky hillsides in Turkey. It can be difficult to grow but is very attractive. Its blooms are creamy white with purplish markings outside at the base, and it is one of the first to flower in spring.

C. korolkowii has blooms in an attractive shade of yellow with a maroon eye.

C. malyi has white blooms with yellow throats and orange styles.

C. minimus is a very good species for gardens and is one of the earliest to bloom in late winter. Its blooms are soft pink, paler inside with darker mauve-pink stripes towards the tips of the petals. It is an excellent rock garden subject and flowers reliably each year in warm districts.

C. pestalozzae is one of the smallest species, originating from Turkey. Its blooms are white or lilac-blue with yellow throats spotted with black.

C. sieberi ssp. *sieberi* has fragrant creamy white blooms with yellow eyes and purple markings outside.

C. sieberi ssp. *atticus* is a good subject for gardens and pots. The rounded blooms are usually soft lilac with lemon eyes. It is particularly tolerant of moist conditions.

C. sieberi ssp. *sublimis* has lustrous lilac-blue flowers, darker at the tips of the petals than at their base, with a golden eye.

C. sieberi ssp. *sublimis* f. *tricolor* has purple blooms with yellow throats and a white band in between.

Several named selections of *C. sieberi* are available. 'Firefly' and 'Violet Queen' are similar, with rounded flowers in shades of blue and golden throats. Both are good reliable garden subjects, tolerating moist soil conditions better than most.

C. tommasinianus is one of the best-known spring-flowering species and is very good for naturalising. Its blooms are silvery grey on the outside and pale lavender inside.

C. veluchensis has large blooms in various shades from lilac to deep purple. It multiplies freely once established.

C. vernus is a lovely species from the mountains of Europe. Many hybrids have been derived from it, producing a range of different flower colours and sizes. The true species has small lavender flowers which appear from winter until spring and is suitable for a well-drained rock garden.

CYCLAMEN
Primulaceae

This is a delightful genus of small plants native to Europe, Asia and North Africa. They have attractive heart-shaped leaves, dainty flowers and corky tubers. Most require partial shade and very good drainage, and they thrive beneath deciduous

trees. A collection of different species can provide flowers for most of the year.

C. hederifolium (syn. *C. neapolitanum*) is a native of southern Europe and Turkey. Its flowers vary in colour from pale to dark pink and pure white. Each flower contains five reflexing twisted petals, and some forms are scented. The blooms appear from early summer until autumn on stems 10–20 cm tall. The foliage can also vary; usually it is plain green but some forms have wonderful silver markings. Leaves are normally ivy-shaped but can be long or oval.

This species is perhaps the easiest of all to grow and is suitable for planting under trees, in rock gardens or in containers. It produces an amazing profusion of small blooms for a prolonged period. The foliage makes a very good ground-cover for about 10 months of the year, usually becoming dormant in early summer. Dormancy sometimes only occurs if conditions are dry at this time.

The corky tubers grow very large with time and can live for 50 years or more. Although they can be stored dry, it is better to replant them as soon as possible after lifting, which should be done during the short dormant period in early summer.

Self-sown seedlings frequently appear, often some considerable distance from the parent plant, the seed having been carried there by ants. The seed-pods ripen in late spring and summer and can be collected at this time. Seed should be sown on the surface of a well-drained mix and the seedlings covered with a fine layer of sand after germinating. Usually the first flowers will appear about 18 months after sowing.

Vine weevils can be a serious pest, eating all the roots and parts of the tubers. Mites can cause spotting of the flowers, and botrytis infection can spoil the flowers in cold wet weather.

Cultivars of this species include 'Album', which has white flowers sometimes with a flush of pink at the top. 'Pink Pearl' and 'White Pearl' are large-flowered selections.

C. africanum is native to Algeria. This species and *C. cilicium* are the earliest to flower in autumn. *C. africanum* resembles *C. hederifolium* but has slightly larger flowers and large leaves, which are generally less patterned. It is also less hardy to

cold. The nodding flowers are lilac-pink with maroon at their mouth and appear on 10 cm tall stems before the leaves in autumn. It is an ideal subject for planting under trees, in rock gardens or in containers. Plants grown from seed take 12–18 months to commence flowering.

C. cilicium is an early-flowering species from Turkey. The tiny nodding lilac-pink flowers appear on 5 cm tall stems in autumn before the leaves emerge. The foliage is green or grey-green with grey and darker blotches, reddish purple beneath. 'Album' is a white-flowered selection.

C. coum originates from the Middle East, where it grows naturally in a wide range of habitats. Flower colour varies, including carmine-red, various shades of pink, and white. The flowers appear throughout winter until spring and are carried on short stems about 3–10 cm in length. The foliage is also variable, ranging from dark green to forms with various silver patterns. It is an ideal subject for rock gardens and pots.

In recent years many new forms of *C. coum* have become available, mainly through the Cyclamen Society in Great Britain, and there has been a resultant upsurge in the popularity of these plants. They thrive in warm climates, naturalising and seeding freely in suitable situations. The small tubers should be planted about 3 cm below the surface of well-drained soil. Seedlings can commence flowering two years after sowing.

C. graecum is native to Southern Turkey and Greece. In mid-summer it produces flowers in shades from pale pink to deep carmine, with two maroon blotches at their base. Some forms have scented flowers, and plant size is variable. Smaller forms carry their blooms on 7 cm stems, and larger forms have stems about 15 cm tall. The foliage is velvety green with silver markings. *C. graecum* thrives in heat, growing naturally in open scrub on rocky hillsides. It flowers best when it receives a dry period followed by rain, the flowers emerging about two weeks after becoming moist. It is a good subject for a rock garden or pots. The tubers are usually round and corky, and about 20 cm across. They should be planted on top of the soil or to about half their depth. Plants grown from seed take about three years to begin flowering.

C. libanoticum is a species from Lebanon and Syria which is now rare in the wild. Flower colour varies from soft pink to carmine, with darker

Opposite, below: *Cyclamen persicum*
Opposite above: *Cyclamen hederifolium* 'Album'

dove-shaped markings. The flowers are carried on 10 cm tall stems from mid-winter until early spring. They have an unusual but not overpowering mousey scent. The foliage is soft green with pale greyish markings. The flowers are very large in comparison to the small 3 cm tubers, which should be planted about 2 cm below the soil surface. Plants take about two years to flower when grown from seed.

C. persicum is an eastern Mediterranean species. It produces dainty flowers of soft pink or white on stems 15–30 cm in height. The flowers appear in winter, and many forms are sweetly scented. The foliage also grows up to about 30 cm tall and is green with silver markings. All modern hybrids have been raised from this species. It is best grown in pots or in a partially shaded position in a rock garden. The tubers are long-lived and in time form clumps which produce several hundred blooms in a good season. They also produce an abundance of seed, which is best sown into a sandy mix as soon as it ripens. Seedlings should be potted on when two leaves have developed, and they will commence flowering in about 12 months.

C. rohlfsianum is an extremely rare species from Libya, with flowers varying from pale pink to dark rose-pink, carried on 10 cm long stems in summer. The broad green foliage is kidney shaped, often with lobes and silver markings. Leaves are usually reddish purple underneath. This species is best grown in pots of well-drained potting mix with limestone added. The pots should be placed in a sunny position. As the tubers age they become very knobbly and uneven. Often these knobs will produce shoots which, when removed with a sharp knife, will form new plants. Even when the flowers are hand pollinated they usually set little seed. Plants grown from seed take three or more years to commence flowering.

CYPELLA
Iridaceae

Cypella is closely related to *Alophia, Herbertia, Gelasine* and *Tigridia*. Another relative, *Hesperoxiphion,* is included here.

Cypella contains about 20 species, originating from Central and South America. Most species are evergreen with sword-like ribbed foliage resembling that of a *Tigridia*. Each flower lasts only one or two days, but an abundance is produced in succession over a long period. The bulbs are usually brightly coloured and generally prefer a sunny position in well-drained soil.

C. herbertii is the species most commonly grown. Its flower colour is variable, often soft orange or buff-yellow with purplish markings around the cup-shaped centres. The flowers have an interesting shape, their three petals broad and rounded at the tips and narrower towards the base. It has a prolonged flowering period, often from spring until autumn. Although not particularly showy, it is a good background plant and provides welcome colour in summer. This is the most easily grown and hardiest species, and generally produces numerous self-sown seedlings. It tolerates full sun but when grown in partial shade can reach 1 m tall, and the flowers do not become bleached.

C. herbertii ssp. *brevicristata* has pure golden yellow blooms. It flowers over the same period as the typical species, although not generally as abundantly, and generally does not grow as tall.

C. aquatilis is a native of Brazil, where it grows along streams and on river-banks. Large open cup-shaped flowers of golden yellow appear in summer. In full bloom it makes the best display of any of the yellow-flowered species. It should be grown near water and should never be allowed

Cypella herbertii

80

Cypella peruvianum

CYRTANTHUS
Amaryllidaceae

This is a large genus native to South Africa, where various species are found growing in a wide range of habitats. These include damp bushy stream-edges, as epiphytes on other plants, and in near-desert conditions. Some species possibly require fire to trigger flowering in the wild.

These are mainly plants for containers, although some species will grow in well-drained soil in the dappled light beneath trees.

Flowers vary in shape from star-like to tubular, and they can be white, pink, red, orange or yellow. The grey or green strap-like leaves vary in width from narrow to quite wide.

C. elatus is the most widely grown species, still much better known under its old name of *Vallota speciosa*. It is also known by several common names, the misleading Scarborough lily being the most popular. It requires good drainage, preferring a position in partial shade. It is a popular cut flower and pot plant, and is one of the easiest species to grow. A few other species adapt well to cultivation, but the requirements of many are so exacting that they will only ever be collectors items.

to dry out. This is the only species to produce pups on its stems.

C. armosa is not the showiest species, but its soft yellow blooms are very attractive. They have an interesting tight form rather than the typical open vase shape, and distinctive pendulous falls. It grows 30 cm tall and is suitable for pots or gardens.

C. osteniana has white flowers. It grows during winter, reaching about 30 cm tall.

C. coelestis (called *Phalocallis coelestis* by some authorities) is one of the few species which dies down in winter. It is also one of the tallest, sometimes reaching 1.2 m. It flowers prolifically in late summer, producing greyish blue blooms with bluish cream markings and yellowish spots. It is robust and very easy. It is also known as *C. plumbea* and is distributed in New Zealand erroneously as *Herbertia platensis*.

C. peruviana, also known as *Hesperoxiphion peruvianum*, is a species from Peru. It differs from other species in having hairs on the inner segments of the flowers. Its bright yellow or orange flowers with reddish dots or lines are up to 8 cm across and appear on 45 cm long stems in summer and early winter. It has the unusual characteristic of producing a flush of bloom every few days, with few flowers appearing between flushes. It is a good garden subject for warm districts but is best grown in pots in colder regions.

C. herrerae (syn. *Hesperoxiphion herrerae*) produces flowers of violet-blue and yellow during summer on stems to about 50 cm.

C. huilense produces white flowers blotched with purplish brown on stems up to 50 cm tall.

Cyrtanthus elatus

Well-drained garden loam or potting mix will suit the following evergreen species:

C. brachyscyphus, orange-red.
C. breviflorus, yellow.
C. mackenii, many colours.
C. sanguineus, red shades, good subject for hanging baskets.

Evergreen types require a short resting period in winter, and water should be withheld without allowing the growing medium to become too dry.

C. guthrieae is a beautiful but rare species from the Cape Province, with flowers in reddish shades. It requires excellent drainage and should be planted in a sandy mix and grown in a semi-shaded position. Sometimes the bulbs remain dormant during the growing season.

C. herrei has large grey evergreen leaves and produces pale orange pendulous flowers in late summer. The huge bulbs require a very sandy soil, semi-shade, and will not tolerate over-watering.

C. obliquus has large twisted grey evergreen foliage and carries orange-yellow-green pendant flowers in spring. It requires high light or full sun and resents over-watering.

C. falcatus blooms in spring from dormant bulbs. The pendant 6 cm long flowers are pale pinkish red and yellow. Broad soft green leaves appear just after flowering.

Many hybrids of great beauty are also available. 'Red Prince' is an easily grown cultivar which multiplies readily and is suitable for gardens or containers. Scented scarlet flowers, ideal for picking, appear abundantly each spring.

Propagation is usually from bulbils, divisions or the black-winged seeds. These should be sown as soon as they are ripe, covered lightly with sand and kept at about 20°C.

The major insect pests are bulb fly, spider mites, thrips and mealy bug. Virus infections are also frequent.

DAHLIA
Asteraceae

DAHLIA SPECIES

Dahlias have established themselves as favourites around the world, but until recently gardeners were interested mainly in hybrids. *D. imperialis* and *D. merckii* are the only two species commonly

Cyrtanthus 'Red Prince'

grown. However, other dahlia species are starting to become available, and are likely to be popular in future. The simplicity of their flower form suits the informal garden styles popular today.

There are about 30 species, which originate from Central America, primarily Mexico. They are usually found in mountainous areas in stony well-drained ground. In cultivation their major requirements are good drainage and full sunlight. They respond vigorously if organic matter is added to the soil prior to planting. Where soils are heavy, raising the planting site with extra topsoil will improve drainage and growth. Species usually sprout later in spring than modern hybrids, and their flowering commences and ends later in the season. Although their blooms are single, they have a lustrous sheen, and the contrast with their central discs is often most appealing.

D. coccinea is the only species to be widely distributed in Mexico, and it is believed to be one of the parents of the modern hybrids. It is extremely variable, flower colour alone ranging through intense scarlet, deep red, apricot, orange and yellow shades. Foliage also varies, although usually the leaves are small and attractive. It has also been found that both diploid and tetraploid forms exist, the tetraploids typically being more robust with larger flowers. Because of their variability, it is necessary to select horticulturally superior forms for garden use. One of the main considerations is the width of the ray florets (petals), those which are broad and overlap one another generally being most satisfactory. Its tuberous roots are usually very long and often skinny.

Two forms of *D. coccinea* are particularly worth obtaining. The scarlet colouring of some is as intense as any in nature, contrasting strikingly with the golden yellow central discs. Because the single blooms are relatively small, usually about 5 cm across, they are never overwhelming despite their brightness. What the flowers lack in size they make up for in numbers, decorating the plants for months from mid-summer. Generally plant height is about 1.5 m, but plants less than 1 m tall occur. A real feature of the best forms is their finely divided dark green foliage. Attractive combinations can be made with *Gaura lindheimeri*, *Coreopsis verticillata* and *Hemerocallis* 'Green Flutter'.

Vigorous forms with yellow flowers are also valuable garden plants, combining perfectly with

Dahlia coccinea

other perennials at the back of cottage gardens. The combination of rich yellow ray florets and golden discs is an eye-catching sight. Many vigorous forms with yellow blooms occur, usually reaching about 1.8 m tall, with flowers more than 6 cm across. *Artemisia* 'Powis Castle' and *Epilobium canum* make stunning companions.

D. pinnata is believed to be the other parent of the modern dahlia. It has relatively large single blooms, usually 8 cm or more across. Flower colour is variable, mainly in shades of mauve. A promiscuous species which crosses freely, its hybrid offspring produce flowers in a wide colour range. As a garden plant it has considerable merit, with its large bold blooms produced abundantly for months throughout summer. The large dark green leaves are serrated along the margins, and the brown stems are usually covered with fine hairs. The tuberous roots tend to be fatter than those of *D. coccinea*. Plant height is generally about 1.5 m. Dwarf asters make most appealing companions.

D. merckii is becoming very popular, its small gracefully nodding blooms carried on long willowy stems above attractive finely divided foliage, making it the perfect cottage garden subject. Usually the flower colour is mauve-pink or lilac, becoming paler as the blooms age. Forms with white flowers also occur. Flowering commences in mid-summer and continues unabated until autumn. At the Auckland Regional Botanic Gardens plants have often reached 1.8 m tall, but this is considered unusual. Compact forms have been selected which do not usually exceed 1 m. These are more acceptable in smaller gardens and make ideal subjects for large containers. This species combines in the garden with almost anything. Because its chromosome number differs from any other species of dahlia, plants grown from seed always come true. It tolerates more cold than any other species. Particularly effective combinations can be made with *Salvia leucantha* and *Tradescantia* cultivars.

A little-known species which deserves greater attention is *D. australis*. Although it is somewhat variable, most forms make handsome garden subjects. The single blooms are about 4.5 cm across, and the ray florets are in vibrant shades of mauve-purple. It is the central disc florets that are most distinctive, usually black and looking stunning when the outer ring of florets produce their golden pollen. Flowering commences in mid- or late summer but continues well into the winter months. Its dark green leathery foliage and compact habit are other features. It dies back later in winter and forms shorter tuberous roots than most species. Plant height is normally about 60–90 cm. It associates well with most perennials, especially *Nepeta* x *faassenii* and *Salvia microphylla* var. *neurepia*.

D. dissecta is bound to become popular when widely available. The flowers are exquisite, almost white with a blush of softest pink. The pointed ray florets slightly overlap, contrasting with golden discs. The blooms appear from mid-summer until autumn on slender stems which sway in the slightest breeze. The most striking feature of this species is its foliage—small, finely cut and dark glossy green. Plant height is about 80 cm.

D. sherffii is a variable species, typically with small pendulous flowers in mauve shades with contrasting golden discs. The plants are usually 80 cm–1.2 m in height, with pale green foliage and often rather sprawling in habit. It is interesting rather than beautiful, as is *D. tubulata*, a variable species that is usually taller and later to flower. The pendulous flowers are normally pale mauve with yellow discs and are carried on long twisted willowy stems. It requires especially good drainage, being very prone to root disease in heavy wet soil. Neither of the above species typically produces healthy vigorous tuberous roots.

Two tree species are also obtainable, *D. imperialis* being the best known. Often exceeding 3 m and sometimes reaching 10 m in height, its large impressive pendulous blooms appear from early winter. These are usually mauve, but white forms

Dahlia imperialis

are occasionally seen. Once flowering is completed, the plants are best cut back to near ground-level.

D. tenuicaulis is perhaps superior for garden use. The pendulous deep lilac flowers are smaller and appear just as *D. imperialis* is finishing. The narrow leathery dark green leaves adorn numerous erect 3 m tall woody canes. Although it is evergreen, pruning hard back after flowering will restrict plant size and ensure maximum flowering. This species is a real feature against buildings or at the rear of gardens, providing welcome colour at a time when little else is flowering. Both tree species require a long growing season and are unsuitable where winters are severe.

Although several *Dahlia* species hybridise, the modern cultivars are derived from only two species, *D. coccinea* and *D. pinnata*. These arrived at the Royal Botanic Gardens in Madrid in 1789, where they are believed to have first crossed. Subsequent crossing of the offspring of this initial pairing resulted in the array of forms now available. Today about 20,000 cultivars are registered with the Royal Horticultural Society.

Crossing *D. pinnata* with *D. coccinea* produces some unpredictable but often useful results. Flower colour can be anything from soft reds to shades of violet, yellow or gold; many bi-colours also occur. Usually the flowers are single and quite large, closest in size to *D. pinnata*. Interestingly, even the F1 hybrids often display some contortion of the ray florets, such as the petal edges rolling either inwards or outwards. It is this modification of the shape of the ray florets which eventually led to the array of flower forms produced by modern hybrids.

A worthwhile cross is *D. australis* x *D. coccinea*. Although the results are variable, most of the seedlings produced are attractive. They range in height from 80 cm to 1.2 m. Flower colours include numerous shades of red, violet and even brown. Often the discs are black with distinctively golden anthers. One wonders what today's dahlia cultivars would look like if species such as *D. australis* had been used as parents sometime in the last two hundred years.

Dahlia seed generally germinates freely, although modern cultivars produce extremely variable offspring. Only a tiny proportion of these are worth retaining. The simplest breeding technique is to grow small blocks of selected parents in isolation, allowing bees to carry out the pollination. As most dahlias are self-incompatible, any seed which is produced is almost certainly hybrid. Although many dahlias will flower throughout summer, seed production is heaviest in late summer and autumn. Seed is harvested and stored during winter then sown the following spring. Seedlings should be evaluated on several occasions and any deemed not worthwhile culled.

Dahlias with double flowers set considerably less seed than those with single or semi-double flowers which expose their reproductive disc florets. For this reason seed-lines which produce double-flowered plants have been difficult to develop. Dahlia species generally set copious quantities of seed.

The most common disease to afflict plants in summer is powdery mildew. This is a particular problem late in the season, and one or two well-timed sprays with fungicide can prolong flowering by several weeks. Species not generally attacked by powdery mildew include *D. merkii*, *D. dissecta*, *D. imperialis* and *D. tenuicaulis*. Some forms of *D. coccinea* and *D. australis* are not usually affected but others are very prone. *D. pinnata*, *D. sherffii* and *D. tubulata* generally become heavily infected if not sprayed.

MODERN DAHLIAS

DWARF DAHLIAS FROM SEED

Growing dahlias from seed is the quickest and most convenient method of producing large numbers of plants. Seed companies have developed many dwarf strains, which are usually offered as seedlings in punnets or small pots by garden centres. Considerable developments have occurred with these strains in recent times, with particular emphasis on extreme dwarfness and early flowering. Traditionally only mixed colours have been available, but seed-lines which produce flowers in single colours are now obtainable. As yet no dwarf seed strain which produces fully double blooms is available. The only seed strain available which produces predominantly fully double blooms is 'Showpiece', developed by Dr Keith Hammett of Auckland. The plants are tall, however, but work is continuing to reduce the height of this strain.

Dwarf seed strains are usually best treated as annuals, although they form tubers which can be retained for subsequent seasons. Seed can be sown in early spring for planting out in early summer. Dwarf dahlias are suitable for bedding, edging perennial borders and for containers. Their spent blooms must be removed regularly to produce a long flowering period. With such a profusion of small blooms being produced, this can be a time-consuming and laborious chore.

'Unwins Dwarf' was the first seed strain to become available, and it has been popular and widely grown for many decades, but it has now been largely superseded by newer developments.

'Figaro', developed in Holland by Royal Sluis, is one of the best modern strains. It is grown in huge numbers in Europe in pots and punnets. The plants are often treated with growth retardants to keep them compact and to induce early flowering. 'Figaro' seedlings reach about 30 cm tall when grown in gardens, and semi-double blooms in a range of colours are produced when the plants are very young. Work is progressing to produce separate colours in this strain, and white and yellow are currently available.

'Rigoletto', the predecessor of 'Figaro' from the same seed company, is slightly taller and commences flowering a few days later.

The 'Sunny' strain, bred in Japan, produces compact plants which flower freely in a range of bright colours. The blooms are semi-double, and separate colours are now available.

'Redskin' is a popular strain with bronze leaves, which provide an attractive background for the brightly coloured blooms. The colour of the foliage varies in the intensity of its colour, but almost invariably some bronze pigmentation occurs. Plant height varies, usually reaching about 40 cm when grown in the garden.

'Diablo' is a recent bronze-leaved introduction which is more dwarf and earlier flowering than 'Redskin'.

'Coltness' is a single-flowered strain which was introduced in about 1922 but which has now been largely superseded.

'Romeo' is smaller and more uniform in size, and is available in several separate colours.

Dwarf dahlias with single flowers are known as mignons. 'Mini Mignon' has a very dwarf habit and flowers freely in a range of bright colours.

Seed strains which produce blooms of collerette form are also available. 'Dandy' was one of the first to be developed but has now been largely replaced by more compact strains such as 'Harlequin'.

A recent innovation is the 'Dahlietta', developed by Royal Sluis of Holland. Ultra-dwarf forms of 'Figaro' have been selected and reproduced clonally by tissue culture. It is now being widely grown, especially in Europe and North America.

SHOW AND GARDEN CULTIVARS

Modern show and garden dahlias exhibit wide diversity, especially in the size and shape of their blooms, as a result of breeding and selection since the early 1800s. The development of today's sophisticated modern hybrids from such simple wild species has been a remarkable achievement. Selected cultivars must be reproduced vegetatively, usually by cuttings or by division of the tubers, to remain true to type.

Most of the breeding work has been undertaken by dahlia enthusiasts whose objective has been to produce superior blooms for the show bench. While this has resulted in near perfection in bloom quality, it has not necessarily produced cultivars which perform well as general garden subjects. The focus of much of the recent breeding work being undertaken by Dr Keith Hammett, in association with the Auckland Regional Botanic Gardens, has been to improve garden performance. The objectives of this programme include reducing plant height, improving foliage appearance, and increasing the abundance and duration of flowering. Cultivars with these characteristics now available still produce blooms of high quality. These are ideal for mixing with perennials or shrubs, and in suitable conditions and with correct treatment they can be maintained in peak flower throughout summer and autumn.

As with other members of the daisy family, each bloom is in fact an inflorescence. Each inflorescence is composed of showy ray florets, which are usually sterile, and an inner cluster of fertile disc florets, which are usually golden yellow. The purpose of the ray florets is to attract pollinators, and they are commonly referred to as petals.

Cultivars are classified by dahlia societies according to the size and form of their blooms.

Dahlia 'Keith H.'

This ensures that blooms of similar type are compared with one another in competitions. A brief description of the main categories follows:

DECORATIVE DAHLIAS have fully double blooms with concealed central disc florets. The ray florets are either flat or slightly incurved (involute).

BALL DAHLIAS are ball-shaped and have involute ray florets, giving them a honeycomb appearance.

POMPON DAHLIAS are miniature ball dahlias.

CACTUS DAHLIAS have double blooms with pointed ray florets which are revolute (curve or roll backwards). This gives the flower-heads a quilled appearance. When the ray florets are revolute at their tips but are flat at their base they are known as semi-cactus dahlias.

WATERLILY DAHLIAS (or nymphaea-flowered) have fully double blooms with relatively few broad ray florets, which are usually flat or slightly incurved. This results in flower-heads which are quite flat and shallow.

SINGLE-FLOWERED DAHLIAS have a single row of outer florets and a prominent cluster of central disc florets.

COLLERETTE DAHLIAS resemble single dahlias but their central disc is surrounded by an inner ring of small ray florets. These are often a different colour to the larger outer ring of ray florets.

Other categories have also been identified but are less common than those described above. Dahlias are further classified according to the size and colour of their individual blooms. Another characteristic of some is fimbriation (laciniation), which is when the ray florets are split at the tips.

Tubers should be planted in late spring once the soil has warmed. The planting site should be well drained, and the beds can be raised if necessary by adding topsoil or gritty material. Organic matter such as compost is also beneficial if worked into the soil prior to planting. Lime should be added to acid soils. Dahlias should be grown in a warm sunny position sheltered from strong winds.

Tubers should be planted so that the eyes at the base of the old stems are just below ground-level.

It is advisable to stake dahlias at planting time (see Cultivation, Supporting Tall Bulbs). When the tubers sprout, a thick layer of organic mulch should be spread over the beds. This can be allowed to build up around the base of the new shoots, encouraging them to produce roots into the mulching material.

Baits should be laid to protect shoots from damage by slugs and snails, and fertiliser should be applied around the base of the plants as they come into growth. If necessary, the new shoots should have their growing tips removed to encourage a dense, compact habit. During the flowering season, spent blooms should be removed regularly to encourage continuous flowering.

Occasional spraying will maintain healthy plants. The major pests are caterpillars, thrips and mites. The worst foliage diseases are powdery mildew and smut. Several combination sprays available will control most pests and diseases. Many of these sprays do not, however, provide satisfactory mite control; if necessary, a miticide can be added to the spray mix (see Pests and Diseases).

If lifting the tubers in winter, the plants should be allowed to die back naturally at the end of the season so that the tubers are well nourished before storage. In early winter, when the old stems and leaves have dried off, the plants can be cut back and the tubers lifted. Tubers should be stored in a position protected from frosts and winter rainfall, in a medium such as sawdust or sand which remains slightly moist so that they do not shrivel. If necessary the tubers can be dipped in fungicidal or insecticidal solutions prior to storage.

Dahlia 'Zomerzon'

Any tubers showing signs of soft rot should be cut off and discarded.

Cultivars can be propagated by cuttings taken from new growth. Tubers can be potted in late winter into a well-drained mix and placed in a heated glasshouse to force new shoots into growth. Soft cuttings containing about three nodes will rapidly form roots and produce green plants which are ready for planting in early summer.

Another method of propagating dahlia cultivars avoids the necessity to sprout tubers in winter and spring. Cuttings can be taken in late summer from healthy shoots and placed in a sandy mix. Once rooted, the plants require extended day length using artificial lighting to prevent them from becoming dormant in winter. This can be simply achieved by using standard incandescent lights controlled by a timer. The lighting should commence in early evening and continue for a period which provides a total day length of about 16 hours. In this environment the cutting-grown plants will retain their foliage. A heated greenhouse is preferable, especially where winters are cold. The plants should be kept only slightly moist until late winter, at which time additional water and fertiliser can be applied to encourage new growth. If required, extra cuttings can be harvested from the new shoots which emerge.

DIERAMA
Iridaceae

Dierama is a South African genus of about 25 species. It is closely related to *Ixia* but does not go dormant. The main feature of most species is their long arching spikes of pendulous flowers, which wave in the slightest breeze and look superb near water. The flowers are bell-shaped and appear over a long period. Well-drained soil which is kept moist in spring and summer is ideal. The clumps resent division and should be left undisturbed once established. Growth is most vigorous during summer.

D. pulcherrimum grows naturally in rich damp meadows in South Africa. Flower colour is usually purplish to carmine-red and occasionally white. The pendulous bell-shaped blooms appear from

Dierama pendulum

summer until autumn on arching stems up to 2 m tall. Although it looks particularly striking planted near water, the soil should never become waterlogged. Rich well-drained soil and full sun are ideal. It forms dense clumps of evergreen leaves which are best thinned out rather than cut hard back when they become overly congested. Seed germinates freely and is the best method of increase. Sections can be separated off the clumps in winter, but these take about 12 months to recover and recommence flowering.

Several cultivars have been selected, but few are currently available. 'Album' has pure white blooms. Hybrids with *D. pumilum* have also been produced, generally intermediate in height between the parents.

D. pendulum is similar to *D. pulcherrimum*, although not so tall and with smaller flowers of a different shape. Its blooms are whitish to pink and purple, and are carried on stems about 1 m tall. *D. pendulum* 'Album' is a white-flowered form.

D. cooperi is a smallish upright species with apricot-pink blooms in spring on stems up to 1 m tall.

D. igneum has mauve-pink blooms which deepen in colour with age. They are carried on stems about 1.2 m tall during spring and early summer.

D. pumilum is another smallish species, with white or yellowish blooms carried on stems usually less than 1 m tall in late summer.

ERYTHRONIUM
Liliaceae

This genus contains about 20 species, most of which are native to the west coast of the United States. All have delightful nodding flowers, and their foliage is often spotted. They thrive in shady positions in rich soils containing plenty of humus. Most species dislike warm humid climates, growing best in cooler regions where the summers are relatively dry. If the corms are lifted, they should be replanted as soon as possible and not allowed to dry out.

E. dens-canis is a European native known as the dog's tooth violet, a reference to the shape of the corms. Flower colour varies from purplish to rose and white. The pendulous blooms resemble those of cyclamen and are carried on 15 cm stems in spring. The green foliage is mottled with white or purple and forms an attractive ground-cover for a short time.

It enjoys a position beneath deciduous trees, requiring moisture when in growth and cool dry conditions in summer. In nature it grows in rich soil in woodlands, meadows and rocky places, often forming large drifts, which make a wonderful sight when in full bloom. The tubers can be divided when dormant, and plants grown from seed will flower after about four years. Slugs and snails are the major pest. Cultivars of this species include 'Pink Perfection', 'Rose Beauty', 'Purple King' and 'White Splendour'.

E. hendersonii is a native of Oregon and California, and is known as trout lily. The flowers vary in colour from dark to pale pink, and they appear in spring on stems about 20 cm tall. The leaves are soft green and mottled with purple. It prefers well-drained soil which is moist in spring when it is flowering and dry during summer. It is a good subject for pots and for garden use, and is most effective when planted in large drifts beneath deciduous trees.

E. californicum is native to California and is one of the easiest species to grow. The flowers are in shades of yellow with orange-yellow markings at the base, and they appear on stems about 25 cm tall in spring. The leaves are mottled with purple. It is a good subject for pots and shady positions in gardens. The corms should be planted as soon as possible after purchase or lifting.

E. revolutum 'White Beauty' is an easily grown and popular form of this dwarf species. It grows about 15 cm tall and the foliage is marbled with green and maroon. The flowers are creamy white with maroon markings in the centre.

Erythronium revolutum 'White Beauty'

EUCHARIS
Amaryllidaceae

This genus contains only a few species, native to tropical South America. They have highly scented white flowers and attractive glossy green leaves. They are suitable for growing outdoors only in very warm climates and are often grown in pots in greenhouses in cooler regions.

E. x grandiflora is native to Colombia and is most commonly grown. The white flowers are very fragrant, carried on stems about 50 cm tall. Winter is the main flowering period in the wild, and the plants must be kept warm at this time. Plants grown commercially for cut flowers can be induced to bloom at intervals throughout the year by controlling temperature. Flowering can also be induced by withholding water for about three months, although fewer flowers are produced using this method. The glossy dark green foliage is very handsome.

Eucharis x *grandiflora*

Generally, it is best to grow the plants in pots, using a well-drained mix. If necessary the bulbs can be stored dry during the cooler months. The bulbs produce numerous offsets, which can be separated and will reach flowering size in about two years. Seed should be sown on the surface and the temperature maintained at about 25°C. Pests include mealy bug, mites and bulb fly. Cold wet conditions can result in the bulbs rotting.

EUCOMIS
Hyacinthaceae

This is a genus of about 10 species from tropical and South Africa, most of which are summer growing. Many are now rare in the wild. The flowers appear in distinctive pineapple-like spikes which usually have a tuft of leaves at their tip, giving rise to the common name pineapple flower. Often the weight of the flowers is so great that their stems collapse. Generally the flowering period is extended, usually in summer, and the fruits which follow are also decorative. Several species are ideal for naturalising in large colonies,

forming a dense effective ground-cover in either full sun or partial shade. They prefer rich well-drained soils and seldom require lifting. The flowers are very good for picking.

E. comosa var. *comosa* (syn. *E. punctata* and *E. pallidiflora*) is a distinctive species from the Cape Province and Natal. The flowers vary in colour, usually greenish yellow with purplish ovaries, and they are sweetly scented. Forms which have pinkish to reddish purple flowers are probably hybrids, possibly with *E. bicolor*. Flowering continues for several months from mid-summer. The plants remain attractive once flowering is finished and the fruit develops, but the stems are particularly prone to collapsing at this stage. The flowers are carried on stems up to 1 m tall and are popular for large floral arrangements. The tuft of leaves at the tip of each flower-spike is inconspicuous in this species. The stems and foliage are often spotted with purple. Increase is usually by separating offsets when the plants are dormant in winter, although seed germinates freely.

E. pole-evansii has a distinctive cluster of leaves carried at the tip of each flower-spike. This is the tallest species, sometimes reaching up to 2 m, and the wide-opening flowers are bright green and

appear for a long period from mid-summer. Once flowering is completed, the greenish fruits are most attractive.

E. autumnalis ssp. *autumnalis* (syn. *E. undulata*) is an easily grown species from South Africa and Zimbabwe. The green flowers become a paler yellowish green as they age and appear on stems about 45 cm tall in late summer and autumn.

E. autumnalis ssp. *clavata* is similar to ssp. *autumnalis* but has larger flowers and undulating foliage.

E. bicolor is a small species from Natal which resembles *E. autumnalis* ssp. *clavata*. Green flowers with purple edgings are carried in spikes about 60 cm tall during mid- and late summer.

E. zambesiaca is a smallish species from tropical East Africa. Its flowers are white or greenish and appear in summer.

EUCROSIA
Amaryllidaceae

Eucrosia are unusual bulbs from South America. Their natural habitat is generally in areas that have seasonally dry periods, but some also grow in mountain rainforests. They have very long stamens which are up to three times the length of the flowers, giving them a unique beauty. They require the same growing conditions as *Phaedranassa*.

E. bicolor occurs in coastal forests and has a short growing season. The flowers emerge before the leaves on stems which are about 35 cm long. The flowers are orange-red with long yellow stamens. After flowering the green leaves emerge. The large bulbs soon form clumps, which should be divided while dormant every second season. They are best grown in pots.

E. aurantiaca occurs naturally in drier areas. The bulbs can become quite large. The flowers are mostly a nice rich lemon-yellow shade, and the long stamens are green. A pink-flowered form also occurs. It requires well-drained sandy soil to be grown successfully.

Opposite, above: *Eucomis comosa* hybrids
Opposite, below: *Eucrosia bicolor*

FERRARIA
Iridaceae

The flowers of these unusual bulbs from South Africa in many ways resemble starfish. Their crisp-edged stars occur in a range of unusual dusky shades of brown, yellow, violet and blue, and the scent can be reminiscent of carrion or sweet almond. They are easy bulbs to grow, although all except *F. crispa* can be difficult to obtain. They enjoy loamy soil in sun or semi-shade, but uncommon species are best grown in pots or containers to ensure success. They will grow in exposed coastal conditions, standing up to salt winds extremely well. The hard flat corms

Ferraria crispa

93

soon build up into large clumps. Even very old corms will produce new shoots when divided and replanted 15 cm deep in early autumn. Seed sown in pots of sandy mix and covered with 2 cm of grit soon produce seedlings, which take about three years to commence flowering. Corms can be stored dry over summer or left in the soil. No pests or diseases usually occur.

F. crispa from the Cape Province has greyish leaves 30–50 cm long and flower-stems 40–70 cm tall. Purplish brown crispy star-shaped flowers are about 5 cm across and produce an unpleasant odour.

F. divaricata ssp. *divaricata* (syn. *F. antherosa*) is about 10–15 cm tall, with sweetly scented soft greenish and blue flowers.

F. uncinata is 20 cm tall, with sweetly scented orange-yellow and green stars with blue blotches. It requires very sandy soil.

FREESIA
Iridaceae

This is a genus containing up to 19 species, which are native mainly to the southern Cape region of South Africa. They grow during winter and become dormant in summer, and many are particularly suitable for naturalising in regions with warm climates. Bulbs should be planted out in late summer and autumn into a sunny position in well-drained soil. They are effective in large groups at the front of borders, in rock gardens and in containers. Many hybrids are available with large flowers in a wide colour range, and these are very popular cut flowers.

F. sparrmannii (syn. *F. alba*) is an easily grown species suitable for small gardens and containers. The flowers are white tinged with purple, especially outside, and the lower petals have a golden yellow blotch. Although the flowers are not particularly showy individually, they are produced so prolifically that they make a great display. The length of the flower-stems ranges from about 20 to 40 cm, and peak flowering is from early spring.

F. corymbosa is a variable species with stems up to 50 cm long. The flowers are usually pale yellow with orange-yellow markings; an attractive pink

form is also available. Its main virtue is its fragrance, which is most noticeable in the evening. It is not the easiest species to cultivate, lacking the vigour of some.

F. leichtlinii grows naturally in sandy soil in the southern Cape region. Flower colour can vary from cream to purple, usually creamy with yellow inside the petals and a purplish flush outside. The flowers are very fragant and are carried on stems about 20 cm long. It is suitable for a rock garden or pots.

F. refracta has greenish yellow blooms flushed with mauve and marked with orange. These appear on stems 15–45 cm long during late winter and early spring.

F. fergusoniae is a pretty little species which produces small sweetly scented blooms on stems up to 20 cm long in spring. Flower colour is a lovely soft yellow with orange markings inside the petals and a purplish flush outside. It is easy to grow in well-drained soil.

F. elimensis is very similar to *F. fergusoniae*.

F. 'Burtonii' is a vigorous free-flowering New Zealand-raised selection which is great for massed garden display and for picking. Fragrant white flowers with yellow markings inside the lower petals are produced abundantly for two months from early spring. This cultivar is particularly notable for the absence of any purplish markings on its flowers.

Numerous hybrids have been raised, mainly derived from *F. corymbosa*. Many of these large-flowered hybrids have lost their scent, and some can grow 80 cm tall. Several varieties with double flowers in shades of cream, blue, lavender-blue, red and yellow are obtainable. They generally have short stems and become readily infected with virus disease, which reduces their vigour. 'Cream Beauty' is scented and robust, and is one of the best of these double-flowered forms.

'Super Emerald' is regarded as the best seed-raised strain for cut-flower production. Flowers in a wide range of colours are carried on long stems. Flowering can commence eight months after sowing the seed, and successive sowings can produce blooms for harvest at any time of the year. Commercial cut-flower production is almost exclusively in greenhouses.

Opposite, above: *Freesia* 'Burtonii'
Opposite, below: *Freesia* 'Super Emerald'

FRITILLARIA
Liliaceae

The common names for *Fritillaria* are snake's-head fritillary and crown imperial. These bulbs have a wide distribution in the northern temperate zones. Many have colourful chequered bells and flower mainly from spring to early summer. They enjoy shady woodland conditions and a well-drained soil with humus such as leaf mould, composted sawdust or bark added. A light dressing of slow-release fertiliser assists with bringing the bulbs up to flowering size.

Bulbs are often very hard to obtain from commercial sources, so seed should be sought from alpine societies, which generally have several species in their seed-lists. Seed should be sown when fresh if possible and placed in a cool shady spot to germinate. Use gritty mix and a light covering of grit to help anchor the seeds. The seed often takes a number of months to germinate, and

Fritillaria pontica

pots should be left for at least two years before they are discarded. The seedlings can take three to six years to reach flowering size but are well worth waiting for. Bulbs when available should be planted as soon as possible after lifting and not stored dry as they soon shrivel and die. They have few pests and diseases, although slugs can eat the soft foliage.

F. imperialis comes from the Himalayas and is called crown imperial or fox lily. This stately species has flowers in red, orange or yellow on 1.5 m stems in spring. The many pendant flowers have a mop of green leaves on top, making them very distinctive, and they have a foxy smell.

F. meleagris, the snake's-head fritillary from Europe, will grow in quite damp shady places. The few grassy grey-green leaves reach 15 cm long. The flower-stem is 10–40 cm tall and carries one or more chequered flowers in a range of colours, including dark purple, violet or pure white. There are a number of named varieties, but these will seed and soon make a colony of mixed colours.

F. pontica, from Southern Europe, has quite dainty green bells with brown tips in spring and is one of the easiest species to grow.

CALIFORNIAN SPECIES

These do quite well in warmer climates if given a dry summer dormant season and watered when the cool autumn weather returns.

Fritillaria biflora

F. affinis, or mission bells, is highly variable. It reaches 50 cm tall with medium-sized nodding bells of yellow, green, red, brown or green-purple. It prefers shade but is quite adaptable.

F. biflora, or chocolate lily, produces one to several mahogany and green bells on stems 15–60 cm tall. This species thrives in full sun.

F. liliacea has small creamy bells on 30 cm stems. It prefers full sun and heavy soil.

F. recurva, the scarlet fritillary, has grassy leaves from which 40–50 cm stems arise in spring. These carry a number of large scarlet-orange bells. It prefers light soils in woodland conditions.

There are many hundreds of other species to try, most of which hold greatest appeal for collectors.

Kingdom. In warmer climates they are relatively difficult to grow, often flowering in the first year after planting and then gradually fading away.

G. elwesii, the giant snowdrop, carries one or two pure white flowers with green tips on stems 20 cm tall. The grey-blue leaves are about 20 cm long. It is one species which will grow and multiply well in warm climates if given a cool partially shaded position. The bulbs should preferably be planted when in leaf, about 10–15 cm deep into well-drained loam. The most serious pest is bulb fly, which will destroy the bulbs.

G. ikariae is an attractive small species which is seldom grown. It has bright glossy green leaves, and the white flowers have green markings on the tips of the inner petals.

GALANTHUS
Amaryllidaceae

Galanthus or snowdrops originate from Europe and the Mediterranean region, and most flower from early winter to late spring. They generally need cool conditions to flower well, and several species and forms are grown in the United

GALAXIA
Iridaceae

This is a small South African genus of very tiny bulbs with grassy foliage. The flowers are large and very bright, mostly in yellow shades but sometimes multi-coloured. They need well-drained potting mix and a bright sunny position,

Galanthus ikariae

and are best grown in pots as the small bulbs can easily be lost. Seed is the best method of increase as offsets are seldom produced. It should be sown on the surface of a sandy mix and kept shaded until the leaves are 1–2 cm long. They can then be given more sun. After three years the first flowers can be expected in autumn.

G. ciliata is a rare species with yellow flowers carried on stems 3–5 cm tall. The leaves have fine hairs.

G. fugacissima is 5–8 cm tall, with cream to lemon-yellow flowers. These are 3–5 cm across, and each opens for one day only.

G. versicolor has pinkish purple bell-shaped flowers with yellow throats which are about 4 cm across. It flowers in winter on stems about 6 cm tall and has grassy foliage.

GALTONIA
Hyacinthaceae

This is a small South African genus, with four species generally recognised. They are related to hyacinths, which they resemble, but they are taller, and flower and grow during summer, hence their common name, summer hyacinth; they are dormant in winter. Lovely pendulous bell-shaped flowers of white or greenish yellow hang from erect stems during mid- and late summer. These make excellent long-lasting cut flowers. The bulbs should be located in a sunny well-drained position and should not be planted too deeply; a covering of about 2 cm of soil is usually sufficient.

G. candicans, sometimes called Cape hyacinth, is the most popular species. Pure white sweetly scented bells hang from upright unbranched stems, which can reach 1.5 m tall. The foliage is greyish green. It is easily grown in a sunny position in fertile well-drained soil. The bulbs are prone to rotting if they become waterlogged during winter. It is very effective when planted in large groups, providing a striking combination with many of the perennials which flower at the same time. Established plants are generally best

Opposite above: *Galaxia fugacissima*
Opposite, below: *Galtonia candicans*

Galtonia candicans 'Moonbeam'

left undisturbed, although offsets can be removed from mature bulbs during winter.

'Moonbeam' produces upright double flowers of ivory-white. Each bloom contains numerous petals and is effectively several flowers combined in one. As the oldest petals age they turn brownish, resulting in the flowers becoming discoloured. It has been found that this cultivar contains double the normal number of chromosomes (tetraploid).

G. princeps grows naturally in wet meadows in Natal and the Cape Province. The distinctively shaped bells of cream tinged with green appear on stems usually about 1 m tall in mid-summer, and the foliage resembles that of *G. candicans.*

G. viridiflora produces unusual greenish flowers on stems up to 1 m tall in summer. It can be distinguished from *G. princeps* by its more glaucous (bluish green) foliage. It prefers a sandy soil and partial shade to prevent the sun damaging the flowers.

Pseudogaltonia contains only one species, *P. clavata*, a native of South Africa. It was previously listed under *Galtonia* and has similar cultural requirements. It grows and flowers in summer and is winter dormant, and it is very poisonous. Pale greyish green flowers are carried on sturdy stems about 60 cm tall. The large bulbs should be planted with their necks above the soil. A sunny well-drained position is best, and established groups should be left undisturbed.

GEISSORHIZA
Iridaceae

This large genus from the winter-rainfall Cape Province of South Africa grows in winter and is dormant during the dry summers. Most species are very attractive although hard to obtain, only a few being widely available. Many are difficult garden subjects, the tiny bulbs tending to get dug up or swamped by other plants. Some of the most desirable species are very slow to multiply. A sunny well-drained position is best, and planting in large groups is most effective. The foliage should be allowed to die off completely in spring before removal.

G. aspera (syn. *G. secunda*) grows naturally in well-drained sandy soil in the Cape Peninsula. Star-shaped flowers of violet-blue with darker stripes are carried on 25 cm long stems from early spring until early summer. It is the best garden species, multiplying freely and making a dainty rock garden or container subject. It requires good drainage, plenty of moisture during autumn and winter, and it prefers relatively dry conditions in summer.

G. bracteata is an easily grown dwarf species which is most effective when mass planted. The tiny cream flowers are flushed with purple and have pointed petals, and are carried on stems about 10 cm long. It is a nice subject for a rock garden or pots.

G. erosa (syn. *G. inflexa* var. *erosa*) grows naturally in moist fields in the southwestern Cape. It is a variable species with flowers of white, blue, yellow, pink or red. The form commonly grown produces carmine-red cup-shaped flowers in spring and is sometimes called red sequins. The slender grassy foliage has prominent veins.

G. furva has bright reddish purple star-like flowers which can be 3 cm across. These are carried in spring on stems about 30 cm long above erect hairy foliage. Some authorities dispute the validity of this species and include it with others, but the form grown is so horticulturally distinct that it requires a separate listing.

G. imbricata has white flowers with fine darker stripes along the petals and a purplish flush outside. Golden yellow stamens complete an attractive contrast. It is the last species to flower, peaking in early summer, and the individual flowers are long-lasting. The flower-stems are about 30 cm tall, and the erect foliage is prominently veined. Seedlings will usually flower in their first season after sowing.

G. ovata is widespread in moist rocky places in South Africa, especially in the Cape Province and often at high altitudes. The large flowers are white flushed with pink inside and pinkish outside, and

Geissorhiza imbricata

Geissorhiza ovata

have large attractive anthers. Peak flowering is in spring. This is quite an easy species to cultivate but not easy to obtain.

G. purpureo-lutea is a good species for rock gardens and containers. Its rounded cup-shaped flowers are particularly large for this genus at about 25 mm across. The creamy flowers are flushed purple outside and have a maroon eye, and are carried on stems 10–15 cm long. It is one of the last to flower, from late spring until early summer.

G. splendidissima produces brilliant violet-blue flowers on stems up to 40 cm long. It flowers profusely throughout spring and is very desirable.

G. tulbaghensis has large attractive flowers of creamy white with a dark eye and blue anthers. It dislikes wet conditions and can be difficult to keep.

The following three species have cup-shaped flowers of blue and red, and are known as winecups. They are deservedly popular.

G. radians (syn. *G. rochensis*) is an attractive species from the southwestern Cape, where it often grows in damp areas of grass. The richly coloured flowers are deep blue with a red centre and a narrow white band in between. It is not easily obtainable and can be a difficult subject even when grown in pots.

G. monanthos is generally more easily grown and reliable. Its flowers are dark violet-blue with pale yellow or reddish centres and appear on stems up to 20 cm long in spring.

G. mathewsii is a rare species with deep purple-blue flowers with reddish centres. These appear on stems about 18 cm long in spring. It differs from *G. radians* in not having a white band between the colours.

GLADIOLUS
Iridaceae

This genus contains about 180 species, which originate from Mediterranean regions, tropical Africa and South Africa. More than 100 species are native to South Africa, where they are mainly concentrated in the winter-rainfall region of the Cape Province. Horticulturally, the South African species are most important, the wide range of hybrids having been derived mainly from these. The flowers of most species are irregular in shape (zygomorphic), but a few have symmetrical (actinomorphic) blooms. Usually the flowers are carried on one side of the stem. Sunny well-drained conditions suit most species.

Most *Gladiolus* produce a corm, which is

replaced annually by numerous new cormlets. These generally develop at the base of the old corm but occasionally on creeping underground stems (e.g. *G. papilio,* which can be invasive). Planting depth for corms is about three times their height.

Gladiolus species can be split into three groups:

WINTER-GROWING SPECIES from the winter-rainfall Cape Province of South Africa. These flower mainly in spring and early summer, and become dormant in summer. They provide the greatest variety of flower shape and colour, and some are also scented. Many species are difficult to cultivate, especially those from moist mountain habitats. Although not all are showy, most provide a beauty and elegance missing from modern large-flowered hybrids.

SUMMER-GROWING SPECIES from summer-rainfall regions of subtropical and tropical Africa. These are usually larger plants than the winter growers, and they are usually more prone to the pest and disease problems which are particularly prevalent during their growing season.

SPRING-FLOWERING, SUMMER-DORMANT SPECIES from the Mediterranean regions of Europe, North Africa and the Middle East.

The vast range of hybrids available can be placed in two main categories:

LARGE-FLOWERED HYBRIDS used for cut-flower production. These should be planted in spring and will flower in summer. They have been derived mainly from summer-growing species such as *G. natalensis* and *G. papilio.* Only *G. cardinalis* of the winter-growing species has made a significant contribution to this group. Their flowers have been exhibited for generations and are separated into various classes according to the shape of the blooms and their arrangement on the spike. A well-drained sunny position protected from strong winds is ideal. When the foliage dries off in autumn it should be cut off, and the corms are usually lifted and stored in a well-ventilated position during winter.

DWARF WINTER-GROWING, SPRING-FLOWERING HYBRIDS, usually referred to as 'Nanus' hybrids (see Miniature Hybrids later in this section).

PESTS AND DISEASES

THRIPS. Insects which damage the foliage and flowers with their rasping, causing silverish markings to appear. They are most prevalent during warm summer months and are a particular problem on summer-growing species. Insecticides such as synthetic pyrethroids give effective control.

MITES. These are also most abundant in summer and can be a particular problem in glasshouses.

RUST. A problem when conditions are warm and humid. Yellowish markings appear on the leaves. Fungicides such as mancozeb are effective if applied as a protectant.

DRY ROT. Causes the foliage to turn brownish and also affects the bulbs, which should be discarded if infected.

PROPAGATION

Fresh seed usually germinates readily. It should be sown immediately prior to the growing season of the particular species: autumn for winter-growing species; spring for summer-growing species.

Seed should be sown into a deep tray of sandy well-drained mix. The seedlings should be left undisturbed during the growing season and transplanted if necessary when they become dormant.

WINTER-GROWING SOUTH AFRICAN SPECIES

G. carneus is one of the easiest winter growers for garden use. It is sometimes called painted lady and occasionally offered as *G. blandus* var. *albidus.* Its flowers are white with purple flakes on the lower petals, and these appear for about four weeks in late spring and early summer. Stem length is variable, usually about 50 cm. It is easy in a sunny well-drained position and is ideal for cottage gardens and rock gardens.

G. alatus is an extremely variable species which has been separated into five varieties. *G. alatus* var. *alatus* is one of the most difficult varieties to grow, producing slightly fragrant hooded flowers mainly in shades of orange, with greenish yellow markings on the lower petals. They are carried on stems about 30 cm long in spring. It is a good subject for a well-drained position in a rock garden or in containers.

G. *alatus* var. *meliusculus* produces larger flowers of softer texture, usually pinkish orange with a reddish throat and greenish yellow markings on the lower petals. It is the easiest variety of G. *alatus* to cultivate. A white form is rarely available.

G. *angustus* usually has creamy yellow upward-facing flowers with reddish inner markings. These are carried on 40 cm tall stems in early summer.

G. *aureus* is known as golden gladiolus, producing blooms of lemon-yellow to bright golden yellow. These appear on stems about 50 cm tall in spring. This primitive and rare species has a delicate appearance, not at all like most other *Gladiolus*. It is generally easily grown in a sunny well-drained location.

G. *cardinalis* grows naturally on rocky ledges near streams and is sometimes called waterfall gladiolus. Its blooms are brilliant scarlet with white markings and appear on 80 cm tall stems in summer. It is generally easily grown in a cool position in moist well drained soil but can become infected with disease where summers are warm and humid. It is one of the main parents of the modern hybrids.

G. *carinatus* is extremely variable, flower colours including shades of blue, violet, pink and pale yellow. Usually they are strongly fragrant, although some blue forms have no scent. The stems are about 70 cm tall. It is not always easy in very humid climates.

G. *carmineus* belongs to a small group of species which produce their flowers in late summer and autumn, before the foliage has appeared (hysteranthous group). It is very easily grown, certainly the easiest member of this group. Its flowers are cerise with white markings on the lower petals, and the stems can be up to 60 cm tall. The floppy untidy foliage lasts for nine months after flowering but must be retained until it dries off.

G. *citrinus* is a rare and unusual species, one of the few with symmetrical flowers. The large blooms are lemon to bright yellow with a dark eye and have a lovely scent. They do not look much like other *Gladiolus*, more like a *Sparaxis*. It is quite easily grown, flowering freely on 30 cm stems in spring.

G. *debilis* var. *debilis* is another of the species

Gladiolus alatus

known as painted lady. A dwarf, seldom exceeding 30 cm, it has pale pink or near-white blooms with reddish markings on the lower petals.

G. *debilis* var. *cochleatus* has delicate white flowers with reddish markings in the throat, somewhat resembling a dainty orchid. It is very pretty but unfortunately susceptible to corm rot in poorly drained soils.

G. *floribundus* is a variable species with flowers of white with purple stripes, or pink with darker markings. These appear on stems up to 50 cm tall in winter and spring. It is not always reliable in gardens and is usually best grown in pots.

G. *inflatus* is a variable species which somewhat resembles G. *alatus*. Flower colour ranges from soft lavender-blue to pinkish cerise shades. Usually the lower petals have yellowish markings with a reddish outline. It flowers in spring on stems under 60 cm tall.

G. *orchidiflorus* is a distinctive species with

strongly scented flowers of various colouring. These can be in shades of grey, green or beige with purplish markings, and they appear in late winter and spring. Plants are easily raised from seed and are best grown in pots of sandy mix.

G. quadrangulus grows naturally in moist sandy soil in the Cape Province. Its flower colour varies, often white with delicate purple veining, especially in the throat. The foliage grows about 60 cm tall, higher than the fragrant flowers. Because the leaves are so fine, they do not detract too much from the blooms. It is usually easily grown and tolerates humid weather.

G. scullyi (syn. *G. venustus*) is a variable spring-flowering species, one of the commonest and most widespread in South Africa. It flowers reliably but is not especially showy, producing very thin flowers with pointed horns. Flowers are mauve and yellow with brownish gold markings on the tips.

G. tristis var. *tristis* has lovely creamy green flowers with brown markings on the lower petals. It flowers from early spring until summer and is strongly fragrant at night. The stems are slender and wiry, usually about 50 cm tall. It grows well in well-drained soil but can be short-lived.

G. tristis var. *concolor* has very pale yellow flowers which are more funnel-shaped.

G. watermeyeri has white upper petals with red veins and yellowish lower petals with white tips. The stems are about 40 cm tall and carry the scented flowers in late winter and spring.

SUMMER-GROWING SPECIES

G. callianthus is more commonly known as *Acidanthera bicolor*. It is a native of eastern tropical Africa and produces large white flowers often blotched with maroon. The hooded flowers hang slightly and have a long tube. It is scented at night, being pollinated by moths in its natural habitat. It has a very long flowering period which can extend to winter. The stems are usually about 60 cm but can be much taller. It is not always easy to cultivate in wet humid climates.

G. natalensis (syn. *G. dalenii*) is one of the most variable of all species and has numerous synonyms. A vigorous form with orange and yellow flowers in autumn and early winter is widely grown. The robust stems can reach 2 m tall but are usually less. It is ideal for large gardens, flowering when there is little other colour and multiplying freely. *G. natalensis* var. *cooperi* has lemon-yellow flowers and is occasionally grown. Other forms of this species flower at various times of the year, mainly in summer, and in a range of colours.

G. ochroleucus var. *ochroleucus* is now listed as *G. stanfordiae* by some authorities. This variable mainly evergreen species grows mostly in summer. In early autumn it produces beautiful blooms with ruffled petals on stems ranging from 45 cm to 1 m tall. A form with pale salmon flowers marked white in the throat is very desirable.

G. ochroleucus var. *triangulus* varies in flower colour from white and cream to pink. An attractive form has pink ruffled petals marked with cerise in the paler throat. It flowers on 40 cm stems in autumn and is ideal for a rock garden.

G. papilio (syn. *G. purpurea-auratus*) is an unusual species with strange hooded flowers that are greenish yellow with purplish markings. They are carried on nodding stems about 1 m tall from

Gladiolus tristis var. *tristis*

Gladiolus natalensis

early summer. Corms are produced on stems which run beneath the soil, and it can become invasive, especially in light soils, but can be restricted by growing in containers.

MEDITERRANEAN SPECIES

G. communis ssp. *byzantinus* (syn. *G. byzantinus*) is a vigorous species with fairly large bright reddish purple flowers carried on stems about 1.2 m tall in summer. It is ideal for naturalising in large clumps and looks effective with grey-foliaged plants.

G. italicus has flowers of pale pink to reddish purple on stems usually about 70 cm tall but is not particularly attractive.

MINIATURE HYBRIDS

These provide a wide variety of flower shapes, often ruffled, and an extensive range of colours. They have various markings and appear on plants which remain quite small. They grow during winter and flower in winter, spring or early summer, and they make wonderful garden subjects where winters are not severely cold. They are derived mainly from winter-growing species.

G. x *colvillei* was the name given to the cross in 1823 between *G. tristis* and *G. cardinalis*. The original selection has bright red flowers, subsequent crosses producing a range of other colours. Other species such as *G. carneus* were later used to produce the hybrids now available.

'Amanda Mahy' produces salmon-red flowers blotched with violet for a long period from late winter until summer. 'Charm' produces pinkish cerise flowers with a lilac and creamy green throat in early winter. 'Comet' is bright red. 'Kates Pink' is pinkish orange with cerise and cream markings in early summer. 'Nymph' is white with cream blotches and rose-red edgings.

G. x *colvillei* 'The Bride' is an old cultivar but still one of the best. Pure white flowers appear in early summer, ideal for combining with old roses.

Gladiolus (miniature hybrid)

GLORIOSA
Colchicaceae

Previously several species were recognised in this genus, but these are now all considered to belong to one extremely variable species, *G. superba*. They are commonly called gloriosa lilies or flame lilies and originate from Africa and India. They are climbing plants with long-lasting flowers which are very good for picking. The large brittle V-shaped tubers should be planted in early spring 10 to 15 cm deep. They should be positioned beneath open shrubs or beside walls where some support will be given to the young emerging shoots. The leaves send out tendrils as they start to climb, and they will eventually reach 2 m tall.

Gloriosa lilies succeed in light loamy or sandy soils, multiplying well in suitable conditions. They tend to grow deeply into soft sandy soils, and this can eventually lead to the plants flowering very late in the season. It is wise to lift and replant at least every two years or locating the delving tubers can become a mining operation. Care must be taken when lifting the tubers as they will die if their tips are broken. The tubers can be stored dry for a long period. Fresh seed when available should be sown into deep pots of sandy mix and covered with 3 cm of sand. They should then be placed in a warm frame or greenhouse until germination commences, which can take several months. Earwigs and caterpillars often chew the soft foliage and flower-buds, which spoils the flowers and renders them unfit for picking.

G. superba has deep orange-red flowers with yellow edges. The oval or pointed petals are reflexed and look like dancing flames.

G. superba 'Carsonii' (syn. *G. carsonii*) is an uncommon species with deep maroon flowers with yellow edges.

G. superba 'Rothschildiana' (syn. *G. rothschildiana*) has bright purple-red flowers with wavy edges. There is also a golden yellow form, which is widely sought but difficult to obtain. This variety has the largest flowers and is extremely good for picking.

G. superba 'Simplex' (syn. *G. virescens*) has flowers which start off greenish and gradually turn through yellow to orange. The plant can have a whole range of different coloured flowers out at one time.

Gloriosa superba 'Rothschildiana'

HABRANTHUS
Amaryllidaceae

Close relatives of *Zephyranthes* and *Hippeastrum,* *Habranthus* or rain lilies are natives of South America, Central America and Texas. They are easily grown small bulbs ideal for rock gardens or pots. Their foliage is neat, and the quantity of flowers they produce is amazing considering the size of their bulbs. Crocus-shaped flowers appear in various shades of pink-white, yellow or copper, successively throughout mid- and late summer, and the leaves are strap-shaped. When wet and dry periods alternate during this time, they will flower a few days after each period of rain. Generally black-winged seed is set, taking only a few days to ripen.

Bulbs should be planted immediately they become dormant in early summer and positioned at or just below the surface of the soil. Well-drained sandy loam and full sun are ideal, and a dressing of sulphate of potash will enhance flowering. As the bulbs seldom go dormant, it is better to plant them immediately after lifting rather than storing them dry.

The usual method of propagation is by division of the bulbils. Seed can be sown directly into the soil in the vicinity of the older bulbs or sown into pots or trays. Flowering will often commence in the second season.

Pests and diseases are relatively uncommon, although bulb fly can occur and thrips sometimes attacks the flowers. Fungal rots are usually only a problem in very wet seasons.

H. tubispathus is much better known by its previous name, *H. andersonii.* It is a popular subject for rock gardens, although this prolific species can become a nuisance in a collection of choice dwarf bulbs. The 10 cm flowers are usually copper in colour, although yellow or pale creamy copper varieties are available.

H. tubispathus 'Rosea' has dainty foliage and dark pink flowers which appear very early.

H. robustus reaches 30 cm tall and has large soft pink flowers.

H. 'Russell Manning' is a popular cultivar, its large pink flowers having rounder petals than the species.

H. brachyandrus has soft pink flowers with a rich

Habranthus tubispathus 'Rosea'

burgundy throat. It reaches about 30 cm tall and is slow to multiply.

Several other species and cultivars are occasionally cultivated, and they are well worth the trouble of obtaining them.

HAEMANTHUS
Amaryllidaceae

This is a medium-sized genus containing over 20 species. Some species previously included here have been shifted to *Scadoxus.*

H. coccineus is a striking South African native known variously as blood lily, Bible plant and elephant's ears. It is grown as much for its large strap-like leaves as for its scarlet flowers, which resemble paintbrushes with their central cluster of golden stamens. These emerge when no foliage is present in summer, prompted by heavy rain or watering. Pinkish red tongue-like buds are carried on spotted stems, opening to display a mass of golden pollen. If fertilised, translucent pink berries are produced which birds will take unless protected. As summer progresses, the large fleshy rounded leaves appear. These lie flat on the ground, forming an effective ground-cover, and last until early the following summer when they dry off as temperatures rise.

The best time to divide and plant the large bulbs is just after the leaves die off. Care must be taken not to damage the fleshy roots. Well-drained soil

Haemanthus albiflos

Haemanthus rotundifolius

is best, and a light dressing of sulphate of potash will enhance the quality of the flowers. Storage of the bulbs is not recommended, replanting immediately after lifting being preferable.

The easiest way to multiply plants is by division, but this is slow. Seed can be used to produce large numbers of plants, which will flower in three to five years from sowing. Seed should be sown on the surface of a well-drained mix at about 20°C.

Slugs and snails enjoy the crisp young leaves and flower-buds. Virus infection can also occur.

H. albiflos is a fairly common evergreen species with hairy leaves which prefers more shade than *H. coccineus*. Well-grown specimens will produce greenish white blooms over a long period. It can be crossed with *H. coccineus* to produce pink-flowered hybrids. It multiplies readily and will grow from leaf cuttings placed in sand in a shady position. It appears to be the only species which can be propagated this way. The other species will grow from the large fleshy leaf bases that make up the bulb, provided they have a strip of basal plate attached.

H. sanguineus is an uncommon species with large rounded leaves, often 30 cm long and almost as wide. The flower-stem is coloured bright red or wine, and the bright red flowers are more substantial than those of *H. coccineus*. It should be grown as for *H. coccineus*.

H. rotundifolius resembles *H. coccineus* when flowering in autumn. The flowers are followed by very large rounded leaves which lie flat on the ground.

HERBERTIA
Iridaceae

Herbertia species produce iris-like flowers in shades of pale blue and violet-blue. They prefer a warm sunny well-drained position and are winter growing. The closely related *Alophia* and *Gelasine* are included here.

H. lahue is the species most commonly grown, often under a variety of incorrect names, and it is often confused with the true *H. pulchella*. Its attractive blooms are lavender-blue with deeper violet blotches at their base.

Alophia drummondii

H. pulchella has flowers in shades varying between blue and purple with a central white stripe and variable spotting. Unlike *H. lahue*, the outer petals hang vertically or nearly so. It grows about 20 cm tall.

Alophia contains about four species with iris-like flowers which are distinguished by the shape of their anthers. *A. drummondii* is the most commonly grown species, producing violet blooms with brown spotted centres. It is summer growing.

Gelasine is another small South American genus with blue flowers. *G. elongata* (syn. *G. azurea*) is the only species usually grown, producing a succession of deep blue flowers with white centres on 50 cm stems. The seed-pods are also interesting and attractive. Although each bloom lasts only about one day, they are produced continuously for quite a long period. The deep green leaves with prominent ribbing are also attractive. Sometimes seed is set so heavily that the stems break.

HESPERANTHA
Iridaceae

This large genus contains about 60 species. Most grow naturally in mountainous regions of South Africa, where they are concentrated in the northwestern Cape. The starry flowers are carried in spikes and are often fragrant. Most species open their flowers at the same time each day, usually late afternoon, and close them the following morning. The flowers remain open longer on overcast days. Flowers are often white, being pollinated at night by moths. Some species open their flowers during the day, and many are brightly coloured in shades of yellow, blue, red, pink and purple. Most species are easily grown but a few are difficult, including some of the most beautiful. They are good plants for warm climates, most thriving in a sunny well-drained position.

H. cucullata (syn. *H. buhri*) is a variable species, the flowers usually being reddish purple outside and white inside. These appear in spring and early summer on wiry stems up to 30 cm tall. The foliage is narrow and erect, and it is a good subject for rock gardens and pots.

H. bachmannii (syn. *H. angusta*) is one of the best species, quite tall at about 30 cm and with tiny corms. Its scented flowers are usually ivory-white with prominent yellow stamens. These appear for about four weeks in spring, facing downwards and remaining open during the day.

H. bauri (syn. *H. mossii*) produces small scented starry pink flowers in summer. These are carried on 20 cm stems and open in the sun. It can be difficult to cultivate, requiring sandy soil.

H. erecta produces small creamy white flowers from reddish brown buds in spring. These open in the afternoon and have a delicate appearance. The stems are about 20 cm tall, and the foliage

Hesperantha vaginata

H. purpurea is a very pretty plant with reddish pink flowers appearing in spring. Although highly desirable, it can be very difficult and is hard to obtain. It requires sandy soil and is generally best grown in pots.

H. vaginata is one of the most striking of all the species. Flowers of bright yellow with black markings are carried on wiry 30 cm tall spikes during spring. They open during the day and close at night.

H. vaginata var. *stanfordiae* has large fragrant flowers of clear golden yellow which open from midday until sunset. It is not always easy to grow.

is narrow and erect. It is a good garden subject, especially for rock gardens, and quickly forms nice clumps.

H. pauciflora is one of the very best species, producing pink to purple flowers which open during the day in spring.

H. pearsonii (syn. *H. latifolia*) is a dwarf species from moist areas in the Cape Province. Rose-pink to purplish blooms appear on 8 cm stems in winter and spring. It hybridises readily and is a good subject for rock gardens and pots.

Hessea discidifera

HESSEA
Amaryllidaceae

This is a small genus of bulbs from South Africa that resemble tiny nerines. They are fairly easy to grow in poor sandy soil and are best planted in pots or in dry sunny rock gardens. When well situated they multiply rapidly, making tight clumps of bulbs which grow with only their lower third beneath the soil. Division of the clumps while dormant in summer is the best method of propagation. Fresh ripe seeds, which set freely, can be sown on the surface of a sandy mix. Seedlings grow fairly fast and flower in three to four years. Pests are few, although in wet conditions fungal disorders can occur.

H. discidifera has 10–15 cm tall stems which carry a number of tiny frilly starry flowers. It has hairy grass-like leaves.

H. gemmata has small starry white flowers, some with a pink tinge, on stems 15 cm tall.

H. zeyheri has very crinkly white flowers and is best grown in pots.

HIPPEASTRUM
Amaryllidaceae

This South American genus is often incorrectly called *Amaryllis*. Modern hybrids with huge trumpet-shaped flowers are most widely grown, especially as pot plants. These, plus some of the species, are suitable garden subjects for warm climates, requiring a well-drained, sheltered sunny position. Once established, the clumps should be left undisturbed for several years. Most are summer growers and should be kept dry in winter and moist from late spring. If kept moist during winter, their foliage often does not die off and flowering the following summer is reduced. Plants growing in containers can be tipped on their sides during winter to keep them dry.

H. aulicum is native to Brazil and Paraguay, and has spotted scarlet flowers with green centres during winter. The foliage emerges after the flowers. It is one of the easiest species to grow.

H. papilio has gorgeous orchid-like cream flowers with maroon and green markings. These are about 10 cm in diameter and appear mainly in early summer.

Numerous large-flowered brightly coloured hybrids are available, producing two to four large trumpets on sturdy stems about 60 cm tall. They prefer rich well-drained soil which contains plenty of humus. The bulbs should be planted with their necks above the soil, and when grown in pots are often placed on top of the mix. The first blooms appear from late spring at about the same time as the leaves, and successive flowers appear sporadically throughout summer. Plants are increased by separating offsets from the mature bulbs in winter. Fresh seed germinates freely and takes at least three years before flowering. If seed is not required, spent blooms should be removed.

Cultivars include: 'Blushing Bride', large rose-pink; 'Intokasa', large pure white with green throat; 'Springtime', soft rose-pink with white centre and tips; 'Wedding Dance', pure white. Many more cultivars in a wide range of colours are also obtainable.

See also *Rhodophiala.*

Hippeastrum 'Intokasa'

HOMOGLOSSUM
Iridaceae

This genus of about 10 species is closely allied to *Gladiolus* and is included in that genus by some authorities. They are winter growers, flowering mainly in spring and becoming dormant during

Homoglossum huttonii x *G. tristis*

111

summer. A collection of different species will provide a long flowering period from autumn until summer. Their requirements are similar to those of the winter-flowering gladiolus from the Cape Province. Flowers are usually coloured yellow, orange or red and are carried in spikes.

Increase is usually by separation of offsets during summer dormancy. Fresh seed germinates readily in a well-drained mix and should be sown in autumn.

H. huttonii (syn. *H. hollandii*) has flowers in various shades, commonly red on the outside with crimson stripes in the throat. It flowers on stems about 50 cm tall for a long period in spring. The foliage is narrow and grass-like. It is a lovely species, easily grown particularly in warm climates. It can be naturalised in well-drained garden soil or grown in containers.

H. merianellum var. *merianellum* produces red or orange-red flowers in spikes up to 70 cm tall during winter. Although very beautiful, it is not always easy to grow, preferring sandy soil.

H. merianellum var. *aureum* is similar but carries yellow or orange-yellow flowers in spring.

H. priorii is similar to *H. huttonii* and is one of the best species for gardens. Its flowers are in various shades of red with creamy yellow markings in the throat and on the lower petals.

Stem length varies from about 30 cm to 80 cm, and the flowers appear in winter and spring.

H. quadrangulare is the last to flower in spring. Its blooms are rose-red and occasionally pink. The stems are up to 75 cm tall, and the squarish foliage is stiff and erect. It tolerates colder conditions than most.

H. watsonium has flowers of reddish orange with narrow pointed petals on stems up to 1 m tall. It flowers during late winter and spring, and is good for picking. The leaves are narrow and grass-like, and it tolerates heavier soil than most species.

H. watsonium was crossed with *Gladiolus tristis* to produce the so-called 'Homoglad' hybrids.

H. huttonii has also been hybridised with *Gladiolus tristis*. Flowers of this cross are usually reddish at the tips and creamy yellow in the throat, and beautifully fragrant at night.

HYACINTHOIDES
Hyacinthaceae

These plants have been shifted through various genera over the years, including *Scilla* and *Endymion*. There are only a few species, these being notable for replacing their bulbs every year. The bluebells, both English and Spanish, belong here. They are good subjects for naturalising, especially beneath deciduous trees and among spring-flowering shrubs such as camellias and rhododendrons. They are most effective when planted in large drifts, preferring rich soil which contains plenty of humus. The bulbs multiply readily, and this is the main means of increase.

H. hispanica (syn. *Scilla campanulata* and *Endymion campanulata*) is the Spanish bluebell. The long bell-shaped flowers are larger and showier than those of the English bluebells and are less pendulous. Also, the anthers are always blue, whereas those of the English bluebell are cream, and the leaves are broader. The flowers are carried evenly around the stems, which are usually about 30–40 cm tall. The flowers are usually blue, although white and pink forms are available, and they appear in spring. It is an ideal subject for naturalising under trees, tolerating heavy soils and multiplying so abundantly that it can almost become weedy.

H. non-scripta is the English bluebell, a native

Hyacinthoides hispanica

of western Europe, where it grows in woods and meadows. Lovely small nodding bells are carried mainly on one side of the 45 cm spikes in spring. Flowers are in shades of blue, pink or white. A cool shady position in rich soil is ideal for naturalising. It is smaller and daintier than the Spanish bluebells and seeds freely. Hybrids between the two often occur when they are grown together.

HYACINTHUS
Hyacinthaceae

This is a well-known genus with tubular bell-shaped flowers carried in spikes. Only three species are now considered to belong here.

H. orientalis is by far the most important species, providing the numerous cultivars popular with gardeners and florists. Their flower colours include white, cream, pink, purple and blue. The starry blooms are heavily perfumed and are carried in spikes about 30 cm tall. Full sun and sandy soil which drains freely are ideal, and they should be placed where their fragrance can be most enjoyed. The bulbs should be planted in late summer or autumn and covered with about 10 cm of soil. Bulbs can be left in the ground but tend to flower better if lifted as the foliage dies off and stored in a well-ventilated situation.

Plants of *H. orientalis* found growing in the wild are quite unlike the modern hybrids. The smallish starry flowers are much more dainty and the spikes less dense. They are usually mauve-blue and occasionally white or pink.

The large-flowered hybrids have largely been developed to flower once and then be discarded. Bulbs are prevented from flowering as they are being grown on and when purchased are ready in size and condition to produce their first flowers. The blooms are so large that the bulbs become completely drained, seldom flowering satisfactorily the following year.

Forcing is a traditional method of bringing potted plants into flower. The bulbs are lightly pressed into the mix, and then the whole pot is plunged into sand or sawdust so that it is covered by about 5 cm. This keeps the plants cool and promotes good root growth. Once the shoots

Hyacinthus orientalis (Roman hyacinth)

appear, the pots are removed and given more light. They can be placed in a well-lit situation inside the house when the first blooms begin to open.

Increase is mainly by separating offsets from the base of mature bulbs when they are dormant.

The major pest is bulb fly. Bulbs that feel soft should be inspected for grubs and destroyed if any are present.

The following is a small selection of the named cultivars which are available: 'Carnegie', pure white; 'L' Innocence', pure white; 'Delft Blue', blue flushed with mauve, 'Ostara', bright deep lavender-blue; 'Lady Derby', soft pink inside, deep pink reverse; 'Pink Pearl', deep pink; 'Eros', deep pink; 'Jan Bos', carmine-red, white centre; 'Amethyst', violet; 'City of Haarlem', primrose-yellow.

Roman hyacinths are forms of *H. orientalis* with slightly larger flowers than the wild types. They

Hyacinthus 'Lady Derby'

HYMENOCALLIS
Amaryllidaceae

Hymenocallis are native to the Americas, from the Southern United States to the Andes. They produce several strap-shaped green to grey-green leaves which can be evergreen or deciduous. In some species a basal leaf-sheath will make a false stem, which can be up to 30 cm tall. The large bulb should be planted in early spring 10–15 cm deep in well-drained rich organic soil in either full sun or semi-shade. They are good for general landscaping among perennials, flowering from late spring until autumn. The flowers are easily damaged by rain, which can be reduced by planting under trees. The large clumps need dividing occasionally to keep them flowering.

The bulbs make a number of offsets, which soon grow large enough to flower if removed and replanted in a nursery bed. The large green seeds, 2–4 cm in diameter, germinate as soon as they are ripe. These should be planted on the top of a well-drained mix and not covered, and they will flower in about four to five years. The flowers are white or yellow and have a cup with long outer segments 5–12 cm wide. They are often scented. There are two to eight flowers per stem, and they can be used as cut flowers but last only a few days.

H. amancaes, from Chile and Peru, likes well-drained conditions. The green strap leaves are deciduous. The flower stems grow 30–60 cm tall and carry three to eight fragrant yellow flowers per head in summer. The cup can be 7–10 cm long with 10 cm wide petals.

H. harrisiana from Mexico has grey-green leaves 15–20 cm long which are deciduous. Three to four white scented narrow spidery flowers are carried in each head.

H. littoralis is a vigorous evergreen species which makes a good garden subject in warm climates. It requires protection during cold winters. The lovely white flowers have long narrow reflexed petals behind a central cup. Several are carried on each sturdy 70–90 cm stem.

H. x *macrostephana,* of hybrid origin, has large scented white flowers. The cup is about 7 cm wide

Opposite, above: *Hymenocallis* x *macrostephana*
Opposite, below: *Hymenocallis speciosa*

are daintier than the large-flowered florists' hyacinths and are regaining popularity. They are easily grown and when naturalised in gardens will flower reliably each spring without any attention. They are ideal in a well-drained rock garden or cottage garden, mixing well with most other bulbs or perennials. The flowers are beautifully fragrant and can be blue, pink or white.

H. litwinowii is native to northern Iran and western central Asia. Pale blue flowers with darker stripes are carried on short stems. It has narrower petals and fewer, shorter leaves than *H. orientalis.* It should be kept dry when dormant in summer.

with 10 cm segments. It is now rare in cultivation but can be found in some older gardens.

H. narcissiflora (syn. *H. calathina*) has two or more deciduous leaves 40 cm long. It produces a false stem up to 30 cm in height from which the flower-stem grows to about 50–60 cm tall. This carries two or more fragrant white flowers with 8 cm cups and 8–10 cm wide segments. This is a parent of a number of hybrids. 'Advance' is pure white and scented. 'Festialis' is white and scented with three to six flower per 45 cm tall stem.

H. speciosa is an evergreen species from the West Indies which requires almost tropical conditions to thrive. Clusters of fragrant white flowers are produced in summer above large glossy evergreen foliage.

The main pest is bulb fly.

IPHEION
Alliaceae

This is a South American genus of small bulbs that are extremely free-flowering and almost evergreen. Most are suitable for containers or rock gardens, although *I. uniflorum* tends to spread rather rapidly and can become a pest in among other small bulbs.

The upward-facing starry flowers are usually carried one per stem, but occasionally more can occur. They divide freely, or seeds can be sown in early autumn in pots of well-drained mix. Two or three years are needed to produce flowering size bulbs. There are no common pests and diseases.

I. uniflorum from Argentina and Uruguay is the most common species. It soon makes a dense mass of bulbs producing a wonderful floral display from mid-winter to spring. Blue is the usual flower colour, and there are several varieties in various blue shades, plus purple and white forms. These include 'Wisley Blue' (pale blue with darker tips), 'Froyle Mill' (violet-purple) and 'Album' (pure white petals with a greenish central vein). There are also a number of striped forms, and pink forms are reported to grow in the wild. All forms of this species have an onion-like smell.

I. sellowianum (syn. *Beauvardia sellowiana*) from Uruguay is a very brightly coloured species which

Ipheion sellowianum

produces masses of yellow flowers over a long period in winter and spring. It has bright green leaves and is very good for pots and containers. This species is non-invasive and non-fragrant. A few seeds usually set, and small offsets that develop around the mother bulb can be separated when dormant.

I. dialystemon from Argentina is an uncommon yellow-flowered species which carries two to three flowers per stem.

IRIS
Iridaceae

Bulbous iris species occur naturally in Mediterranean areas of Europe, Africa and Asia. They are seldom grown in regions with warm climates and damp summers as they are prone to disease in these conditions. The bulbs often rot if they are too moist during the dormant summer period.

SMALL BULBOUS IRISES

Reticulata types are easy to grow, and provided they receive a dry ripening period, they will flower satisfactorily. Most grow only 15 cm tall. A rich well-drained loam is ideal. The bulbs should be planted 10 cm deep in containers or rock gardens in autumn. Bulbs have a tendency to split into numerous 'pips', which take three to four years to reach flowering size. A number of pests and diseases can attack them, including ink spot, fusarium, virus and eelworm. Bulbs can be stored dry in paper bags when dormant.

I. reticulata from Turkey and Iraq grows naturally on rocky hillsides. The variably coloured flowers open on 10–15 cm stems in winter to early spring. The foliage looks tidy at flowering time and grows 20–30 cm tall. Many different forms are widely grown, and a collection of these delightful bulbs can be planted in troughs or in sink gardens. Colours range from dark to pale blue, wine, red and white.

I. danfordiae produces flowers of bright yellow with soft green spotting early in the season. It is very prone to splitting. The bulbs should be planted firmly, 10 cm deep, and fed with sulphate of potash. The plants flower best if they receive a good summer baking.

I. histrio has attractive soft blue flowers, larger than the other reticulata types, which open from late winter to spring. It is best grown in pots and responds well to a dry summer baking.

JUNO IRIS

These are fairly rare but generally grow well in full sun and well-drained gritty soil. The bulbs have thick fleshy roots which should not be damaged. They are best left in the soil and not stored dry, and should be kept just slightly moist and cool during the summer resting period. They can be lost in the garden, often rotting in heavy soils. Their growth habit makes them ideal subjects for containers, which should be reasonably deep to accommodate their root system.

I. bucharica from central Asia is the species offered most frequently. The broad green leaves are 30–40 cm long. It produces several flowers of creamy white with yellow markings on the falls.

LARGER BULBOUS IRIS

I. tingitana from Morocco requires a hot summer baking to flower well. Some growers place the bulbs on a sheet of iron in summer to promote flowering. The bulbs are then planted in late summer to flower in autumn. It grows 40–60 cm tall and is a good source of cut flowers in late winter. It requires a fertile soil rich in humus to grow and flower well. Bulbs should be planted in autumn about 12 cm deep, and each produces two to three large violet-blue flowers. It is one of the parents of the Dutch iris, and it can be badly affected by virus disease.

Iris bucharica

I. xiphium, the Spanish iris, is native to parts of Europe and northwest Africa. Usually the flowers are in shades of blue or violet, with a band of gold on the falls. The flower-stems are about 60 cm tall. This species and *I. tingitana* are the main parents of the Dutch irises.

Dutch irises are grown extensively for cut-flower production and are widely used in gardens. They grow during winter, and different varieties flower from early to late spring. They become dormant in summer, and the bulbs can be divided at this time. They should be replanted by autumn about 10 cm deep. A large number of cultivars in a wide colour range are available. 'Wedgwood' is commonly grown and has soft blue flowers with yellow blotches in early spring. 'Professor Blaauw' has deep violet-blue flowers with golden blotches. 'Pride of Holland' has golden orange blooms, and those of 'White Beauty' are white with orange blotches. Numerous others are also offered.

I. latifolia (syn. *I. xiphioides*), the so-called English iris, is actually native to Spain and the Pyrenees. In the wild the flowers are usually violet-blue with a central yellow blotch on the falls. The main flowering period is from early to mid-summer. It prefers well-drained soil rich in humus, and it must be moist during the growing season.

The bulbs do not store well, and they should be planted about 15 cm deep in late summer or autumn. The shoots may not appear until spring. Many cultivars are available in a range of flower colours. 'King of the Blues' has dark purple-blue flowers and is commonly grown; others include 'Mont Blanc' (white), 'Prince Albert' (silver-blue) and 'Prince of Wales' (blue).

IXIA
Iridaceae

This is a large genus of some 50 species, commonly called corn lilies, native to the winter-rainfall Cape Province of South Africa. All grow during winter and are dormant in summer. Most prefer a sunny well-drained position and are most

Opposite, above. Dutch iris

Opposite, below. *Ixia maculata*

effective when planted in large clumps. The narrow upright leaves also provide valuable texture in a garden. The starry flowers are carried on spikes, the weight of the numerous blooms often causing the stems to collapse. Usually the flowers have a black eye, and often they open in the sun and close when it becomes cool and shady.

Foliage diseases can be a problem in humid districts. In heavy soils the leaves can remain wet for long periods, allowing fungal spores to germinate and infection to begin. New leaves are often infected as they emerge in such conditions. Disease is seldom a problem in sunny dry positions, especially where there is sufficient air circulation to dry moisture from the leaves before spores can germinate.

Increase is usually by the separation of offsets when the plants are dormant in summer. Seed germinates freely and should be sown in autumn. Sandy free-draining mix should be used in deep trays, allowing the seedlings to grow throughout their first season without requiring transplanting.

I. viridiflora is the best-known and most beautiful species. Known as the green corn lily, it has uniquely coloured blooms of greenish blue or turquoise with a dark eye. These are carried from late spring on slender 90 cm tall spikes, which sway in the slightest breeze. It often thrives for a few years and then suddenly dies out. This is usually caused by excessive summer rainfall and is less of a problem in very sandy soils. Increase is usually by lifting, in summer, the numerous cormlets which are produced. Fresh seed germinates readily. 'Elvira' is a late-flowering form with pale blue flowers.

I. campanulata (syn. *I. crateroides*) is an attractive easily grown species, sometimes called red ixia. Usually the flowers are brilliant carmine-red and occasionally white. They face upwards from 40 cm tall stems in early summer.

I. dubia has brilliant golden yellow flowers with a reddish reverse and tiny reddish eye. No blotches appear in the throat, whereas the similar *I. maculata* has large blotches.

I. maculata has large orange or yellow-orange flowers which are blotched in the throat. The buds have reddish or brownish shadings outside. The flowers are upward-facing and appear on 40 cm stems in spring. It is an outstanding subject for gardens.

I. monadelpha has flowers of unusual colouring,

usually blue or purple. These are carried on 40 cm stems in spring.

I. paniculata (syn. *Morphixia paniculata*) has creamy yellow starry flowers flushed with red or pink outside and in the throat. These appear in late spring and early summer on stems up to 1 m tall. This distinctive species is easily grown in gardens but can become blemished in bad weather.

I. paniculata 'Alba' has white flowers flushed with palest blue outside, carried on slender stems. It flowers mainly in early summer and is an excellent garden subject.

I. polystachya (syn. *I. flexuosa*) has soft lilac-pink upward-facing flowers. These appear on erect 50

cm stems in late spring. It forms dense clumps of narrow erect grassy foliage and is an excellent garden subject.

I. rapunculoides produces masses of mauve-blue flowers on 50 cm stems in winter. It is one of the first to flower, continuing in bloom for a long period.

I. rouxii has flowers in a range of colours with variable markings. The form usually grown has turquoise-green flowers with dark centres on 50 cm stems. It is the only species which resembles *I. viridiflora*, but it flowers later and is less vigorous. Neither species tolerates too much rain at flowering time.

A number of cultivars are available. The more reliable include: 'Conqueror', deep golden yellow flushed reddish orange outside; 'Uranus', golden yellow with a dark eye on 45 cm stems; 'Vulcan', rich orange-red.

Ixia, pink form

LACHENALIA
Hyacinthaceae

This is a genus of more than a hundred species, all natives of South Africa. Most are found in the winter-rainfall Cape Province, growing during winter and dormant for a long period in summer. Different species can be had in flower over a long period from autumn until mid-summer, with most species at peak in spring. The last few to flower come into bloom after the leaves have died down. Many are scented, often for only a short period each day. They are particularly suitable for growing in warm climates, although many species are specialist plants with difficult requirements. Several are suitable for naturalising in gardens, and most are good container subjects.

In gardens they are particularly effective when planted in clumps. Most prefer full sun but a few do well in partial shade. Generally they require well-drained soil, although many grow in heavy soil in their natural habitats. Species which grow naturally in deserts and semi-deserts are the most difficult, often rotting in cultivation; winter-rainfall species are the easiest. The soft bulbs vary considerably in shape and are not very large.

Seed germinates easily if sown into a sandy mix as soon as it is ripe. Mature bulbs produce

Lachenalia contaminata

numerous offsets, which can be separated when dormant. These are best placed into a sandy mix just below soil level. Some species can be propagated by leaf cuttings or by splitting the bulbs at their base.

L. aloides is a variable species from the Cape Province which has been separated into several varieties. All grow about 25 cm tall. It is the most widely grown species, suitable for sunny or partially shaded positions with well-drained soil. The flowers are in shades of greenish yellow to golden orange and hang from maroon-spotted stems. Each bulb produces one or two leaves, which are also heavily marked.

L. aloides var. *aloides* usually has yellow flowers with red tips during winter and spring.

L. aloides var. *aurea* is most widely used for naturalising. Golden yellow flowers hang from purplish brown stalks during winter and spring. It is taller than most varieties and can be left undisturbed in well-drained soils.

L. aloides var. *tricolor* has flowers in three colours. The outer petals are pale yellow and green with reddish orange tips. It flowers abundantly slightly later in the season.

L. aloides var. *quadricolor* produces flowers in four

colours: reddish orange becoming yellowish and green with maroon tips. Its colourful blooms appear abundantly in late winter and spring. It multiplies rapidly in well-drained soils.

L. aloides var. *vanzyliae* has unusual colouring, lustrous white flowers flushed at the base with pale blue and green at the tips. It usually grows vigorously and multiplies freely in gardens.

'Pearsonii' is a widely grown selection with bright scarlet-orange flowers edged with red. It was raised in New Zealand and has long been considered to be a hybrid but is now thought to be a form of *L. aloides*. It should not be confused with the species *L. pearsonii*.

L. bulbifera produces striking tubular flowers in various shades of reddish orange with green tips. It is one of the showiest species for gardens and pots, flowering from mid-winter until spring. It is extremely vigorous, stems often reaching 30 cm tall and the bulbs multiplying freely. 'Crimson Joy' has pendulous flowers which are pinkish crimson outside, yellowish inside, violet at the tip and with greenish markings. 'Scarlet Bloom' is a vigorous selection of *L. bulbifera* which flowers for a similar period.

L. rubida is similar to *L. bulbifera* but is earlier

121

Lachenalia orchioides var. *glaucina*

Lachenalia reflexa

to flower in the autumn. It is extremely variable, usually producing reddish speckled flowers which earn it the name of the strawberry lachenalia. It does not flower abundantly and can be slow to multiply.

L. contaminata is sometimes called wild hyacinth in South Africa. Its waxy white flowers often have reddish brown tips and spots. The small flowers are bell-shaped rather than tubular and appear for a long period during spring. It is unusual in producing up to 10 grass-like leaves per bulb, most species producing only two. It is easily grown, multiplying freely, and is most effective in massed plantings.

L. mutabilis is a variable species, usually with iridescent pale blue flowers tipped with yellow. These are carried in slender spikes with several unopened sterile golden flowers on the top. It has a long flowering period, commencing as *L. bulbifera* finishes. It multiplies freely and is excellent for naturalising in large colonies.

L. orchioides is a variable species which usually grows naturally in shady mountainous places in the Cape Province.

L. orchioides var. *orchioides* is the most widespread variety, usually with pale blue flowers becoming greenish yellow at the tips. Its flowers are strongly scented and appear in spring on sturdy stalks about 30 cm tall.

L. orchioides var. *glaucina* (syn. *L. glaucina*) has blue flowers with purplish tips in spring and is less strongly scented.

L. pallida (syn. *L. glaucina* var. *pallida*) is popular and easily grown, favouring moist well-drained soil. Flower colour is variable, the form most commonly grown being lemon-yellow with greenish markings. The unopened flowers at the top of each 20 cm spike are purplish. It flowers mainly in spring and is ideal for naturalising in rock gardens.

L. reflexa has spikes of greenish yellow flowers which are unusual in being borne almost upright. It flowers during winter and is very easy and desirable.

The species mentioned so far are the most widely available and generally the easiest to grow. A selection of other desirable species follows.

L. arbuthnotiae produces dense spikes of soft yellow flowers with green markings. These are carried on spotted stems about 30 cm tall in spring. It is a beautiful species but not one of the easiest. It does not multiply freely, and sometimes the bulbs do not come into growth in their second season. This can often be overcome by soaking the bulbs in tepid water for several hours in autumn prior to planting.

L. carnosa has cream flowers flushed with lavender-purple at the tips. These are carried on 25 cm tall stems in early spring.

L. elegans grows naturally at high altitudes and should be cold-hardy. The variably coloured flowers can be pale blue, pink, white or yellow. A form commonly grown has pale blue flowers with brownish tips and flowers in late spring.

L. hirta var. *hirta* is also variable, typically producing bluish flowers with yellow shadings and brownish tips. An unusual green-flowered form is popular when available.

L. juncifolia is a variable dwarf species, usually white flowered with various markings of purple or rose. Although it multiplies freely by offsets, it can easily be lost.

L. liliflora has large creamy white flowers flushed with purple at their tips. These appear in spring on 25 cm stems. It is vigorous and usually does well in gardens.

L. mathewsii produces yellow bell-shaped flowers with greenish spots on short stems. It is one of the best for gardens, growing vigorously and making a bold display.

L. mediana typically has pale blue and white flowers with reddish purple markings. These appear in short slender spikes in spring. It is easily grown and multiplies readily.

L. orthopetala produces white bell-shaped flowers with brown markings and contrasting red stamens. The flowers face upwards on short 25 cm stalks in spring. It is one of the few species which produce numerous grass-like leaves per bulb. It is easily grown and is suitable for rock gardens or pots.

L. purpureo-caerulea is one of the last to flower, producing purplish blue flowers in early summer. Masses of raised pustules give the foliage a sandpaper appearance. It is generally easily grown and usually best in pots.

L. pusilla is very unusual, producing several white flowers at ground-level among a rosette of prostrate leaves. It does not look much like a lachenalia at all, resembling a *Polyxena* or *Massonia* in appearance. A collector's plant, it requires sandy soil and is very prone to slug and snail damage.

It is one of the first to flower in autumn.

L. pustulata gets its name from the large blisters on the upper surface of its foliage. Its flower colour is variable, including vivid violet-blue with purplish tips and pale yellow with greenish tips. It is a good subject for pots or gardens, flowering freely in spring.

L. rosea is a late-flowering species, producing rose-pink blooms on 20 cm stems in spring. It is attractive and easily grown in pots or gardens.

L. trichophylla has yellowish flowers which are often flushed with pink during spring. It is grown mainly for its large hairy shield-shaped foliage, which is quite different from that of any other species. It is an interesting novelty for growing in pots.

L. unifolia produces flowers in various unusual colourings. The form usually grown has blue shadings at the base of the flowers with a white band and is tipped with green and maroon. The leaves have a swollen stem-like base and are striped with reddish brown and white. Often more than one leaf per bulb is produced in cultivation.

L. viridiflora is a beautiful species with flowers in various shades of greenish blue. It is very early flowering, producing short spikes from early winter. It requires good drainage and is usually grown in pots.

L. zeyheri has delicate white flowers tinged with pink in spring. It resembles *L. contaminata* and is just as easy to grow.

LAPEIROUSIA
Iridaceae

This fairly large genus has many colourful members, mostly native to South Africa and extending into tropical Africa. They are closely related to *Anomatheca* but generally have narrower leaves. They all need a warm sunny position with well-drained soil, or sandy potting mix if grown in containers. The species from South Africa usually flower in late winter to spring. The foliage is narrow, often grassy, and green or grey-green. They are generally free from pests, although aphids occasionally appear, and botrytis can be a problem in the colder months if they remain wet

for any length of time. The corms are fairly small and produce a few offsets, but seed is the best method of propagation. Seed should be sown in sandy soil in pots as soon as ripe and will often flower after 12 months.

L. corymbosa from the Cape Province of South Africa is a wonderful plant with soft blue or darker blue flowers with attractive white markings. These are carried in large clusters of 20 or more on 15 cm tall stems. This species is best grown in pots as it flowers from mid-winter to spring, and heavy rain can spoil the blooms.

L. oreogena from Nieuwouldtville produces an abundance of tiny dark violet and white flowers. These appear on 15 cm stems in mid- to late winter and are quite stunning on a sunny day.

L. silenoides is a small difficult species which needs sand or sandy soil. It has brilliant rosy red flowers, and the bulbs need a good summer baking. Unfortunately, the seed takes a long while to germinate.

L. jacquinii has very nice violet flowers with cream markings carried on 10 cm stems. It is another species that should be grown in pots.

L. ixioides has star-shaped flowers in shades of blue, purple or white. Six or more highly scented blooms appear on 50 cm tall stems in late spring.

L. purpurea produces five to eight flowers per head in shades of soft violet with maroon-purple stripes in the centre of the petals. They are carried on stems 30–50 cm tall.

L. coquimbensis has tight heads containing three to seven scented flowers per stem of showy violet-blue with white stripes in the centre of the petals.

LEUCOJUM
Amaryllidaceae

Snowflakes are closely related to and often confused with snowdrops (*Galanthus*). The most obvious difference is that the petals of snowflakes are all the same length, whereas snowdrops have three short and three long petals. Snowflakes are much easier to grow in warm climates than snowdrops. They prefer a cool position in rich

LEUCOCORYNE
Alliaceae

These South American bulbs, commonly known as glory of the sun, have scented long-lasting flowers which are very good for picking. They are also ideal for pots and containers, growing in the winter months and flowering in late winter and spring. They need a well-drained loamy soil or potting mix and become dormant in summer, when they should be allowed to dry out. Bulbs should be repotted in autumn and watered when the weather becomes cooler to start them into growth. A few bulbils are formed around the old bulbs, and when separated these take about two years to mature. Seed can be sown in pots of sandy soil in autumn. Seedlings take three or more years to reach flowering size. Generally they are pest free but can rot if they become too wet during warm weather.

Opposite, above: *Leucocoryne corymbosa*

Opposite, below: *Leucocoryne purpurea*

Leucojum aestivum 'Graveteye Giant'

moist soil and are among the easiest of all bulbs for naturalising.

L. aestivum grows naturally in moist areas of Europe and parts of Asia. The white flowers have a distinctive green spot near the tip of each petal. Clusters of six or more flowers are carried on stems about 45 cm long in winter and spring. It is outstanding for naturalising, forming large dense clumps which never require any attention. It is one of the few bulbs to thrive in heavy moist soils and tolerates full sun or shade. It is ideal for naturalising in clumps on farms as it is poisonous and never grazed by animals. It makes a nice combination mixed with daffodils. Numerous offsets are produced by the large bulbs, and these can be separated when dormant in summer. Because this species is so easily grown, it is generally disregarded by most gardeners, who perhaps consider it common.

'Gravetye Giant' produces larger flowers on taller stems and is more striking than the typical species. It begins flowering slightly later but continues for a long period.

L. autumnale (syn. *Acis autumnale*) produces tiny white nodding bells flushed with pink at their base and with yellow anthers. These are scented, and several appear on each 25 cm stem in late summer and autumn before the grassy leaves have emerged. It is a good substitute for snowdrops (*Galanthus*) in warm climates.

L. roseum resembles *L. autumnale,* but its lovely pendulous bells are rose-pink. This tiny species is ideal for rock gardens.

L. vernum is native to central Europe, where it often grows in great quantities in shady situations. Relatively large white flowers with green spots on the petal tips are carried on stems about 30 cm tall. It thrives in moist soil and is best left undisturbed once established.

LILIUM
Liliaceae

Lilies form part of the history and culture of many nations. The genus contains about 80 species, mostly native to North America, Asia and Europe. Most produce several showy flowers on a single stem.

The large number of species and vast number of hybrids have a range of differing requirements, and generalising is not easy. Some are particularly difficult to grow, while others seed freely and can sometimes become weeds.

Full sun is required by most lilies, although a few with pale flowers are grown in partial shade to protect their flowers from bleaching. In shade fewer flowers normally develop, and disease problems can be worse.

Well-drained soil with plenty of humus added is ideal. Planting bulbs in heavy soils is a common cause of failure. Adding coarse gritty material such as gravel and sand will improve drainage and promote vigorous healthy growth.

Usually lilies should be planted in autumn, although some need to be put in earlier (e.g. *L. candidum* and *L. longiflorum*). The usual planting depth is twice the size of the bulb, which is about 6–10 cm below the soil. The bulbs should not be allowed to dry out when lifted, and their roots should be damaged as little as possible. It is very important not to damage the basal plate of the bulbs. Many growers dust their bulbs with fungicide prior to planting to help prevent fungal rots developing. Tall lilies require staking, especially when heavy with flower.

Lilies come into growth in spring, and they should be fertilised with general garden fertiliser or blood and bone at this time. As most produce stem roots just below the soil surface, they should be mulched to prevent these from drying out. It is recommended to keep 'their heads in the sun and their feet in the shade'. Roots can be kept cool also by planting ground-covers which are not too competitive (e.g. *Ajuga, Pratia puberula*).

The flowers of lilies are usually large and often fragrant. Colours include white, yellow, orange, purple, pink and crimson. They are often multi-coloured with various spots and markings.

It is important not to cut the stems back too early in autumn, allowing them to die back naturally so that the bulbs are nourished as much as possible. When the foliage has turned brown they are ready for pruning. Seeds should be removed as soon as possible, unless required, so that energy is not wasted in their development.

The usual method of increase is by division of the bulbs in early winter. Some species form small bulbils in their leaf axils, and these can be separated and planted immediately into well-

Lilium formosanum

drained sandy soil. They will usually flower in about two years.

Seed is a good method of propagating some lilies and produces new plants which are free from virus. Most species will germinate a few weeks after sowing; others can take up to two years. A few species, such as *L. formosanum,* will flower late in their first summer from a spring sowing.

When used as cut flowers, lilies should be picked as soon as the flowers begin to open. The complete stem should not be harvested, ideally leaving some stem which contains foliage so that the bulbs can continue to develop. Pollen can be a problem, staining clothing and furniture. If it is allowed to dry it can be brushed off the stamens prior to arranging.

Lilies can be very effective when grown in containers, and this is often the best method where soils are heavy. Bulbs should be planted in autumn into large deep containers of free-draining gritty mix to a depth of about 10 cm. Slow-release fertiliser applied in spring will produce vigorous healthy growth. The plants should be repotted using fresh mix every few years.

A range of different lilies will produce a succession of flowers throughout summer. *L. candidum* (madonna lily) begins in early summer, followed in mid-summer by *L. longiflorum, L.*

martagon (Turk's cap lily) and *L. regale.* Various hybrids flower from mid-summer, and in late summer *L. formosanum* produces its large trumpets.

The usual cause of poor health is unsuitable growing conditions. Diseases which affect lilies include virus, which produces yellow streaks on the leaves and weak growth. It is usually spread by insects, especially aphids, and infected plants including the bulbs should be destroyed.

Fusarium basal rot causes the scales and bulbs to become blackened. Dusting bulbs with fungicide prior to planting will reduce infection. Poorly drained soils should have sand added prior to planting.

Botrytis attacks the foliage and the stems, often causing new shoots to turn brown. Later in the season rusty blotches can develop on the leaves, followed by typical grey mould. This is a secondary infection, the result of prior damage from hail or wind. The plants usually survive but are often considerably weakened. The best control is prevention by planting in a sunny, well-drained position with good air circulation. Fungicides are available commercially which will control it for a time.

Insects which can attack lilies include thrips, aphids, mites and nematodes. See the Pests and Diseases section for their control.

LILIUM SPECIES

L. auratum is the golden-rayed lily of Japan. The flowers are large and fragrant, and it is the parent of numerous hybrids. It is often considered to be difficult, but it is usually quite easy in well-drained soil. It is a good garden subject for growing among shrubs and perennials. The flowers are white with yellow or reddish streaks and crimson spots. Several varieties are available:

L. auratum var. *platyphyllum* is vigorous with large flowers and fewer spots.

L. auratum var. *virginale* has white flowers with yellow streaks.

L. bulbiferum is the fire lily. The flowers are orange with deeper tips and maroon spots. It can be grown in most soils, and increase is by separation of offsets when dormant.

L. candidum is the madonna lily, valued for centuries for its beauty and symbolism as well as its food and medicinal properties. The flowers are pure white with golden anthers. Unlike most lilies, the bulbs should be planted just below the surface of the soil as the stems do not form roots at their base. It also prefers lime added to the soil and is prone to virus and botrytis infections.

L. chalcedonicum is the scarlet Turk's cap lily. It carries bright scarlet flowers with recurved petals on stems to about 90 cm tall. It resents disturbance and is susceptible to botrytis infection in humid conditions.

L. davidii is a graceful species from China, with scentless flowers of orange with dark spots and reflexed petals. It is easily grown in a sunny position and produces numerous small bulbs on its underground stems. It crosses easily and is the parent of many hybrids.

L. formosanum from Taiwan is a wonderful garden subject in warm climates. It is best to produce new plants from seed each year. Seed should be sown in early spring, and seedlings planted in early summer will flower late in summer. It is an ideal subject for mixing with perennials, providing valuable late colour. Clusters of large white funnel-shaped flowers are carried on stems up 1.8 m tall. These are fragrant and often flushed with purple outside. A form with pure white flowers is also available, and this is to be preferred. Numerous seeds are produced in large pods in autumn, and these should be collected when ripe and stored in a paper bag during winter. This species is not too particular as to soil type, growing easily in average well-drained soil in full sun.

L. formosanum var. *pricei* is a dwarf form of the species, also native to Taiwan, where it grows in the mountains. The flowers are almost as large as the typical species and are flushed with purple outside. They are huge in comparison to the short 40 cm stems and look rather incongruous.

L. hansonii from Japan is one of the Turk's cap lilies. Its orange-yellow flowers have reddish spots and are sweetly scented, and several are carried on each 90 cm stem. It is easily grown in most soils in full sun or partial shade.

L. henryi belongs to the speciosum group, producing orange nodding blooms with reflexed petals. It is easily grown and quite late flowering. It dislikes acid soil, so lime should be applied prior to planting. Usually 10–20 flowers are carried on each stem.

L. lancifolium (syn. *L. tigrinum*) is the widely grown tiger lily, one of the oldest species in cultivation. The form commonly grown produces reflexed reddish orange flowers with purplish spots. These hang from stems about 1.5 m tall in mid-summer. It is extremely easy to grow, multiplying freely from numerous bulbs produced at the base of the stems.

L. longiflorum is known as the Christmas lily in the Southern Hemisphere, flowering in mid-summer at Christmas time. It produces numerous blooms with a sweet honeysuckle fragrance and is one of the most significant of all lilies, with its large trumpet-shaped pure white flowers and easy culture. Many cultivars are available. *L. longiflorum* var. *eximium* has very reflexed petals and is widely grown. Well-drained light soils with leaf mould added are ideal. The plants often die if they become waterlogged.

L. martagon is the Turk's cap lily. It has a wider natural distribution than any other lily, occurring from Portugal to Poland, Russia and Mongolia. Usually the flowers are purplish with darker spots and a waxy texture. As many as 50 hang from stems which can reach 1.8 m tall. Numerous cultivars are available in a range of red, purple and pink shades. *L. martagon* var. *album* has white flowers without spots.

Opposite: *Lilium martagon*

128

L. pardalinum is a native of coastal California, where it grows in relatively high-rainfall areas. One of the most dependable of species from this region, it is extremely variable in height and flower colour. The Turk's cap type flowers are in various shades of golden orange to scarlet with spotted yellow throats. The stems can reach about 80 cm tall but are usually shorter.

L. philippinense is a smallish species with numerous large trumpets appearing in late summer. These are white flushed heavily with purple outside. It is a good subject for warm climates and is easily grown from fresh seed.

L. pumilum is a small species producing dainty nodding flowers of brilliant scarlet with reflexed petals. These are carried on slender stems, usually about 50 cm in height but sometimes taller. The foliage is grass-like, and it prefers sandy well-drained soil. Several different colour forms are available. This species tends to be short-lived, and new plants should be raised regularly from seed.

L. regale, the regal or royal lily, is a native of China and one of the best of the trumpet-shaped lilies. Clusters of white trumpets flushed purplish outside are carried on stems about 1.2 m tall in mid-summer. The petals bend backwards to produce flowers about 15 cm across. Narrow dark green leaves are carried along the stems. Numerous small bulbils develop at the base of each stem, and division of these when dormant is the usual method of increase. Seed also germinates freely and usually produces flowering plants in the second season. Free-draining soil and full sun are required. It is the parent of numerous hybrids and deservedly the most popular species.

L. speciosum is a valuable late-flowering species with many colour forms available. The fragrant Turk's cap flowers vary from rose to carmine in the centre, with white edging and spots. The flowers hang from stems up to 1.6 m tall and are among the last to appear in late summer. It prefers a soil rich in humus and a position in partial shade.

L. speciosum var. *rubrum* has deeper-coloured flowers.

L. x *parkmanii* is a popular hybrid group derived from crossing *L. auratum* with *L. speciosum*. The recurved petals are crimson with white margins. Numerous selections are available.

Lilies have been classified into nine divisions:
DIVISION I. Asiatic hybrids (small early-flowering hybrids).

Lilium 'Zephyr'

DIVISION II. Martagon hybrids (Turk's cap lilies derived from *L. martagon* and *L. hansonii*).

DIVISION III. Candidum hybrids (derived from European species such as *L. candidum*).

DIVISION IV. American hybrids.

DIVISION V. Longiflorum hybrids (derived from *L. longiflorum* and *L. formosanum*).

DIVISION VI. Trumpet hybrids (tall lilies with large trumpets derived from Asian species).

DIVISION VII. Oriental hybrids (derived from Far Eastern species; usually late flowering).

DIVISION VIII. Miscellaneous hybrids.

DIVISION IX. True species.

For an extensive list and description of cultivars, refer to specialist lily books.

LITTONIA
Colchicaceae

L. modesta, a climbing lily from South Africa, is the species most commonly grown. It is closely related to *Gloriosa*, which it resembles when in bud but from which it is easily distinguished when the flowers are open. It has much the same requirements, needing a well-drained soil for the forked tubers to delve into. Some support is necessary for the 60–150 cm tall stems to climb up.

The foliage is soft green and has tendrils on the tips. These will cling to twigs or other foliage. The golden yellow flowers are somewhat bell-shaped and about 5 cm across. The peak display is in mid-summer, with numerous flowers appearing for a few weeks. They are very good for picking. After flowering large green pods develop, and these eventually split open in late autumn to display orange-brown seeds. The seed-heads will last in dried arrangements for quite some time. The seeds can be sown in a light sandy mix and covered with 2 cm of coarse grit. Some seed can remain dormant for a number of seasons, but most will germinate after three to four months. Seedlings form small tubers that flower in two to three years. The tubers can be stored dry during the cold wet winter months and should be planted in spring or early summer in a sunny or partially shaded position. Some forms produce larger flowers than the type, and these should be obtained if available.

Littonia modesta

LYCORIS
Amaryllidaceae

Lycoris are splendid autumn-flowering bulbs when their requirements are met. The large number of species and hybrids make excellent garden subjects and provide a good supply of cut flowers. They also perform well when grown in containers. They resemble nerines, with heads of 5–20 flowers carried on strong stems. Flower colour ranges through shades of yellow, cream, pink, violet, blue and red. The strap-like leaves can be 30–50 cm long and 3–5 cm wide.

The tendency for the bulbs to split into several small pips can be overcome by firmly planting them just below the soil surface as soon as they become dormant. Free-draining sandy soils are ideal, and organic manure and compost must be avoided. Roots can rot if kept too wet.

Water should be withheld from late spring to mid-summer. As the nights cool towards autumn, heavy watering will induce flowering.

Cut flowers should be harvested just as the first buds begin to open, and they will continue to

open in water. They last 10 or more days if placed in a cool room. Virus can be spread by contaminated cutters when picking flowers.

It is best to replant the bulbs in a semi-shaded position as soon as possible after lifting. They can be stored for a number of weeks if kept dry, but if they become moist, flowers will sprout and spoil inside the storage container.

Lycoris multiply readily and require dividing every three to five years. They can also be propagated by twin scaling early in their dormancy. When available, seed can be sown into a sandy medium, just covered, and kept at about 20°C. The first flower will appear between four and seven years from sowing.

L. aurea, the golden spider lily, originates from limestone areas of China. It can often be a difficult species to get into flower. As with all *Lycoris,* it requires a hot dry resting period during summer to promote flowering. Dressings of potash and lime are also helpful. Applying slow-release fertiliser during the growing season will encourage the bulbs to rapidly reach flowering size.

Other species and hybrids include:

L. albiflora, shining white.
L. incarnata, soft flesh-pink.
L. radiata, red.
L. radiata, var. *pumila,* red.
L. sprengeri, vivid rose, purple, carmine and Prussian blue.
L. straminea, pale straw-yellow with freckles.
L. 'Blue Pearl', electric-blue

MASSONIA
Hyacinthaceae

These unusual natives of Namaqualand typically have two prostrate succulent rounded leaves and flowers which resemble paint brushes. They are seldom grown but reward enthusiasts with excellent winter colour. Well-drained sandy soil is necessary, and they usually perform best when grown in containers. It is advisable to plant only

Opposite, above. *Lycoris aurea*
Opposite, below: *Lycoris radiata*

one plant per pot as the leaves are best without others growing over them.

M. depressa is a species from the Cape. It is appropriately called pigs' ears because of its rounded succulent leaves. These can be 20 cm across and often have purple markings, although some are plain green.

White to pale pink flowers appear in early to mid-winter. These comprise clusters of stamens and small petals, and are covered with copious glistering nectar. The large droplets of nectar attract bees and ants, and there is sufficient for small rodents to drink. These could well be the normal pollinators in their near-desert homeland.

This species, as with most others, is worth growing for its handsome foliage alone. The large leaves are inviting to touch but surprisingly cold.

When dormant during summer the bulbs are best left in their pots and kept dry. Watering should re-commence in late autumn.

Propagation is usually by seed, which sets fairly readily, and seedlings take at least two years to reach flowering size. As they are related to lachenalias, they could possibly be propagated by leaf cuttings (see *Lachenalia* section for this procedure).

The only disease problem is botrytis, which can infect the flowers, but this is not usually a problem in a well-ventilated greenhouse.

M. pustulata is another species from the Cape, commonly referred to as bristly pigs' ears. It is altogether a prettier species and deserves to be more widely grown. The rounded leaves are 5–10 cm across, with striations and some purple markings, and are covered with a variable number of pustules.

In early winter, clusters of soft pink stamens appear. These are sweetly apple scented and long lasting. They are smaller than those of *M. depressa* and do not require as large a pot.

M. angustifolia is now classified as *Neobakeria angustifolia* by some authorities. Native to the Cape, it produces two upright dark green ribbed leaves about 5 cm wide and up to 20 cm tall. Brilliant orange star-like flowers with clusters of orange stamens are covered with orange pollen. They are carried on 10–15 cm long stems in early winter. Water should be applied from late summer, taking care not to apply too much. From mid-spring the plants should be dried off and kept dry throughout summer. Generally, two clones are

Massonia angustifolia

MELASPHAERULA
Iridaceae

This genus contains only one species, *M. ramosa* (syn. *M. graminea*), from the Cape Province of South Africa. It is a winter grower, producing delicate papery flowers of creamy yellow in winter and spring. It is best in a warm sheltered position in well-drained average garden soil and spreads rapidly, soon forming dense clumps. It makes a nice foil for other showier plants and is long-lasting when picked. Increase is normally by separation of the small black corms when dormant in summer. These should be planted by autumn.

MORAEA
Iridaceae

needed before seed will be set. Seedlings take two to three years to reach flowering size. Botrytis can develop on old flowers, sometimes spreading to the rest of the plant and causing serious damage.

M. echinata has white flowers and is seen on rare occasions. Very few other species are in cultivation.

Moraea is a very large genus of corm-producing plants. Most species are native to South Africa, and a few are from tropical Africa and Madagascar. Some are evergreen, while others go dormant in the summer. They enjoy a sunny position and well-drained sandy soil, although a few can be grown in boggy situations. The flowers are often large and brilliantly coloured, and some are scented. Individual flowers can last from only a few hours to several days, but each stem carries a large number at any one time for many weeks. Each bulb produces one or more long leaves. Strong 'contractile' spring-like roots often pull the small corms quite deeply into the soil. The corms can be stored dry over summer and replanted in autumn. The smaller species are best grown in pots of sandy mix, and some larger species are suitable for use in gardens or big containers.

Potted plants can be placed in a sunny position inside the house when in flower. This will also protect the blooms from rain damage during their winter and spring flowering period. The small seeds ripen in late spring and should be sown in early autumn into a sandy mix, lightly covered with sand or grit. They usually germinate as the temperatures become cool, forming tiny corms in the first season and taking three to four years to commence flowering. They will often pull to

Melasphaerula ramosa

the bottom of the pot in the first season, and they should be replanted 5 cm deep the following autumn or they can remain dormant for an entire season.

M. aristata is a rare species in its natural habitat in South Africa but fortunately grows well in cultivation. The 35–40 cm tall stems can be single or branched, and the long-lasting flowers are white with a hint of smoky blue. The eye is deep peacock-violet. This spring-flowering species has hairy leaves and can often be found growing in old gardens.

M. atropunctata is a winter-growing native of the southwestern Cape. The distinctive cream flowers are heavily overlaid with dark brown and are carried on 25 cm stems from early spring. Although little known, this attractive species is easily grown in well-drained garden soil.

M. fugax (syn. *M. edulis*) is a variable species with small edible corms. It grows well in sandy soils and produces single or branched stems 10–30 cm tall. The fragrant flowers open at midday and appear for a long period from late winter to late spring in a range of colours, including white, yellows, lilac, blue and soft lavender shades. It makes a nice small pot plant for a sunny position and can be grown in rock gardens.

M. gigandra, as with many beautiful plants, has now become rare in the wild. It will grow quite well in damp soils, even clay, but is also easy in pots or containers. The plants can have single or branched stems 40–60 cm tall. The large flowers are 6–8 cm across and occur in a wide range of colours, usually in deep blue shades with peacock eyes. This species flowers in spring and is highly desirable.

M. loubseri has only recently been discovered but is now well established in cultivation. The branched stems are 35–40 cm tall and carry large dark violet-purple flowers in spring. It is best grown in pots of sandy soil.

M. neopavonia is another rare species. It can be difficult to grow, requiring well-drained soil with some clay added. The 50 cm tall stems can be branched and carry large orange to orange-red flowers. The eyes can be iridescent green, black or speckled. *M. neopavonia* var. *lutea* has bright citron-yellow flowers and is slightly taller than the species.

M. polystachya has a wide distribution in South Africa. It is one of the easiest species to grow and perhaps the most valuable in the garden. Plants readily self-sow, seedlings often appearing in unexpected places. The branched stems grow 40–80 cm tall, and the mauve to pale blue flowers are the first to open in early autumn. Peak

Moraea aristata

Moraea villosa hybrid

flowering is during autumn, but some blooms continue to open until late spring. A huge number of flowers are produced over the season. It thrives in sun but will also grow in quite shady places. The bulbs will pull themselves down into the soil and can sometimes remain dormant for several years. Seed is produced abundantly.

M. spathulata grows naturally on damp streamsides in South Africa. The 60–100 cm tall single flower-stems carry 10 cm wide bright yellow flowers with darker yellow markings. In gardens it can be grown in a wide range of soils. The evergreen foliage can be rather untidy, growing more than 1 m long and sprawling. This summer-flowering species is best planted among shrubs or perennials.

M. tripetala produces single or branched stems about 50 cm tall, which carry flowers in a range of colours, including rich royal-blue, pale blue, yellow or pink, in spring. This species is easily grown in sandy soil.

M. vegeta is a dainty species which is easy to grow. The branched stems are 20–30 cm tall and have masses of buff flowers with yellow eyes in late winter. It is best grown in pots as the flowers do not stand out against a background of soil.

M. villosa has beautiful flowers which give the species its common name, peacock iris. It resembles *M. aristata* but has smooth leaves without hairs. Flower colour is variable, including violet, mauve, lilac, pink, pale orange or white with blue peacock eyes. The large flowers are carried on stems 30–50 cm tall in spring. It is an easily grown species in sandy loams and will often self-sow when established.

MUSCARI
Hyacinthaceae

This is a genus of about 30 species of small bulbous plants which are generally very easy to grow. Most produce blue flowers in spring, and many are useful for naturalising in large groups at the front of a garden. Some species have a strong musky fragrance. They are commonly known as grape hyacinths.

Increase is usually by division of the dormant

bulbs in summer, and most multiply rapidly this way. Plants can also be raised from seed. The dormant period is often not very long, many species commencing into growth in late summer. Bulbs can be stored dry if necessary and should be planted by autumn.

The following species are all winter growers which flower in spring.

M. armeniacum is commonly grown and very vigorous. The scented flowers are in shades of blue or purplish blue and have white tips. It is vigorous, with flowers reaching about 10 cm tall, and it soon forms dense clumps in the garden. Several cultivars are available: 'Cantab' has pale blue flowers on short stems; 'Blue Spike' has double blooms of soft blue; 'Heavenly Blue' has sky-blue flowers and is vigorous and easily grown; 'Barbara' is a small form with pale ice-blue flowers.

M. aucheri (syn. *M. tubergenianum*) is a dwarf species with flowers in shades of blue. Those at the base of the spikes are bright deep blue, and those above are paler. The combination is most attractive, as are the turquoise-blue buds. It is easily grown and very free-flowering. 'Iceberg'

Muscari latifolium

has pale ice-blue flowers with darker sterile flowers at the top of the racemes.

M. azureum is a lovely little species with bell-shaped flowers. It carries its blooms in dense heads, those at the base of the racemes blue and those above paler. A white-flowered form is also available. This species is ideal for rock gardens and shallow containers. It does not produce many offsets and so is slow to multiply.

M. botryoides is the true grape hyacinth, a dwarf species with sky-blue rounded flowers in dense racemes. It is early flowering and slow to multiply. 'Album' is the very desirable white form of this species, with sweetly scented blooms from early winter. The flowers become soft lilac with age.

M. comosum (tassel hyacinth) has stems up to 50 cm tall, the flowers at the top being blue and those below greenish brown. 'Plumosum' produces large clusters of deep mauve-blue feathery sterile flowers and is known as the feathered hyacinth. It has broad shiny grey-green leaves and 30 cm tall stems, and is very good for picking.

M. commutatum is a distinctive species with dark blackish violet flowers on stems about 15 cm tall.

M. latifolium is a distinctive species from Turkey with one broad leaf at the base of each stem. The lower flowers are very dark violet, and the upper flowers are blue, appearing on stems up to 3 cm tall in late spring.

M. muscarimi (syn. *M. moschatum*) produces sweetly scented flowers, purplish when they open and becoming yellowish as they age. The stems are usually about 15 cm high, and the erect arching leaves are a little taller.

M. neglectum produces racemes of deep blue bells with white frilly edging on 20 cm stems, those at the top being paler than the very dark navy-blue blooms at the base. It is extremely vigorous, too invasive for garden use in many places.

NARCISSUS
Amaryllidaceae

This well-known genus, commonly known as daffodils, contains numerous species and countless hybrids which vary considerably in their appearance. Many species can be difficult garden subjects in warm climates, whereas others naturalise easily and flower reliably. Generally, a cool position in rich well-drained soil is best. Many *Narcissus* make ideal companions for the large number of blue-flowered bulbs which flower at the same time (e.g. *Hyacinthoides, Muscari* and *Scilla*). If naturalised in grass, they are most effective when planted in large drifts of one variety. It is important to leave the grass unmown until the foliage of the daffodils has dried off, despite it looking untidy. This can take six or more weeks after flowering has finished.

Bulbs should be planted in late summer or autumn at a depth of about twice the size of the bulbs. Drainage in heavy soils should be improved by incorporating gritty material such as sand prior to planting. A dressing of fertiliser such as blood and bone should be given in autumn as growth commences.

Many *Narcissus* make excellent container subjects, especially those with numerous flowers carried on short sturdy stems. Many of the miniature hybrids are particularly suitable for this purpose.

The most serious pest is bulb fly (narcissus fly), which attacks a wide range of bulbs (see Pests and Diseases).

Bulbs often rot if left in heavy soil when dormant. This is especially a problem in regions with high summer rainfall. Either the bulbs can be lifted and stored over this period or the soil drainage improved, as previously described.

NARCISSUS SPECIES

This section includes naturally occurring hybrids.

N. bulbocodium is the lovely and extremely variable hoop petticoat. The plants vary in size, and in their flower colour and flowering time. They bloom mainly in winter and spring, and have narrow grassy foliage. They are popular for naturalising in grass and are ideal for rock gardens and pots, but they prefer a cool shady position in well-drained soil. Seed is the best method of increase as the bulbs multiply quite slowly.

N. bulbocodium ssp. *vulgaris* var. *citrinus* has lovely pale lemon blooms striped with green at their base. It grows readily in moist well-drained soil and is ideal for rock gardens.

N. romieuxii (syn. *N. bulbocodium* ssp. *romieuxii*) is distinguished by its large widely flared trumpets of lemon-yellow. It is one of the easiest and most

reliable forms of this species for gardens.

N. cantabricus is the white hoop petticoat, previously listed as a form of *N. bulbocodium* but now considered to be a separate species. It produces soft cream fluted flowers of thin texture with golden anthers. These appear for a long period from early winter, with occasional blooms appearing until spring. It is a good garden subject, more easily grown than 'Nylon', which it resembles. The edges of the trumpets are less wavy, and the flowers appear slightly later. *N. cantabricus* var. *folius* has papery white flowers from early winter.

N. cyclamineus is a lovely species with pendulous bright golden yellow flowers which have a long tubular trumpet and distinctively reflexed petals. It grows about 20 cm tall and is best planted in a cool moist position beneath trees. The numerous hybrids derived from it are more vigorous and suitable for general garden use (see Miniature Narcissus section below).

N. x *incomparabilis* is a naturally occurring hybrid between *N. pseudonarcissus* and *N. poeticus.* It has slightly fragrant flowers with yellow petals and a golden trumpet.

N. jonquilla is the well-known jonquil, easily grown and ideal for naturalising. Several strongly scented deep yellow flowers are carried on each stem in early spring. A number of selections of this species are available.

N. x *medioluteus* is a naturally occurring hybrid between *N. tazetta* and *N. poeticus* which is naturalised in much of Europe. It performs very well in warmer climates, where it is sometimes found naturalised around old farm homesteads. Clumps which have been established for decades continue to flourish and flower reliably without attention. The fragrant flowers usually have creamy white rounded petals and small golden cups. Several garden forms are available.

N. papyraceus 'Paperwhite' produces masses of pure white trumpets in winter. It is ideal for naturalising, especially in warm climates.

N. poeticus has white or pale cream petals and lemon cups with red edging. It is a charming little species, flowering in late spring. Although it is usually easily grown in cool moist positions, it often flowers poorly in warm climates.

N. pseudonarcissus is the extremely variable Lent lily. Usually its petals are creamy white and the trumpets pale yellow, and the flowers appear on

Narcissus cantabricus

tall stems in spring. It is one of the most robust species, ideal for naturalising. It grows well in moist soils beneath trees and is best left undisturbed once established.

N. requienii (syn. *N. juncifolius* and *N. assoanus*) has quite small golden yellow flowers with cup-shaped centres. These are carried on 20 cm stems in winter. It is a lovely little species with narrow upright foliage and is easily grown in pots or gardens.

N. tazetta produces clusters of fragrant yellow flowers with shallow orange-yellow cups. It is suitable for naturalising in warm climates. Hybrids derived from this species are more commonly grown.

N. triandrus (angel's tears) has creamy white or yellow nodding flowers with reflexed petals. It is easily grown in moist well-drained soil and is ideal for rock gardens. The bulbs multiply quite slowly, and rapid increase is best from seed. It is the parent of many hybrids.

MINIATURE NARCISSUS

A wide range of miniature *Narcissus* is available. The small selection which follows are all attractive and generally reliable in warm climates. A large number are more suitable for container growing than for gardens. Although many are hybrids, they are listed under the parent which they most resemble.

N. BULBOCODIUM CULTIVARS

'Nylon' is a hybrid between *N. bulbocodium* and *N. romieuxii*. It produces numerous creamy white flowers early in the season. It is weaker than either species, tending to die out in gardens, and is usually best grown in containers.

'Elfhorn' is much smaller and later flowering than the species.

'Jessamy' is an early-flowering form with cream flowers which become paler. It is good for gardens.

'Nivalis' is the tiniest hoop petticoat, with narrow golden yellow flowers. It grows well in free-draining soils.

N. CYCLAMINEUS CULTIVARS

'Beryl' has a neat orange cup and reflexed white petals. It is very attractive and easily grown.

'Jack Snipe' has creamy petals and a golden cup.

'Jenny' resembles 'February Gold', with pure-

white petals and a long primrose-lemon trumpet.

'Jumblie' has deep golden blooms with an orange-gold cup and reflexed petals. It is very easily grown and free-flowering.

'Little Gentleman' has very attractive butter-yellow blooms with long trumpets.

'Peeping Tom' has pure yellow blooms which resemble a large version of the species.

'Tête à Tête' is regarded as the best of all by many enthusiasts. It does well in gardens, producing an abundance of flowers from winter. These have lemon-yellow petals and orange cups.

'Yimkin' is a small desirable cultivar with tiny golden blooms.

N. JONQUILLA CULTIVARS

'Baby Moon' carries several soft yellow scented flowers on each stem. It is very free-flowering.

'Lintie' has fragrant flowers with yellow petals and an orange cup on 25 cm stems.

'Sundial' is an outstanding miniature selection with dark lemon petals and an orange cup. These appear on 15 cm stems very early in the season.

N. POETICUS CULTIVARS

'Actaea' is an early-flowering hybrid with large white rounded petals and a small golden cup edged with red. It is early flowering.

'Flore Pleno' has scented double white blooms.

N. poeticus has been crossed with *N. tazetta* to produce the 'Poetaz' hybrids. 'Geranium' is one of the best of these, with fragrant heads of white flowers with reddish orange cups in spring. It is robust and one of the best cultivars for naturalising in warm climates.

N. TAZETTA CULTIVARS

'Erlicheer' has double creamy white flowers which are strongly perfumed, appearing on sturdy 45 cm stems from mid-winter. It is among the most easily grown and reliable of cultivars and is ideal for planting among early-flowering camellias.

'Minnow' carries several creamy flowers with yellow cups per stem. It is easily grown.

'Soleil d'Or' carries clusters of small blooms from early winter and is one of the most cheerful

Opposite: *Narcissus* 'Geranium'

Narcissus 'Hawera'

of sights at this time. Its petals are bright golden yellow, and the small cups are orange.

N. TRIANDRUS CULTIVARS

'Hawera' is perhaps the best of all the miniature hybrids for naturalising in gardens. Every spring it produces an abundance of lemon-yellow blooms with reflexed petals on stems about 35 cm tall. It is great for rock gardens and does not mind moist soil. It was raised in New Zealand by Dr W. Thompson in the 1930s.

'Liberty Bells' has nodding flowers of clear lemon.

'Mary Plumstead' is slightly paler and smaller than 'Hawera', and flowers about two weeks later.

A vast array of large-flowered cultivars is also available. These are popular for exhibition and have been placed by enthusiasts into various classifications according to the form of their flowers and their parentage. They are so numerous that they are not discussed here; many specialist books on the subject are available.

NELUMBO
Nelumbonaceae

N. nucifera is an aquatic plant from Australia and Asia. It is suitable for regions with warm climates, growing well in shallow water which warms quickly in spring. It does not grow well in deep

Nelumbo nucifera

water, except in very warm climates, as the water takes too long to warm up. It can also be grown in sturdy round containers placed in a trough of water. In summer, large impressive pink blooms appear. The first frosts of winter kill off the foliage, but it resprouts the following spring. It is not difficult to grow but can be hard to obtain.

The plants can be increased by division of the tuber, ensuring some roots and leaves remain with each section. Division should take place in early spring just before growth commences.

NERINE
Amaryllidaceae

Nerine is a large genus of bulbs, all originating from South Africa. They grow in a range of habitats from mountains to moist soils and dry scrublands. Most of the species in cultivation prefer well-drained sandy soils and a sunny position. The majority flower in autumn, although three uncommon species flower in early summer. The foliage varies from grassy to thick and strap-shaped, in shades of green or grey-green. A few are almost evergreen, while others go totally dormant during hot weather.

Bulbs can be stored dry but are best replanted as soon as possible after lifting. They will grow for many years in a clump, but flower quality and numbers decline after about five years. At this stage they should be divided and replanted with one third of the bulb below soil level. The soil should be well dug and extra sand or grit added, plus sulphate of potash at 50 g and agricultural lime at 25 g per square metre. If growth is slow, a small quantity of slow-release fertiliser can be used. If strong nitrogenous fertiliser or composts are used, flowering can be suppressed for several years. These can also encourage fungal problems, as can blood and bone.

After planting in summer, growth commences as the weather cools, and the first rains trigger the flowers. The flower-stems grow very fast, and the first flowers will appear about two weeks after the buds emerge from the bulbs. The species have a colour range from brilliant red to pink shades and white, and they are good cut flowers. All will grow from seeds, which must be sown fresh on top of sandy mix in pots or boxes. These should be placed in a shady area until the young plants are established. The first flowers can be expected after three to nine years from sowing. Twin scaling can be used to build up special plants, as can simple division of the bulblets.

N. bowdenii flowers late in the season, mostly in rather harsh shades of pink. It is very hardy in cold climates and is popular for cut flowers, with 60–80 cm tall stems.

N. bowdenii 'Wellsii' has small pale pink flowers on stems 1 m tall. *N. bowdenii* 'Fenwicks Variety' has pink flowers on 80 cm tall stems. There are a number of pink *N. bowdenii* cultivars suitable for cut-flower production.

N. filifolia has very grassy foliage and thin spidery flowers of rose-pink on 30–40 cm stems. It is usually quite early flowering.

N. flexuosa 'Alba' is a commonly grown white form which often fails to flower. It is widely grown by some nurserymen as it multiplies rapidly. There is, however, another white form which flowers well, although it is slower to divide. This is the one to try to obtain as it can make a fine show in late autumn. It is best planted in semi-shade under trees with filtered sunlight. *N. flexuosa*, with rose-pink flowers, is rare in gardens.

N. fothergillii, the spider lily, has stems 40–60 cm tall carrying orange-scarlet flowers, which sparkle in the sun. This species has blue-grey leaves, and it flowers in early autumn.

N. fothergillii var. *major* has reddish orange flowers on stems 60–80 cm tall.

N. fothergillii var. *minor* has orange flowers on stems 30–50 cm tall.

N. humilis has slightly larger flowers than most other smaller species, carried on 20–30 cm tall stems. The flowers are usually soft pink but in some forms can be salmon-pink and rose.

N. krigei, the curly-leaved nerine, has rose-pink flowers in early summer on 45 cm tall stems. It has distinctive spirally twisted leaves.

N. laticoma has many pale pink flowers on a 15 cm stem growing just above the curved leaves in summer. Neither of these summer-flowering bulbs is free-flowering, and they are far from common.

N. masonorum, Miss Mason's spider lily, carries dainty heads of small pink flowers on 30 cm tall stems.

N. pudica has almost white bell-shaped flowers on 40 cm stems, and its neat blue-grey foliage is quite different from most. This species is not often seen but is one of the original parents of the modern hybrids. These species plus others are extremely good for container growing or for larger rock gardens.

N. undulata is a very dainty spider flower which can give a wonderful display when mass planted. The soft pink flowers are produced abundantly on 30–40 cm stems. *N. undulata* var. *alba* is as yet uncommon but even more desirable for pots and containers.

N. sarniensis grows 40 cm tall and has rose-red flowers. It is seldom seen in cultivation, but as the main parent in three hundred years of nerine breeding, it has possibly been the most important. There are a few white forms which have been found in South Africa.

Nerine fothergillii var. *major*

143

Nerine seedling

N. sarniensis hybrids have beautiful flowers, but for many years they have been fairly hard to obtain, many of the newest and best having been kept in private English collections. With the advent of World War Two, a number of bulbs were sent to various countries, and it is the progeny of these earlier imports that are now becoming widely grown.

Nerines thrive in mild climates, multiplying rapidly and producing long-lasting flowers in an amazing array of colours. For commercial production they should be grown under protection in a greenhouse. The soil should be a well-drained loam with plenty of sand added and the bulbs planted in raised beds that are wide enough to allow access for weeding, picking, spraying and other jobs. This care will produce flowers that are of excellent quality for cutting for local or export markets. They can be grown in containers of sandy mix or in a sunny position in a flower garden, positioned where they will not get overgrown by larger plants, which will suppress flowering.

There are many named varieties too numerous to mention. The colour range is now vast, including white, pinks, rose, salmon, orange and scarlet. Many now have a violet or lilac overlay, and some are in colours reminiscent of the Victorian era such as velvety rust, wine, violet-grey and mulberry. Many have frilly petals, and stem length can vary from 40 cm to 1.3 m.

ONIXOTIS
Asphodelaceae

This small genus is still much better known under its previous name, *Dipidax*.

O. triquetra is the species most commonly cultivated. It is native to the Cape Province of South Africa, where it grows naturally in damp ground and is sometimes called waterflower. The corms grow deeply in the soil.

The shallow bowl-shaped flowers can be white or occasionally pink with a small maroon eye. The first blooms open in winter and continue to appear until late spring. They are carried in spikes about 45 cm tall and last well when picked.

The reed-like foliage is almost as tall as the flowers and provides valuable texture in mixed plantings. The bulbs pull themselves down deeply into the soil, and when grown in pots they need to be lifted occasionally and replanted nearer to the surface.

This species thrives in moist soils but also grows well in drier conditions. It is extremely versatile and can be grown in full sun or partial shade. It is most effective when used in large groups, especially near water.

The corms can be dug up and separated when dormant in summer. Seed germinates easily if sown as soon as it is ripe in mid-summer. The seedlings grow very quickly, and most will commence flowering in their second season. No pests or diseases usually occur.

Onixotis triquetra

ORNITHOGALUM
Hyacinthaceae

This large group of bulbs originates from a wide area, including Europe, Asia and Africa, and many of the species are suitable for warm climates. In South Africa they vary from dwarf to tall plants, with sturdy stems and long-lasting flowers. They are extremely good for picking and make an attractive display in the garden during spring and summer. Well-drained loamy soil suits most species, but those which naturally grow in deserts require sandy soil. If it is cool and damp at flowering time, botrytis often spoils the flowers; thrips can be a problem in warmer weather. *Ornithogalum* stocks are often infected with virus, which debilitates the plants; the bulbs should be burned to prevent further spread. Propagation is by division of the clumps when they are dormant or by seed sown in autumn into trays of sandy mix. The seedlings can be left for up to two years before planting them just below the surface of the soil. Another method of propagation for some of the species is by leaf cuttings, with numerous bulbils forming on sections of mature leaf in just a few weeks. Cut leaves should be placed into trays of sand in a semi-shaded position for five months. Bulbils will develop which are large enough for planting the following autumn. Bulbs can be stored dry for up to two years if necessary.

O. arabicum, or black-eyed Susan, originates from the Mediterranean region. It is a strong-growing species with bold strap-shaped green foliage. Stems about 50 cm tall carry white starry flowers with dark green-black eyes. These are about 5 cm wide and are carried in flattish heads. It is an easy species to grow, flowering from early spring to summer, and is very good for picking. The bulbs multiply readily and will self-seed when happy. *O. arabicum* var. *corymbosum* carries many flowers in each head.

O. dubium, from the Cape Province, has succulent strap-shaped leaves which lie flat on the surface of the soil. They appear in early autumn and are followed in late winter by 30–50 cm flower-stems. Brilliant starry flowers about 5 cm across can be yellow, orange or apricot. They often have a dark eye but will sometimes be a single colour. Flowers will continue to open over a long period, and seed often ripens while fresh flowers are still opening on the same stem. The bulbs should be planted just below the surface in sandy soil. Adding fertiliser high in potash will enhance the colour of the flowers. Occasionally some bulbs remain dormant, missing a whole growing season and recommencing normal growth the following season. Soaking the bulbs in tepid water for four hours can improve this. After soaking, the bulbs must be planted as soon as possible as roots emerge in about eight hours. The foliage dies off at flowering time.

O. longibracteatum is a South African species with large white flowers with golden eyes which open from greenish buds. They are carried in erect racemes about 80 cm tall during summer. It is easily grown in well-drained soil.

O. maculatum from the Cape Province produces stems 10–50 cm tall. These carry a few yellow or orange flowers with black tips in late spring. While this is not a common species, it is well worth growing as a pot plant or for cut flowers.

O. montanum is a species from Europe with white starry flowers which have a broad green stripe on the reverse of each petal. It flowers in late spring on stems about 20 cm tall. The flowering can be so abundant that the bulbs

apparently deteriorate and the plants are lost. It is best grown in pots or in rock gardens.

O. saundersiae from Natal can reach 2 m tall and is known as the giant chincherinchee. It makes a bold show from mid- to late summer, with creamy flowers with dark eyes carried in large flat heads. They are very good cut flowers or landscape plants, with 80 cm tall sword-shaped leaves. The large bulbs should be planted in spring about 15 cm deep into well-drained soil in sun or semi-shade. It is best to lift the bulbs each season as they will commence growth too late for flowering to occur if left in cold wet soil during winter. Sowing seed in September is the quickest method of building up a large number of bulbs. Seedlings take about three to four years before flowering commences.

O. thyrsoides derives its common hame of chincherinchee from the noise its stems supposedly make when rubbing together. The thick shiny stems grow 15–60 cm in height. The flowers are carried in a tapering spike and are about 5 cm across. They can be white or pale yellow and usually have a darkish brown-grey eye. They open from early spring to summer and provide an abundant supply of cut flowers. This species is also a very useful garden subject.

Ornithogalum montanum

OXALIS
Oxalidaceae

This is a very large genus which has unfortunately gained a bad reputation because of the invasive tendencies of some species. Many are delightful plants which do not become weeds. Some of those which can become troublesome can be safely contained if grown in pots. Many species make a superb display when grown in shallow containers. Not all are bulbous, and some of these make well-behaved garden subjects; a number are, in fact, difficult subjects to cultivate, with no possibility of them ever becoming weeds. Those with woolly covered bulbs tend to be the most difficult, often rotting when dormant. These need to be grown in containers in a sandy mix.

It is sensible to try new species in pots first to see how they perform before considering planting them out. Those most likely to prove troublesome are those which produce bulbs most freely and those which seed very freely. Many do not produce seeds at all in New Zealand and Australia, and few are potential weeds in regions with severe winters.

Most of the species are natives of South Africa and South America. The majority of those in cultivation are natives of South Africa, most of which grow and flower during winter. A range of these species can provide a succession of flowers from early autumn until late spring. A few species also flower in summer. All require full sun and sandy free-draining soil or potting mix. They should be kept dry when dormant in summer and moist when growing during winter. The flowers only open in sunshine, making a brilliant display before closing late in the day. Typically the buds and old flowers are distinctively twisted.

The foliage of most species is very attractive. It can be of three types:

CLOVER-LIKE, usually with three or four rounded leaflets.
NEEDLE-LIKE, narrow and pointed.
FINGER-LIKE, usually fleshy.

The following species are South African natives unless otherwise mentioned.

O. purpurea is an extremely variable species with large flowers in a range of colours including pink, yellow and white. Flowering commences in autumn, and the large foliage is clover-like and sometimes mottled. It is vigorous and is a wonderful subject for shallow containers. It is occasionally found naturalised in lawns, where it is very pretty without becoming too invasive. The form most commonly grown has very large soft pink flowers with a small yellow eye. The large leaves are bright green, and it commences flowering in autumn.

'Alba' is a superb form with large pure white blooms which glisten in the sunlight. It has a long flowering period, commencing in autumn and continuing well into winter. It has slightly hairy green leaves.

'Nigrescens' is distinguished by its mottled bronze foliage. Its flowers are soft pink with a yellow eye and appear several months later than the previous cultivars.

O. deppei is a Mexican species with large rose-pink flowers on tall strong 30 cm stems in summer. The four clover-like leaves have distinctive red rings. 'Alba' has pure white flowers.

O. depressa (syn. O. inops) is a dwarf species with pale lilac-pink flowers in late summer. The foliage is clover-like. It is suitable for pots or rock gardens and requires well-drained sandy soil.

O. eckloniana has variably coloured flowers. The form usually grown has large (5 cm across) flowers of pale lilac with a circular lemon eye which appear in autumn. It is vigorous with large clover-like leaves carried on reddish stems.

O. enneaphylla is a South American species from the Falklands, Southern Chile and Patagonia. It has fragrant flowers of white or pink on short stems. It is best in a sunny well-drained position.

O. fabaefolia usually produces large flowers of brilliant yellow in autumn. Forms with white and mauve flowers also occur. It is vigorous although not usually invasive and is superb in large shallow containers.

O. hirta is a variable species with flowers of white or lilac-purple. The form usually grown has rose-purple flowers with a yellow throat in late summer. It is a tall-growing vigorous species (30 cm), ideal for containers and hanging baskets.

O. karrioca is a rare dwarf species with apricot-orange flowers with a lemon throat carried on 6 cm stems. Although the flowers resemble those of O. massoniana, its minute needle-like foliage is very different.

Oxalis massoniana

early winter, and the foliage is clover-like. It is a vigorous grower but not invasive. A form with purple mottled foliage is available.

O. massoniana produces soft orange flowers with a lemon eye from scarlet buds in autumn. It is a lovely species, ideal for containers.

O. megalorrhiza is an unusual South American species. It has a succulent trunk, woody at the base, with fleshy foliage and leaf-stalks. The leaves are maroon above and greyish beneath. Clusters of small golden yellow flowers are carried on 12 cm long reddish stalks in summer.

O. namaquana is sometimes called rabbits' ear oxalis because of the appearance of its finger-like foliage. It is extremely beautiful, producing large flowers of brilliant yellow in spring, giving rise to its other common name, yellow splendour. It requires a warm well-drained position and is generally best grown in containers, although it is not invasive.

O. obtusa is a variable species, the form commonly grown having soft pink flowers with darker veining and a yellow eye. Forms with white and yellow flowers also occur. The leaves are clover-like with some markings.

O. polyphylla (syn. *O. pentaphylla*) is a variable species with small cup-shaped flowers, usually of lilac-pink, sometimes white or purplish. It blooms in autumn and has needle-like foliage.

O. versicolor is a striking species with candy-pink striped buds which look like peppermint sticks. These are pure white or purplish white when open. It is not very vigorous and can be lost in gardens but does well in pots.

A few of the invasive species, which should be avoided if possible, follow.

O. pes-caprae (syn. *O. cernua*) is the yellow-flowered rampant weed so common in many districts. It has bright green clover-like foliage and is difficult to eradicate.

O. corniculata is the terribly invasive creeping oxalis which has become a problem in many parts of Australia and New Zealand. It has tiny yellow flowers and small clover-like leaves. Although it does not form corms, it seeds prolifically and is extremely difficult to control. It is a particular problem in rock gardens and containers, and has been largely spread on potted plants obtained from garden centres. A form with bronze foliage (var. *atropurpurea*) is just as rampant as the green-leaved form.

O. laciniata is a native of cold wild grassy screes in Argentina and Patagonia. Flower colour is variable, steel-blue, crimson or white with a darker eye, and the foliage is needle-like. It is one of the most beautiful of all species but can be very difficult to grow. It should be worth trying in regions with cold climates.

O. lobata is a dwarf species from South America, producing masses of lovely buttercup-yellow flowers in late summer and autumn.

O. luteola has blooms of clear shining golden yellow which are particularly beautiful when in bud. The flowers are fluted as they unfurl and flat when open. It blooms abundantly in autumn and

Oxalis obtusa

148

PAMIANTHE
Amaryllidaceae

P. peruviana is an evergreen bulb native to Peru. In mid-summer large flared creamy flowers with greenish stripes appear, becoming paler as they age. These have a beautiful fragrance and are carried on stems about 50 cm tall. The strap-like leaves are slightly shorter than the flowers. This species is not hardy and should be given protection during winter. Because it is evergreen, the soil should be moist throughout the year but only slightly so in winter.

The bulbs are best grown in pots, planted with their necks at about soil level. The flowers are self-fertile and are followed by ornamental seed-pods. Seeds take about seven months to ripen after flowering, usually being ready for harvest in mid-winter. The black papery seeds germinate in a few days if sown as soon as they are ripe. As this is in winter, they must be given warm conditions such as a heated bench or greenhouse. Bulb fly, thrips and mealy bug are occasional pests.

PANCRATIUM
Amaryllidaceae

Pancratium is known as the sea daffodil or sea lily, and it comes from the Mediterranean. It is similar to *Hymenocallis,* with minor botanical differences, the most obvious being in the seeds. *Hymenocallis* seeds are large and fleshy, whereas *Pancratium* seeds are thin and papery. The bulbs need well-drained sandy soils in full sun, and they should be planted 10–15 cm deep in early spring. Twelve or more flowers are carried on 30–50 cm stems in late summer. Division of the large bulbs is the best method of propagation. They can also be grown from their black papery seeds, which should be planted on edge just below the surface of a gritty seed mix as soon as ripe.

P. maritimum has scented white flowers on 45 cm tall stems and evergreen foliage.

P. illyricum, known as Corsican sea daffodil, has strap-shaped deciduous leaves and produces 10–15 fragrant white flowers, which are long-lasting and make good cut flowers.

Pamianthe peruviana

P. canariense from the Canary Islands produces 8–12 scented white flowers. The leaves are grey-green and deciduous.

The main pests are bulb fly and thrips.

PHAEDRANASSA
Amaryllidaceae

This is a small genus of interesting bulbs from Ecuador, Colombia and Peru with unusual flowers. Although they are not true lilies, they are often called queen lilies because of their beautiful blooms. They are very good plants for growing in warm climates. In the wild they grow mainly in pockets of humus among rocks and on cliff sites, and some are found in mountain rainforests. They grow well in containers, hanging baskets or large pots if a well-drained potting mix is used. Dry resting periods of at least eight weeks should be given at various times of the year to induce flowering. When watering is recommenced the bulbs will produce flowers if they are large enough. This process can be repeated at intervals throughout the year to produce a succession of flowers.

The large bulbs grow on or near the surface of the soil and should be repotted occasionally into fresh potting mix. This is best done in early summer so that the bulbs become settled before the weather becomes cooler. The bulbs produce offsets, which can be separated during dormancy. The large papery seeds should be planted on the surface of a sandy seed mix as soon as possible when ripe. Germination will often take only a few days when temperatures are warm. Seedlings should be kept growing continually and repotted when they fill their pots. They can reach flowering size in 18 months. The bulbs can be stored dry for short periods, but it is better to keep them in their containers.

P. cinerea, the queen lily from Ecuador, has large bulbs which grow in clumps on or just below the surface of the soil. It enjoys a free-draining open potting mix and is best grown in pots. The fleshy pink tubular flowers with green tips will emerge after a dormant period at any time of the year. They are carried on 30–40 cm stems and set a large number of seed-pods, which are quite attractive.

Phaedranassa cinerea

They last for several weeks when picked. Large oval grey-green leaves emerge after flowering is completed.

P. dubia is the other species that is occasionally grown. The tubular flowers are more carmine-pink in colour with green tips, and fewer in number than *P. cinerea.* The leaves are green with just a hint of grey.

POLIANTHES
Agavaceae

This is a genus containing about 13 species, mainly native to Mexico. They have succulent leaves and funnel-shaped flowers of reddish orange or white. They prefer full sun and good garden loam. The clumps can be lifted and divided in autumn or winter and the old spent bulbs discarded. Younger bulbs should be replanted about 5 cm deep and 20 cm apart. Rosettes of strap-like leaves soon emerge, and the flowers appear in summer. Several flowers are carried on stems 30–100 cm tall, and many species are fragrant.

P. tuberosa, the tuberose, is the best-known species. It has been grown as a cut flower for centuries, highly valued for its strongly scented waxy white flowers. The fragrance can be overpowering in confined spaces. The flowers appear in summer on long stems. Different forms are available, some with a pink flush to their blooms, others with variegated foliage. Double-flowered forms are popular, particularly 'The Pearl', which holds its blooms for a long time before they drop. The essential oil extracted from tuberose flowers is used extensively in the making of perfume.

P. geminiflora (syn. *Bravoa geminiflora*) carries pendulous tubular flowers of reddish orange on slender 50 cm tall stems. It commences flowering in early summer, with occasional blooms appearing until autumn. The pale grey-green foliage forms dense clumps. It is easily grown in average garden soil and is suitable for cottage or rock gardens. The blooms are also good for picking, lasting well in water with buds opening successively for a long period.

Polianthes howardii

P. howardii produces dark rose flowers with green stripes in summer. These are carried on stems about 60 cm tall. It is native to Mexico.

P. nelsonii is another Mexican native. It carries white flowers on 30 cm stems in autumn.

POLYXENA
Hyacinthaceae

These small autumn-flowering bulbs originate from the Cape Province of South Africa. They have succulent grassy or broad leaves about 10 cm long. Flower colour is variable, including pink striped with white, violet or pure white. They can be scented or unscented and make a good display in late autumn or early winter. The bulbs are easily grown in well-drained mix in pots or in sunny rock gardens. They should be planted just below the soil surface in late summer. The bulbs will multiply slowly or they can be increased by sowing seed in pots in autumn. They can be left in the pots for two seasons, and if repotted in their third year they should flower. The plants should be kept dry during summer. They are generally pest-free when grown in suitable conditions.

P. ensifolia produces flowers of white, or white turning pink with darker stripes, or violet. They are carried on stems about 5 cm tall in early winter. Some forms are apple scented. The leaves can be grassy or broad.

P. corymbosa differs in producing racemes of soft pink flowers with darker stripes. This is the earliest species to flower, and it is faintly scented.

RANUNCULUS
Ranunculaceae

This large genus contains about four hundred species, including many which produce tubers and become dormant during periods of adversity.

R. asiaticus is the species most commonly cultivated, and many forms with various flower colours have been developed. These are all derived from the species which grows wild in the Mediterranean area. They prefer well-drained

loam and dry summers, or they can be stored dry when dormant. The claw like tubers should be planted with their claws facing downwards in early autumn. Seed can be sown in mid-summer in trays and seedlings planted out in autumn. These will often flower in their first season.

R. cortusifolius from Crete is a very large species that enjoys shade and a fairly dry root run. It grows well near shrubs, where the root competition keeps the soil dry. The large rounded leaves, about 30 cm wide, start into growth in late autumn. Strong stems about 1 m tall carry numerous golden buttercup flowers. This extremely showy species is easily grown from seed. Fresh seed should be sown in summer into trays of seed mix and seedlings planted out in autumn. The plant dies down in summer.

R. ficaria is a small species which grows naturally over a wide area in Europe and Asia. It is extremely variable and spreads by small tubers. The flowers can be bright yellow, gold or cream, and both single and double forms occur. Flowering is from mid-winter to late spring. Damp soil in a semi-shaded position is ideal. Every small section of tuber will grow, and it can become invasive. It grows only 10–20 cm tall and is a good container subject.

Several seed strains of *R. asiaticus* are available, popular commercially for producing flowering plants for sale in spring and summer.

'Tecolote Hybrids' is a vigorous strain with exceptionally large double flowers. Recently dwarf strains suitable for small pots have been produced.

containers or terracotta pots. These should be placed in a warm sunny position such as a deck or terrace. The flowers will also remain open if grown in a well-lit room inside. In the garden they can be grown through very flat plants that also prefer dry conditions, such as thymes. It is important to mark their position in the garden carefully as the tiny rhizomes can easily be lost or dug out, or the plants swamped by vigorous neighbours.

R. baurii is the species most commonly grown, with variable starry flowers in a range of colours from white and pink to deep red. *R. baurii* var. *platypetala* is a wonderful white-flowered form. Many other selections are also available, some of which seem insufficiently distinct to warrant naming. Cultivars include: 'Albrighton', red; 'Fred Broom', creamy pink petals, cerise at base and paler margins; 'Knockdolean', true red, one of the best; 'Margaret Rose', rose-pink; 'Morning Star', white flushed with violet on the petal tips; 'Pictus', creamy white, faint cerise eye; 'Ruth', has larger flowers of similar colouring to 'Fred Broom' and is one of the very best pinks; 'Snow', white; 'Two Tone', pink and white, fading to white; 'Susan Garnet', deep pink.

R. deflexa is a minute species with pink, reddish pink or white flowers. Its foliage is relatively broad.

R. rubella has flowers usually in bright pink shades. Its narrow leaves are less hairy than those of *R. baurii*.

RHODOHYPOXIS
Hypoxidaceae

This is a genus of lovely dwarf bulbs which are ideal for growing in containers or rock gardens. They grow in summer and become dormant in winter, and flower for a prolonged period from spring until late summer. They prefer well-drained sandy soil or potting mix and should be kept dry in winter and moist during their growing season. They are superb when mass planted into shallow

Opposite, above: *Polyxena ensifolia*

Opposite, below: *Ranunculus cortusifolius*

Rhodohypoxis baurii 'Ruth'

RHODOPHIALA
Amaryllidaceae

These are close relatives of *Hippeastrum*, under which many of the species were formerly listed. Rhodophialas typically have much narrower leaves and small bulbs with distinctive narrow necks. They flower mainly in summer and have similar cultural requirement to hippeastrums.

R. bifida produces heads of small (35mm across) lustrous pinkish red trumpets with maroon lines in the throat and prominent golden anthers. These appear on 35 cm stems before the leaves in late summer. It is easily grown in a sunny position in ordinary well-drained garden soil. The bulbs pull themselves deep into the soil, unlike hippeastrums.

R. advena (syn. *Hippeastrum advenum*) has smallish trumpets of soft orange to bright red with greenish central stripes. It is one of the hardiest species but is often reluctant to bloom. It is best grown in pots or raised beds. The leaves emerge after the flowers.

R. pratensis (syn. *Hippeastrum pratensis*) has bright red or purplish flowers marked with yellow at their base. Usually heads of three to five flowers are carried on 30 cm stems from early summer. The leaves emerge at the same time as the flowers.

Rich sandy soil which is moist in summer and dryish during winter is ideal.

R. chilense produces a succession of small narrow trumpets in various lustrous shades. These appear on stems about 40 cm long in flushes during summer. Flower colour is variable, including cream, creamy pink, soft lemon-apricot, reddish and yellow.

R. colonum has small blooms in shades of red on stems to 50 cm tall. These appear in summer. It is one of the easiest species to grow and flower.

ROMULEA
Iridaceae

These small bulbs are widely distributed throughout Europe, Mediterranean regions and parts of Africa. Most have brightly coloured flowers and grassy leaves, and they are ideal for growing in rock gardens. Some are vigorous and can become a nuisance, but other smaller species need to be planted in pots of sandy mix if they are to be successfully grown.

A well-drained soil containing plenty of grit or sand is best. The bulbs are often tiny, and they can be stored dry over summer. In autumn they should be planted 5 cm deep in a sunny position.

Rhodophiala colonum

154

A careful watch should be kept for mice or rats, which are extremely fond of the bulbs. Sparrows often eat the young flower-buds. Bulbs are very slow to multiply, but seed often sets abundantly. This should be sown in pots of sandy mix in autumn and covered with a thin layer of sand. Most species germinate well and grow to flowering size in about two years. A few species require longer to germinate, sometimes even taking several years. A sequence of dry hot, wet cold, and damp warm periods over a year may help break dormancy. Seed which is not quite ripe will often germinate readily. Botrytis can spoil the flowers in cold wet periods.

R. bulbocodium from the Mediterranean is an easily grown species which will naturalise when well suited to its position. The flowers can be soft blue to violet and are about 4 cm across. They are borne on 10–15 cm stems in spring.

R. clusiana has larger flowers of soft violet with yellow centres and is well worth obtaining. It is regarded by some authorities as a form of *R. bulbocodium*

R. flava from South Africa produces an abundance of 3 cm wide starry flowers in winter. These occur in a wide colour range including yellow, cream, white, blue-lilac and, rarely, pink. The outside of the petals can have a greenish brown colouring.

R. hantamensis is native to the Hantam mountains in South Africa and is a little jewel of a plant. The small 4 cm starry flowers are violet-purple with darker markings and are carried on 6–15 cm tall stems in winter. It is rare in cultivation, the seed being difficult to germinate. It is best grown in pots of well drained mix.

R. monticola grows naturally high in the mountains of South Africa. This small species has 3 cm wide funnel-shaped yellow flowers with darker veins. These are carried on 15 cm tall stems in mid-winter. It is a good subject for pots or sunny rock gardens.

R. multisulcata is a South African species with smallish buttercup-yellow flowers. It prefers moist soils.

R. rosea is an easily grown attractive species from South Africa. Starry flowers of cerise-pink with golden eyes open in the sun. They are at their peak in early summer and nestle among erect grassy leaves. 'Alba' has pure white flowers with a greenish eye and prominent golden stamens, and

Romulea rosea

can be invasive in cultivation.

R. sabulosa is known as the satin flower, the sheer brilliance of its flowers making it one of the most desirable of all bulbs. A native of South Africa, it grows well in a sandy loam or pots. Wiry stems about 20 cm tall carry in winter a number of open bell-shaped satin-red flowers. These have yellow and black markings in the centre and are about 7 cm across. The size and number of the flowers produced is remarkable considering the tiny bulbs are only about 10 mm across. The bulbs are slow to multiply. Seed, when available, will take three years to reach flowering size from sowing.

Romulea sabulosa

R. saldanhensis is a South African native with golden yellow flowers with slender dark lines inside the cup. It grows about 10 cm tall.

R. tabularis from South Africa has small starry flowers in various blue shades in late winter. It is best mass planted as a ground-cover on the sunny side of trees or shrubs. It self-sows in suitable conditions and can become a nuisance. Some of the tiny-flowered species have become weeds in certain parts of Australia and the United States of America, and garden escapes have naturalised in some sandy areas in New Zealand.

SANDERSONIA
Colchicaceae

This South African genus contains only one species and is now very rare in its natural habitat. *S. aurantiaca* is generally uniform in its appearance, although some variation in the shape of its bells occurs. It somewhat resembles *Gloriosa,* with soft green leaves growing along the flower-stems, but the flowers are quite different.

The stems grow 30–70 cm tall and require support to prevent them collapsing when in flower. The stubby tubers are finger-like and very brittle. They should be handled carefully to avoid damage, which can cause the whole tuber to rot. For garden use the tubers should be planted in spring about 10 cm deep in well-drained soil in sun or semi-shade. Small sticks or canes can be used for support. The normal flowering time is in summer, but for commercial cut-flower production the tubers can be cool-stored and planted at intervals to produce flowers the year round in a greenhouse. The rich golden bell-shaped flowers are in high demand for floral work.

Seed is the usual method of propagation. It can be difficult to germinate, and it is best sown in trays when ripe and left outside exposed to the weather during winter. In early spring a layer of sand about 2 cm deep should be spread over the trays, and they should be moved to a warm place (about 20°C) for germination to occur. Plants grown from seed often flower in their second year. Tubers can be cut through the joint from where the old stem was formed and both halves planted. Caterpillars are the major pest.

SCADOXUS
Amaryllidaceae

Most *Scadoxus,* or blood lilies, are native to tropical Africa and seldom cultivated.

S. multiflorus ssp. *katherinae,* a native of South Africa and Zimbabwe, is the most popular. A vigorous species which reaches about 1 m high, it is an ideal subject for a shady garden. It thrives under trees, benefitting in high-rainfall climates from the relatively dry soil beneath them. It is almost evergreen, with new leaf-shoots arising in late winter just as the previous season's growth is dying off. Flower-buds develop at the base of the leaves, and the rounded heads of salmon-orange star-like flowers appear on long stalks in mid-summer. Bright red fruits will appear if pollination occurs, ripening in mid-winter and lasting several weeks. This is a superb cut flower for large arrangements.

The best time to plant is late winter, just as new growth begins. Well-drained soil is essential, and a small quantity of organic matter will be tolerated. When grown in pots they should be kept slightly moist in a shady place over winter and watered freely in summer. They should be repotted annually. The bulbs must not be allowed to dry out if stored.

Scadoxus germinate freely if the seed is fresh. This must be sown on top of the mix, not covered, and gentle heat of about 20°C will assist germination. Young plants will commence flowering as early as 18 months after sowing, but with maturity much larger flower-stems are produced. Division is another method of increase, but it is very slow.

Slugs and snails are the main pests, making ugly holes in the leaves. Thrips can cause distortion of the flowers. Conditions which are badly drained will lead to root rot and poor growth.

S. puniceus from Natal is quite different in its growth habit, the flower-stem arising in mid-winter before the leaves appear. Large paintbrush-like heads in soft orange-green to reddish orange are carried on strong stems, followed by large red

Opposite, above: *Sandersonia aurantiaca*
Opposite, below: *Scadoxus multiflorus* ssp. *katherinae*

fruits in summer. Dormancy begins in autumn, and planting or repotting should take place in early winter. The shade of large evergreen trees will provide protection during winter. Although the bulbs multiply slowly, fresh seed germinates readily.

SCHIZOSTYLIS
Iridaceae

This is a small genus of evergreen bulbs from the Cape Province of South Africa. They are free-flowering and prefer damp soils in a sunny

Schizostylis coccinea 'Alba'

situation. They make excellent subjects for the edge of bog gardens, where they soon form extensive clumps which flower for most of the year but look their best in winter. The flowers are good for picking, lasting well in winter. The clumps can be divided at any time of the year, and the old foliage should be cut back by half before replanting. The foliage and flowers can be badly damaged by thrips, which can completely spoil the floral display. Spraying occasionally with insecticide and removing old foliage will help to keep the plants clean.

S. coccinea, Kaffir lily, is commonly grown in gardens. The green sword-shaped leaves can grow 30–60 cm tall, while the flower-stems can be 30–90 cm in height. Each stem can produce 10–30 flowers. Some forms have very rounded petals, looking like small tulips, while others are star shaped. 'Alba' has white flowers. 'November Cheer' is an English-raised variety with soft pink flowers.

There are many seedling forms available, ranging in flower colour from salmon-pink to very pale pink. Old varieties include 'Mrs Hegarty', with rose-pink flowers, and 'Viscountess Byng', with pale pink blooms.

SCILLA
Hyacinthaceae

Scilla is an exceedingly large genus which occurs naturally in a wide area including Europe, Asia and South Africa. Many attractive species from the Mediterranean and South Africa grow well in warmer climates. The bulbs of all the species should be replanted as soon as possible after lifting in autumn. They should be planted into well-drained soil, and in semi-shaded positions the floral display is longer. Seed should be sown as soon as it is ripe. Some species take several months to germinate. Trays of well-drained mix should be used, and the seedlings should be kept growing for as long as possible as larger species take up to seven years before commencing flowering. The bulbs multiply slowly. The plants are not generally attacked by pests and diseases when growing in suitable conditions.

S. natalensis from South Africa is a highly

desirable species for large gardens. It forms very large clumps, and when located among rocks where the huge papery bulbs can be seen it is very effective. In early summer the flower-spikes emerge and quickly grow to 1 m or more. They are covered with hundreds of soft blue stars, which appear continually for several weeks. The flowers are followed by 40 cm long grey-green leaves, which often have a purple sheen. The flowers are useful for large floral displays. The bulbs should be planted with their lower third below soil level in autumn or winter. They multiply extremely slowly, in some cases one bulb increasing to only eight over a period of 20 years. Seed is therefore the quickest method of increase. It must be fresh when sown as old seed does not germinate. It should be sown on the surface of a sandy mix, and germination will commence in one to three days. Small bulbs will form before winter, at which time they will become dormant, coming into growth again the following spring. Between four and seven years are required for bulbs of flowering size to develop.

S. peruviana is a Mediterranean species which is useful for planting in large colonies, quickly forming clumps of bulbs with thick waxy leaves. The flower-spikes start off as rounded heads of stars and gradually elongate until they are about 40 cm long. Violet-blue is the most common flower colour, although sky-blue and white forms occur; a reddish violet form is reported, but it has not been seen by the authors. The bulbs can be divided in autumn and replanted to half their depth in rich loamy soil or in containers of potting mix. Seed sown about 2 cm deep when ripe takes a few months to germinate and three to four years before reaching flowering size. Root cuttings about 5 cm long taken in early summer and inserted into sand will usually form small bulbs. The dried seed-heads can be used in floral art.

S. scilloides is a small species from China and Japan, with dainty heads of pink flowers carried on 15 cm tall stems. It makes a nice display in autumn when grown in pots or in rock gardens. This is a very easy species to grow from seed, and it is not usually subject to pests and diseases.

S. verna is a small species about 20 cm tall, which grows naturally in coastal places in western Europe. Small starry lilac-blue flowers with deep lavender anthers appear just above the narrow foliage in spring. It is sometimes called sea squill.

Scilla natalensis

SPARAXIS
Iridaceae

These showy winter- and spring-flowering bulbs from South Africa are very effective when planted in large groups to produce a bold display. They thrive in sunny positions in open areas, alongside hedges, and in difficult positions which become quite dry. Bulbs multiply readily, producing bulbils which will flower the following season. The strap-like leaves are about 2 cm wide and 20–40 cm long. Plants hybridise freely and produce numerous self-sown seedlings, which flower in their second season. Seed can also be sown in trays and grown on for two seasons before planting out in autumn, about 5 cm deep. If a number of species are grown together they produce hybrid seedlings with a wide range of flower colours. Bulbs can be stored dry over summer, and they are not generally attacked by pests and diseases.

S. bulbifera is the most common species in the wild, with large colonies occurring in the Cape Province of South Africa. Easily grown, it produces white or creamy white flowers on 30 cm stems in spring.

S. elegans (syn. *Streptanthera cuprea*) has flowers which are usually soft salmon-pink, although rarely white forms do occur.

S. fragrans from the southwest Cape produces 20–35 cm tall flower-stems which carry 5 cm wide starry yellow flowers with black eyes. These are highly scented. It is an ideal species for growing in containers and placing indoors when in flower so that the scent may be enjoyed.

S. grandiflora has large flowers in a wide range of colours, including shades of violet, yellow, pink, purple and white. It tolerates damp conditions, in its natural habitat often growing in wet clay soils.

S. grandiflora ssp. *acutiloba* has upward-facing golden yellow flowers.

S. tricolor is sometimes called the harlequin flower. It produces many colour variations in bright hues, including orange, purple or pink with a yellow throat plus a zone of dark red or purple.

Many selections and hybrids are available. 'Purple Glory' has mottled flowers of violet and purple with yellow throats. 'Golden Glory' has flowers in a nice combination of lemon with yellow throats and cream petal tips, carried on tall stems.

cultivation, but if obtained it can be sown in pots of sandy mix and covered lightly with sand. Seedlings should be grown on in the pots for two or more seasons before repotting or planting out. Some species start to flower very early in the autumn, and others continue the display through winter, spring and early summer. They can be stored dry and are not usually attacked by pests or diseases.

S. alba grows naturally in damp places. It is one of the earliest species to start flowering, the leaves and flowers appearing after the first autumn rains. Short stems about 5 cm tall carry pure white flowers flushed purplish on the outside. It is an extremely easy species to grow and multiplies very quickly. It grows well in containers and makes a good ground-cover in large tubs containing trees, but it is a bit too rampant to be planted among small choice rock garden plants. It is quite commonly grown, usually under incorrect names including *Hypoxis alba* and as various species of *Zephyranthes* and *Cooperia*.

S. capensis makes a stunning show on a bright day when the flowers open in the sun. It is sometimes called golden stars, the 30–45 cm tall stems carrying flowers which vary in colour, including white, golden yellow and rarely pink. They usually have iridescent dark green or peacock-blue central eyes, although rarely the

SPILOXENE
Hypoxidaceae

These small bulbs from South Africa have starry flowers and grassy leaves. The flowers open only in the sun, remaining closed on dull days. Most grow naturally in slightly damp areas in full sun or semi-shade. They soon form clumps by sending out stolons which form bulbs a short distance from the mother bulb. The clumps can be dug up and divided in autumn, although the small bulbs can be easily missed as they are difficult to distinguish from the soil. Seed is seldom set in

Opposite, above: *Sparaxis bulbifera*
Opposite, below: *Sparaxis* hybrid

Spiloxene capensis

flowers are unmarked. It is an easily grown species in well-drained loam.

S. canaliculata is very similar to S. capensis in its size and in the colour of its flowers, but the central eyes are dull brown.

S. trifurcillata has bright yellow starry flowers in spring and early summer. These open in the sun and close at night. It is known as fairy stars, and it thrives in moist soils.

Hypoxis are closely related to Spiloxene but they are worldwide in their distribution. They have strong grassy leaves which can be covered in silvery hairs, and they have yellow starry flowers. Most flower from summer to autumn. A few are in cultivation, and these grow easily in loamy soil or in containers.

H. argentea from South Africa has attractive silver foliage about 20–30 cm tall and small yellow starry flowers.

H. rooperi is one of the best South African species, producing large bright yellow flowers which last well when picked. It requires full sun and well-drained soil. Once established, the plants multiply rapidly and can be left undisturbed. Plant height varies from 30 to 50 cm.

Sprekelia formosissima

to orange-red and are about 12 cm wide and 15 cm long. They appear in summer. It is a good subject for gardens or containers, and the flowers are very good for picking. Recently a new dwarf species has been discovered in Mexico. It has brick-red flowers and is ideal for growing in pots.

SPREKELIA
Amaryllidaceae

This is a genus in which only one species, S. formosissima is generally recognised. It is closely related to *Hippeastrum,* with which it can hybridise. Native to Mexico, where it grows naturally in stony soils, it often forms large clumps in full sun or beneath shrubs. The bulbs multiply readily in well-drained soil, and they can be divided in autumn and replanted 10 cm deep; they can be stored dry for a number of months. The black papery seeds germinate freely if sown when fresh on the surface of sandy mix. They should be covered lightly with a dressing of sand after they have germinated. The seedlings take about three years to reach flowering size. Pests include bulb fly, thrips and virus diseases.

S. formosissima is sometimes called the Jacobean lily. It has strap-shaped leaves and flowering stems 25–30 cm tall. The flowers vary from dark red

STENOMESSON
Amaryllidaceae

This is a South American genus native to Colombia, Ecuador and Peru. The species produce numerous tubular flowers, mostly in orange-red shades on stems 30–40 cm tall. A dry resting period is required to promote flowering. The flowers often emerge before the large grey-green leaves, usually in summer. They are best grown in containers of potting mix which contains humus. No pests generally occur.

S. miniatum (syn. Urceolina peruviana) is the species most often encountered, and then only occasionally. It should be grown more widely in regions with warm climates, where it will succeed outdoors. Its pendulous orange bells have protruding stamens tipped with gold anthers. Several flowers are carried on each 35 cm stem, and they appear over a long period from early summer until autumn. The dark green strap-shaped foliage can be almost evergreen in mild districts, but where winters are cold it dies off completely. It is a good subject for sunny well-drained gardens and for containers. The main pest is bulb fly.

S. pearcei has yellowish orange tubular flowers in early summer. Five or more are carried on each 40–60 cm tall stem. The bulbs produce numerous pips or bulbils, which can be separated and potted up individually for growing on.

S. aurantiacum produces a number of orange pendant bell-shaped flowers in summer. The leaves are dark green. Papery seed is often available and should be sown in pots of sandy mix, placed in a warm area (20–25 °C) until the seedlings are about 5 cm tall. They should then be hardened off and will take two to four years to reach flowering size.

STERNBERGIA
Amaryllidaceae

This genus contains five species, which originate mainly from regions with hot dry summers. The flowers resemble those of *Crocus,* mainly yellow and appearing in autumn, and are commonly known as autumn crocuses. The bulbs are poisonous and require good drainage to prevent rotting. The autumn-flowering species are good garden subjects, providing colour when little else is in bloom.

S. lutea is the best and most common species, native to Mediterranean regions. In autumn its golden yellow cup-shaped flowers are a most welcome sight. The large flowers are carried on

Stenomesson miniatum

163

Sternbergia lutea

STRUMARIA
Amaryllidaceae

These dainty autumn-flowering bulbs, commonly called desert snowflakes, are related to nerines. They produce heads of white to pale pink star-like flowers about 3 cm across for about three to four weeks.

After a dry dormant period during summer, liberal watering will induce them into growth. First to appear is a small reddish funnel device, presumably to direct moisture towards the bulb in their near-desert habitat. Foliage grows from the middle of the funnel, and flower-stems quickly follow from the sides of these funnels. Twenty or more flowers can be carried in each head. Individual flowers last for several days but fade quickly if pollinated.

Seed is produced freely, and after a few days will fall off if knocked. They are best left on the stem to get as large as possible before collection. Seed should be sprinkled onto the surface of the sowing medium in early autumn and protected from wet and cold during winter. Germination takes only a few days, and flowering commences after about two to three years.

A very well-drained sandy soil is required, and pure sand with a small amount of nutrient gives

10 cm tall stems and emerge after the first autumn rains. It grows easily in a sunny position in the garden, thriving in well-drained soil. It is a great substitute for *Crocus* in regions with warm climates, and it is surprising that it is not more widely grown. The bulbs should be planted in late summer, the foliage appearing with the flowers and persisting until spring. Increase is usually by separating offsets from the dormant bulbs in summer. The most common problem is rotting of the bulbs where drainage is poor. Occasionally they can also become infested with bulb fly.

S. clusiana originates from the Middle East. It has much larger golden yellow blooms than *S. lutea,* and they are slightly ragged at their tips. Flowers are carried almost at ground level and emerge before the grey-green foliage.

S. sicula produces starry golden blooms just before the foliage emerges in autumn. Its leaves are narrower than those of *S. lutea,* and it is very vigorous.

The other two species are spring flowering and seldom grown.

Strumaria rubella

Synnotia villosa

good results. Fungal root rot often results from excessive summer moisture.

S. rubella produces heads of soft pink flowers for a long period in autumn. These are carried on stems about 30 cm long. Although not common, it is the species seen most often. The bulbs should be planted on or just below the soil surface. The bulbs multiply readily, and new plants can be easily raised from seed.

S. truncata is seen occasionally, but few other species are cultivated.

SYNNOTIA
Iridaceae

This genus from the winter-rainfall Cape Province of South Africa is closely related to *Sparaxis*. They are winter growers, most flowering in spring and becoming dormant in summer. They are great garden subjects in warm climates, thriving in a sunny well-drained position and preferring dry summers. They flower reliably and abundantly each year, and are best left undisturbed once established. The distinctive bulbs are bottle-shaped and have a honeycomb-like covering when mature. They should be planted in late summer and can be lifted and stored dry in summer if required.

S. villosa produces lemon flowers with purple tips on stems about 40 cm tall during spring. The flowers resemble those of *S. variegata,* with which it is confused, but they contain more yellow and less purple; sometimes they are completely yellow. The small leaves tend to lie flat on the ground. It is a good subject for gardens or containers.

S. villosa has been crossed with *Sparaxis grandiflora,* producing seedlings which look like small-flowered *Sparaxis*.

S. variegata var. *variegata* has purple flowers, usually with white stripes, on 45 cm tall stems. It differs from *S. villosa* in containing more purple in its flowers, which appear later in spring. It is also more upright, slightly taller and more difficult to grow.

S. variegata var. *metelerkampiae* is slightly shorter and has an orange spot at the base of the petals.

S. parviflora has small flowers, creamy yellow inside and flushed slightly with purple outside. These are produced in spring.

TECOPHILAEA
Tecophilaeaceae

These small bulbs from Chile are now extremely rare in their natural habitat owing to over-collection. They are not difficult to grow but are hard to procure. Because they are so rare and beautiful, they deserve the very best treatment.

The bulbs can be stored dry for a few weeks in the summer and in autumn should be planted about 5 cm deep in containers of gritty potting mix. They should remain cool until growth commences and the crocus-like flowers appear, from mid- to late winter. The plants should not be over-watered in warm conditions. The bulbs multiply slowly, and the best method of increase is to sow fresh seed in a gritty mix in autumn, lightly covered with a 1 cm layer of grit. The seedlings should be grown on for about three years, when they will reach flowering size. Pests are not usually a problem, but botrytis often damages the flowers in cool damp conditions. This can be prevented by giving the plants plenty of light and fresh air.

T. cyanocrocus, the Chilean crocus, has 10–15 cm tall flowering stems which usually carry one or two deep blue flowers. The foliage is grassy. This species is now believed to be extinct in the wild. The plants tolerate some frost. Snails often eat the flowers.

T. cyanocrocus var. *leichtlinii* has pale blue flowers with large white centres.

T. cyanocrocus var. *violacea* has deep purple-blue flowers.

T. violiflora from Chile has numerous smaller flowers of lilac, purplish blue or, rarely, white on 10 cm tall stems.

THYSANOTUS
Asphodelaceae

Members of this genus produce exquisite flowers with three purple petals and fringed margins, giving rise to the common name fringed lilies. They are delightful small perennials, with different species varying greatly in their requirements. Few species are generally available.

T. multiflorus is a robust species from Western Australia, one of the easiest to grow in gardens. It requires a well-drained soil, with sand or other gritty material added if necessary. If performs best in a position which is protected from the midday sun by rocks or adjacent plants. In these situations plants may flower continually from late spring until autumn. Numerous buds are carried in the flower-heads, and these open over a long period. The fringing on the soft violet petals resembles eye-lashes. The flowers are carried on stems 30–45 cm tall above tufts of grassy foliage. This is an ideal subject for sandy coastal gardens and containers, and it survives light frosts. Plants can be divided in spring if the foliage is cut back by

Opposite, above: *Thysanotus multiflorus*
Opposite, below: *Tigridia pavonia*

Tecophilaea cyanocrocus

at least half and the segments replanted into containers of sand until new roots form. The plants resent excessive manure or fertiliser, and a few grains of slow-release fertiliser is sufficient to produce healthy growth.

T. tuberosus is a dainty species which produces purple flowers in spring and summer above grassy leaves. It prefers a sunny well-drained position and is ideal for rock gardens or containers.

T. patersonii is a climbing species which will twine around other plants or a trellis, or cascade over rocks. Soft violet fringed flowers appear throughout spring and early summer before dying down to a small tuber.

TIGRIDIA
Iridaceae

This is a genus of about 30 species, commonly known as jockey caps, which originate from Mexico through to South America. They grow and flower in summer, and many are useful for mixing in gardens with summer-flowering perennials. They grow naturally in regions with dry winters and require very good drainage. Plenty of coarse gritty material should be added to the soil if necessary. Some species are particularly difficult, and these need to be lifted in winter to prevent rotting. When stored in winter the bulbs should not be allowed to dry out or they become prone to rotting when repotted in spring. A well-drained material such as slightly moist sand is ideal for storing the bulbs to prevent desiccation. The bulbs should be replanted the following spring in a sunny position. Most species can be left in the ground when dormant if the soil is well drained. When growing during summer they require moisture, but this should be withheld if possible when the foliage begins dying off in autumn. They often self-sow in dry places such as cracks in concrete paths.

T. pavonia is the best-known species, believed to have been cultivated by the Aztecs over a thousand years ago. Numerous selections of this species are offered in a wide colour range, including red, purple, rose, pink, orange, yellow and white. Most have spots or markings, mainly in the centre of the flowers, but some are not spotted. This species is popular for garden use because of its showy and relatively large blooms. These appear in summer and are stunning when at their peak, but this is often for a short period. The sword-shaped foliage contributes interesting texture, especially when adjacent to fine-foliaged plants. It is usually easily grown in a sunny well-drained position.

Seed germinates freely if fresh and should be sown in spring. Seedlings usually flower after two years and produce a vast array of different colours. This species could be hybridised with some of those with smaller blooms to further increase the colour range.

T. dugesii is one of the loveliest species, golden yellow flowers spotted with maroon appearing in mid-summer. Usually two or three blooms are carried on each 12 cm stem. It can be difficult and is best grown in containers of sandy mix.

T. durangense is another small species, but it is much easier to grow. Small pale violet-blue flowers with darker mauve spots are carried on 15 cm stems in mid-summer. It can be grown in well-drained garden soil and is most effective when planted in clumps. It can also be grown in containers but does not usually flower for as long.

T. multiflora is a smallish species from mountainous areas in Mexico. Erect flowers in shades of purple-brown are carried on 30 cm stems in summer. It is easily grown in pots or well-drained sunny positions in the garden.

T. vanhouttei is a tall Mexican species, producing blooms that are interesting rather than beautiful. Creamy yellow flowers with reddish purple spots are carried on stems up to 1 m tall. It is not always easy to grow and requires free-draining soil.

T. violacea is a small Mexican species with flowers of various colours. These are usually violet-purple with pale shadings and purple spots, and they are carried on 15–30 cm tall stems.

TRACHYANDRA
Asphodelaceae

This genus contains about 65 species, which occur naturally from southern and eastern tropical Africa to Ethiopia. Most are native to the Cape Province of South Africa, and few are in cultivation.

Trachyandra hirsutiflora

T. hirsutiflora, from South Africa, has hairy triangular leaves 45 cm or more in length. These are followed in late winter by numerous 60 cm tall spikes of white starry flowers with brown stripes. The lower flowers set seed, which ripens before the top flowers have opened. They need a well-drained soil, or they can be grown in pots placed in a sunny or semi-shaded position. Fresh seed germinates freely in a sandy mix, and the seedlings will flower in their second year.

TRITELEIA
Alliaceae

This genus and *Brodiaea* are closely related, and botanists have shifted species from one to the other on numerous occasions. *Triteleia* is a genus of easily grown bulbs, native to California, which produce flat heads of many starry flowers in spring. The foliage dies off at flowering time, and bulbs can be stored dry during summer. In autumn they should be planted 10 cm deep in well-drained soil. They prefer a sunny position in gardens or large containers. They make good cut flowers. The bulbs multiply freely, or seed can be sown into trays of sandy mix in autumn. They often take two years to germinate, especially those species which grow naturally at high altitudes.

T. ixioides is sometimes called coastal pretty face. There are a number of forms of this species, the most common producing heads of yellow flowers with grey stripes on stems 20–40 cm tall. Some forms have very pale lemon flowers, and others have a reddish maroon flush outside the petals.

T. hyacinthina produces tight heads of white starry flowers which are sometimes tinged with blue, carried on 30–50 cm tall stems. There are many hybrids between these species which grow extremely well in the garden.

T. laxa (syn. *Brodiaea laxa*) is native to California and Oregon. Flower colour is usually pale blue to violet-blue, and these are carried in loose heads on strong wiry stems, usually about 50 cm in height but up to 1 m tall in some forms. It is generally easily grown in well-drained soil in full sun.

Hybrids developed in Europe from *T. laxa* are widely grown. 'Queen Fabiola' is the best and most popular, producing blooms which are larger and more intensely coloured than the species.

Triteleia ixioides

169

Flower colour is lilac becoming deep violet-blue at the petal tips. It flowers in early summer on stems about 70 cm tall and is most effective when planted in clumps.

T. bridgesii has heads of pink or lavender starry flowers with white eyes, carried on stems only 10–20 cm tall.

TRITONIA
Iridaceae

This genus contains up to 28 species, native to tropical and South African and mainly from the winter-rainfall Cape Province. They are close relatives of *Crocosmia* and *Ixia*. They provide a wide range of flower colours, mainly orange and often fading to pink, with most species flowering for a long period in spring and some in summer. A sunny position in well-drained soil suits most. Larger species are best planted in bold groups in the garden, and small species are suitable for rock gardens or containers.

T. crocata is widely grown in cultivation although now scarce in the wild. It is one of the most attractive species, with flowers in a range of colours. The form commonly grown has bright orange flowers on 30 cm stems in early summer. Other forms have blooms in reddish and pinkish orange shades, with or without prominent veins. It is the only really easy species for growing in gardens, many of the others resenting moisture when in flower. Occasionally disease can infect the foliage, but this is not generally a problem in well-drained sunny positions. A range of brightly coloured cultivars is available, mainly hybrids between this species and *T. squalida*. The corms are usually left in the ground when dormant in summer, but they can be lifted and stored dry if required. Fresh seed germinates easily and should be sown in autumn.

T. squalida is an unusual species, not as showy as *T. crocata* but still very attractive. Its soft shell-pink blooms have wine markings in the throat and almost transparent petal edges. They are carried on stems about 35 cm tall in late spring. It can be grown in pots or gardens and prefers a sunny well-drained position.

T. bakeri has cream flowers with brown veining

outside and blooms during spring and early summer. It grows 30–45 cm tall and is generally easily grown and suitable for gardens. It can, in fact, become somewhat weedy, with plants appearing in various parts of the garden.

The following species are relatively difficult to grow. They may appeal to collectors and should be grown in containers.

T. deusta ssp. *miniata* has showy flowers of deep persimmon-orange with dark maroon-spotted throats, carried on 30 cm stems in spring. It is prone to disease in humid climates and should be grown in containers kept in a warm dry position.

T. deusta ssp. *deusta* has larger flowers with darker central markings.

T. lacerata (syn. *T. crispa*) has small starry flowers with interesting veining in early summer. They are cream inside and deep rose outside. The leaves grow about 30 cm tall and are undulating and crisped. This small species is not usually too difficult if grown in pots in well-drained mix.

T. lineata has cream or pale yellow cup-shaped flowers with dark veining which appear on 45 cm stems in late spring. The foliage is almost evergreen in some situations. It is not particularly showy and can be difficult, requiring a sunny dry position and free-draining soil.

T. securigera has small orange or yellow-orange flowers with rounded petals. It is one of the first to flower in spring on stems about 30 cm tall. This small species is very pretty but can be difficult to keep.

TROPAEOLUM
Tropaeolaceae

This is a genus containing more than 60 species of South American plants, including the common nasturtium (*T. majus*). It also contains bulbous species, some of which remain evergreen in warm climates; in colder regions they become dormant in winter. Generally they are best left undisturbed once established. Seed should be sown in spring and usually germinates easily. Many species are attractive climbers, and others can be used in the

Opposite, above: *Tritonia crocata*
Opposite, below: *Tropaeolum tricolorum*

170

garden or in containers. Many are good for picking. They require good drainage and tolerate full sun or partial shade.

T. tricolorum is a tall climbing species from Chile and Bolivia. Flower colour is variable—red, violet, blue or yellow with greenish margins and yellowish inside. It flowers in summer and is ideal for covering a trellis in a warm position, preferably in partial shade.

T. pentaphyllum is a climbing species which produces masses of pink flowers tipped with green, followed by dark purple fruits. It is commonly called ladies' legs, the flowers resembling pink legs with green shoes. In cold regions the tubers can be lifted in autumn and replanted the following spring.

T. azureum is a slender climbing species from Chile. The flowers vary in shape, usually being open and rounded. They are lavender-blue with a white eye and appear mainly in spring.

TULBAGHIA
Alliaceae

Tulbaghia species are native to Africa. They are not difficult to grow and flower for a long period when in suitable situations. Dainty flowers are carried on slender stems, and these are suitable for using as cut flowers. The robust clumps are usually evergreen and fit well in perennial gardens. They are also very good subjects for coastal gardens, resembling small *Agapanthus*. Some species have an onion smell when bruised, while others are sweetly scented, especially at night. Clumps can be divided, some having a small rhizome, others producing tubers. This should be done between mid-spring and early summer, as the plants tend to decline when divided in cool wet weather. They should be replanted into well-drained loamy soil in full sun or semi-shade. Seeds should be sown in pots of sandy mix, and flowering usually commences after 6-12 months. commences after 6-12 months.

T. cominsii has been only recently introduced into cultivation. It is one of the smaller species and grows well in containers. The tidy foliage reaches about 15 cm tall and smells slightly of onion. The flower-stems grow 30 cm tall and

Tulbaghia fragrans

carry 10 or more sweetly scented pale lilac flowers. Some flowers have a green stripe on their petals.

T. fragrans is one of the best species for floral work. Ten or more sweetly scented pale-violet, pink or white flowers are carried on 30–45 cm tall stems in spring and summer. The plants often flower again in autumn or winter if it is mild but can be damaged by frost. The foliage is grey and grows 20–30 cm tall.

T. natalensis is a tidy species with dark purple flowers carried on 30 cm tall stems from early to late summer. The flowers are not scented, and the 15–25 cm long shiny leaves have an onion fragrance. It makes an attractive container plant.

T. violacea is extremely easy to grow and soon forms large clumps of shiny green leaves about 30 cm long. The flowering stems are about 40 cm tall and carry 10–20 violet-purple flowers during most of the summer. This species has a strong onion smell and is frost-hardy. A variegated form has recently become available.

TULIPA
Liliaceae

Tulipa is a large genus of hardy species which flower abundantly in cold climates but do not always flower reliably in warmer regions. Generally they are best when planted deeply, about 12 cm below the soil surface, although they will pull themselves down if planted higher. The best time to plant most tulips is early winter, in a sunny position in free-draining fertile soil.

Many of the species which follow flower more reliably in warm districts than the modern large-flowered hybrids.

T. bakeri is a delightful dwarf species from Crete, ideal for growing in warm climates. Usually the flowers are purplish and carried on 15 cm stems. A delightful form with white flowers flushed reddish outside is available.

T. saxatilis is another native of Crete, where it grows in rocky places. The lilac-pink flowers have gold markings at their base and open up very wide. Up to four blooms are carried on each stem in late winter and spring. Its flowers are paler than those of *T. bakeri* and resemble but are larger than those of *T. cretica*. It multiplies freely in a sunny well-drained position, often forming large clumps, and is best left undisturbed once established.

T. cretica, also from Crete, has pink or white flowers with a yellow eye; they become star-shaped when fully open. It grows well in free-draining gritty soil in full sun and should be kept dry during summer.

T. batalinii has pale lemon-yellow flowers on stems about 30 cm long above rosettes of leaves. 'Bronze Charm' is a bronze-flowered hybrid which flowers in spring.

T. celsiana has bright golden yellow starry flowers which are flushed with red.

T. clusiana has flowers which are white inside and reddish pink outside, and they become star-shaped when fully open. Several cultivars are available, including 'Cynthia', which has golden blooms flushed with reddish outside. This species can be naturalised if planted into gravel or scree.

T. fosteriana has scarlet-red flowers with black blotches on 20 cm tall stems. These have rounded petals and the flowers open wide in the sun. Several forms of this species are cultivated, including 'Cantata' (soft red and cream) and 'Red Emperor', which has reddish flowers on 45 cm stems.

T. greigii has cup-shaped flowers of bright scarlet, and the base of the petals is bright yellow with darker markings. The broad undulating foliage is most distinctive, with purplish markings and stripes.

T. hageri produces red flowers with darker markings inside from greenish buds. The flowers are about 10 cm across and appear in spring, and the leaves have distinctive red margins. It can be naturalised under trees.

T. kaufmanniana has variably coloured flowers, usually creamy yellow flushed reddish outside. The leaves are bluish green with undulating margins. It is easy in well-drained soil which remains dry in summer. Numerous forms are available in a range of colour combinations.

T. linifolia has scarlet-red flowers with pointed petals in spring. The undulating leaves have red margins.

T. maximowiczii grows naturally in rocky hillsides in central Asia. Its flowers are reddish with bluish markings in the centre. It is easy in

Tulipa maximowiczii x *T. batalini*

a sunny position if kept dry or lifted during summer.

T. sprengeri has reddish flowers which are reddish orange outside. They are carried on 45 cm stems in late spring and open very wide.

T. sylvestris has large golden yellow blooms flushed greenish outside, carried on 35 cm stems in spring. It is easily grown and can be naturalised in grass. It makes a good garden subject and multiplies freely.

T. tarda grows naturally in stony places in central Asia. Canary-yellow petals are tipped with white and are greenish outside. The flowers are small and unusual in shape. It is easy in well-drained soil which remains dry in summer.

A vast range of tulip hybrids is available. In warm climates these generally flower well in the first spring following planting and then refuse to flower in subsequent years. Lifting the bulbs each year and replanting them into fresh soil which has not contained tulips for several years improves flower production. The large and small bulbs should be separated, and they should be replanted in different locations. Interested readers are referred to the wide range of specialist tulip books available for detailed information on these. One cultivar is, however, worth mentioning. This is 'Oxford', which produces lovely glistening red flowers reliably each spring in warm regions. It makes a stunning sight when planted in large groups and is ideal for containers.

URGINEA
Hyacinthaceae

This genus contains many species which are widespread from the Mediterranean to South Africa. Few are worthy of cultivation, and most prefer sandy well-drained soil.

U. maritima is the most commonly grown species. It is particularly tough, one of the last survivors in some parts of the Mediterranean coast, where it grows naturally in sandy soils. In

Double tulip

late summer robust erect stems about 1 m tall carry numerous starry white flowers with brown stripes. The lovely large grey-green triangular leaves reach about 40 cm tall. These resemble *Eremurus,* but it is easier to grow. The flowers are good for picking and are grown commercially for this purpose in North America.

The bulbs are very large, and only the lower half should be planted into the soil. Huge clumps eventually develop which can be left undisturbed for years. Bulbils form around the base of the parent bulbs, and these can be separated when the plants are dormant in summer.

Another method of increasing stocks is to separate scales from the parent bulbs and place these 25 mm deep in sand. Bulbils develop from the scales, and they can be broken off and grown on in a sandy mix. The old scales can be put back into the sand and will continue to produce more bulbils.

Seedlings take about seven years to commence flowering after sowing.

VELTHEIMIA
Hyacinthaceae

This is a South African genus containing two variable species which are often confused. They grow during winter, and most become dormant in summer, although a few forms are almost evergreen. In winter and spring they produce waxy flowers, which resemble dwarf pokers (*Kniphofia* spp.), and attractive foliage. The tubular flowers are upright when in bud and pendulous when they open, and make attractive long-lasting cut flowers. The bulbs should be planted on top of the ground, or at least with the top third showing. They are beautiful plants, well suited to growing in warm climates, and are generally most successful when grown in containers in sandy well-drained mix. They can look stunning in terracotta pots when in full bloom. In the garden they require a warm sheltered position in well-drained soil. Moisture is required during the growing season but should be withheld in summer. Established clumps flower best if left undisturbed. Increase is usually by separation of the bulbs when dormant in summer. Fresh seed

Urginea maritima

germinates very readily in sandy mix and should be sown as soon as it is ripe. This is usually in early summer, but if sown then the seedlings will not become dormant if they are kept moist.

V. capensis grows naturally in winter-rainfall regions and has flowers in lovely soft pink shades with greenish tips. These appear in winter on stems up to 40 cm tall, sometimes commencing before the rosettes of bluish green foliage have appeared. It flowers before *V. bracteata* and is ideal in containers in full sun or partial shade.

V. capensis 'Rosalba' has beautiful flowers tipped with soft yellow and with soft pink at the base, a gorgeous pastel mixture. The leaves are very ruffled along their margins.

175

V. bracteata has flowers in various shades of pale rose-pink with greenish tips. Several outstanding colour forms have been selected. The blooms hang delightfully in dense racemes during late winter and spring. The flower-stalks are usually mottled and about 45 cm tall, often longer when growing in shade. The large fleshy leaves have undulating margins. It is more robust than *V. capensis* and prefers a well-drained position in partial shade. The bulbs of *V. bracteata* are not covered with the thin dry scaly tunics typical of *V. capensis*.

WACHENDORFIA
Haemodoraceae

This is a genus of five species from South Africa, only two of which are commonly grown. Most grow during winter and are summer dormant; only one, *W. thyrsiflora*, is evergreen. The flowers are golden and carried in panicles of various size. The reddish corms should be planted about 2 cm below soil level when they are dormant. Plants can be increased by division or from seed, which germinates easily.

W. paniculata is widespread in its native Cape Peninsula. Golden yellow flowers are carried in panicles about 40 cm tall which appear in late spring. These continue flowering for a long period, often until summer. It dies down during summer and should be kept dry at this time. It can be divided when dormant, and self-sown seedlings frequently appear. It is easily grown in sun or partial shade, provided the soil is well drained, and is particularly suitable for rock gardens.

W. thyrsiflora grows naturally in wet, often swampy, places in South Africa. It is very tall, often about 1.2 m, and extremely easy to grow in moist heavy soils. Sometimes it can be too easy, forming large clumps and producing numerous self-sown seedlings. Once established, it is best left undisturbed. It is rather coarse in appearance and not to everyone's taste, but it is still a useful plant for the back of a sunny garden. It flowers for a long period from spring until summer,

Opposite, above: *Veltheimia bracteata*
Opposite, below: *Wachendorfia paniculata*

producing an abundance of golden yellow flowers on erect stems. The stiffly upright sword-like foliage is evergreen and provides useful texture in gardens. The leaves can become stunted and get black edges in dry sunny positions.

W. brachyandra is a little-known species from the Cape Province, with dull brownish yellow flowers in spring.

WATSONIA
Iridaceae

This important genus contains more than 50 species, all natives of South Africa and most from the winter-rainfall Cape Province. It is one of the most valuable and easily grown of all bulbs in warm climates, and many species are ideal for naturalising in gardens.

Most species grow in winter and become dormant in summer, and a few are evergreen. The flowers of different species vary greatly in their size, shape and flowering period, but most bloom in spring or summer on erect stems. The foliage is also erect and sword-like, providing valuable vertical emphasis in gardens. When combined with fine-foliaged plants such as *Artemisia* 'Powis Castle', they can be particularly effective.

Watsonias require full sun and well-drained garden soil. Large clumps benefit from lifting and dividing of the corms when dormant every few years. Increase is usually by separation of the corms. Seed of winter-growing species should be sown in autumn into deep trays of sandy mix, and the seedlings are best if not disturbed or lifted in their first growing season. Summer-growing species should be sown in spring.

A wide range of species and hybrids is available. Tall vigorous varieties are suitable for naturalising in large gardens, and dwarf forms make good container plants.

Rust infection of the foliage occasionally occurs but is not generally a problem in sunny well-drained positions which are not too sheltered.

DWARF WINTER-GROWING SPECIES

W. laccata is still most commonly available under its old name, *W. brevifolia*. This small species has flowers in various shades and is one of the most desirable. The forms commonly available have upward-facing lilac-pink flowers clasped against 40 cm tall stems. The erect veined leaves are bluish. It is a good garden subject in light well-drained soils and is ideal for containers.

W. humilis (syn. *W. roseo-alba*) is another very attractive dwarf species, ideal for small gardens and pots. The flowers are usually white flushed with pink and face upwards, a desirable characteristic in any small plant. They appear on 40 cm stems in late spring and early summer.

W. meriana is a small variable species from the winter-rainfall Cape Province, where it generally grows in moist situations. Distinctive tubular flowers are carried on stems about 90 cm tall for a long period from late spring until early summer. The form usually grown has pink flowers, but they can also be purplish, orange or red. A rare yellow sport is reported; dwarf forms also occur.

This very desirable species also contains a most undesirable and invasive member. *W. meriana* 'Bulbillifera' produces numerous small corms on its flowering stems and has become a serious weed in many places. It is often seen growing prolifically alongside streams and other moist places.

W. aletroides is one of the most attractive dwarf species. The narrow tubular flowers hang from stems about 50 cm tall in spring and are very distinctive. Usually they are pink with a white tip, or reddish and occasionally purplish. This species requires good drainage.

TALL WINTER-GROWING SPECIES

W. borbonica is much better known under its previous name, *W. pyramidata*. It is very tall, often about 1.8 m in height, and is one of the best for gardens. The flowers are usually pink, sometimes white, and are at their peak in early summer. It is a dramatic specimen when grown at the back of a garden.

W. borbonica ssp. *ardernei* has widely flared pure white flowers. These are carried on tall stems for about two months from late spring. It is vigorous and ideal for naturalising.

W. versfeldii can be confused with the more common *W. borbonica,* but it produces larger flowers slightly later in the season and has broader leaves. The upward-facing flowers are rose-pink and appear in early summer. They are carried on stems up to about 1.8 m tall above long arching sword-like foliage.

W. marginata has flowers in shades of mauve to

Watsonia hybrid

magenta and occasionally white. It flowers in early summer and is variable in height. Tall forms can reach 1.8 m, and there are dwarf forms only 40 cm tall; most plants are intermediate in size between these. The bluish foliage has a distinctive brownish yellow margin.

SUMMER-GROWING SPECIES

W. densiflora grows naturally on rocky slopes in summer-rainfall regions of South Africa. The flowers vary in colour from lilac-pink to reddish and are rarely white. They appear in dense racemes on stems about 90 cm tall in summer.

W. fourcadei is one of the most attractive of the summer growers. It is evergreen and produces flowers of pink, orange or red in summer. These are carried on stems up to 2 m tall above clumps of evergreen foliage.

W. galpinii is a rare species from the Southern Cape, where it grows in moist shady places. It produces dense racemes of upward-facing flowers on stems up to 2 m tall. These appear for a long period in summer and are usually pinkish or orange-red. It is evergreen and very slender in appearance.

W. latifolia grows naturally in summer-rainfall regions of South Africa at high altitudes. The flowers are small and usually reddish orange, with long tubes and narrow petals. Peak flowering is in mid-summer, and the stems are about 1.5 m tall. The foliage is very broad and handsome.

W. pillansii (syn. *W. socium*) is similar to *W. latifolia* but has narrower leaves, and the flower colour ranges from orange to scarlet. The flowers are carried in dense racemes on stems about 1.2 m tall in summer. It forms large clumps of evergreen foliage and is a striking garden subject. It prefers well-drained soil which remains moist in summer.

WORSLEYA
Amaryllidaceae

W. rayneri, commonly known as Empress of Brazil, is the only member of this genus. A large spectacular native of Brazil, it is unfortunately rare in cultivation. In mid-summer clusters of gorgeous violet-blue flowers appear on stems up

Worsleya rayneri

to 1.5 m tall. They resemble *Hippeastrum* blooms, each lasting up to ten days if not pollinated. Fertilisation only occurs when two clones are present. Also attractive are the arching sickle-shaped evergreen leaves. In its natural habitat it hangs from acidic basalt cliffs, constantly bathed in mist from waterfalls.

Successful cultivation depends on providing suitable conditions. A position in bright light, not necessarily full sun, is best. Large raised beds of well-drained acid soil mix give excellent results. Containers make a suitable alternative, provided a well-drained and aerated acid potting mix is used. The medium should be watered sparingly in winter, gradually increasing the moisture supply as temperatures rise until flooding regularly in mid-summer. This will produce rapid growth and one, occasionally two, flower-spikes per bulb. In regions with high winter rainfall, the plants should be covered or moved to a greenhouse. The bulbs should not be stored.

Planting is best done in summer when the plants are in full growth, allowing the roots to rapidly fill the bed or container. A yearly application of acid fertiliser in spring will encourage vigorous growth. Plants in containers require repotting when root-bound.

Fresh seed, when available, provides an easy method of increase. It should be sown at 20–25 °C and covered lightly. Germination takes about four weeks, but it will be about nine years before the first flowers appear. Bulb cuttage or twin scaling are other methods, but these necessitate the sacrifice of mature bulbs. Established plants produce a few offshoots each year.

Root rot can be a problem, particularly in winter if drainage is inadequate. Greater bulb fly will hollow out larger bulbs, causing them to produce offsets but reducing flower production.

WURMBEA
Colchicaceae

This genus occurs in Australia and South Africa, and most species require moist sandy soil. Male and female flowers are produced on separate plants, and the small bulbs are edible. In the wild larger forms have been observed, and these would be well worth introducing to gardens. The bulbs can be left in their pots while dormant, during which time they should be kept cool and moist. In autumn they should be repotted into fresh sandy mix about 5–10 cm deep.

W. dioica is a dainty Australian species, known as early Nancy, which is suitable for rock gardens or pots. The flower-stems are 10–20 cm tall and carry a number of scented pink or white starry flowers in late winter. Only a few grassy leaves are produced.

W. recurva is a South African species which flowers in late winter. It has recurving leaves about 15 cm tall and flower stems 15–20 cm tall. These carry up to 40 dark purplish black flowers, which are vanilla scented.

W. capensis from South Africa grows naturally in damp areas. This small species grows 12–20 cm tall and produces 10 or more chocolate and white starry flowers about 2 cm wide. These are carried in spikes during spring. It is a suitable subject for the edge of small ponds or for growing in pots.

W. spicata produces creamy white and purplish starry flowers in late winter and spring. It is best grown in pots as the bulbs are very small.

Wurmbea spicata

Zantedeschia hybrid

Burchardia umbellata, from Australia, is commonly called milkmaids. It is very similar to *Wurmbea* but is slightly larger in all parts. It is also closely related to *Androcymbium.* Snails and other pests often eat the seed-heads, and seed is seldom available.

ZANTEDESCHIA
Araceae

This genus contains six species, all native to South Africa. They are generally easy to grow in well-drained soils.

Z. aethiopica, the white calla lily, often incorrectly called arum lily, so enjoys the climate in New Zealand and Australia that it has become a weed in many places. It grows mainly in damp streamsides but also invades bush and other vulnerable habitats, overwhelming native plants even in quite dry situations. It manages to do this because it grows mainly during the wet autumn and winter period. Unwanted material should never be dumped on roadsides or remote places as small pieces of rhizome and seeds soon develop into large clumps.

The flowers, if grown well, have potential to be exported as cut flowers. There are a number of forms and varieties.

Z. aethiopica var. *childsiana* is a dwarf variety which provides a useful supply of long-lasting scented cut flowers. It is also a good garden subject, especially in moist soils, and is very effective when planted in large drifts beneath deciduous trees. Other forms vary in their height and scent, and a pure green form is reported.

Z. aethiopica 'Green Goddess' has creamy flowers blotched and edged with green. It grows to the same height as the species, often about 1.5 m tall in rich soils, and is popular for floral work.

Z. aethiopica var. *odorata* has scented white open flowers about 15 cm long on stems about 1.5 m tall.

181

A form of *Z. aethiopica* which originates from Natal has soft pink scented flowers on stems about 1 m tall. It grows true from seed and flowers 12–18 months after sowing.

Z. albomaculata varies in size and in the colour of its flowers. The flower-stems can reach 45–60 cm tall and carry flowers about 15 cm long. These can be white, cream, lemon or golden yellow. A beautiful apricot form of this species is called 'Helen O'Connor'. The foliage has white spots where chlorophyll is absent, and it flowers in summer. Plenty of moisture must be present during the growing season, but the soil must be well-drained.

Z. pentlandii has magnificent rich golden yellow flowers with a black eye. The flowers can vary from 12 to 20 cm in length, and they are carried on stems 45–60 cm tall. The leaves are usually plain green and arrow shaped, and are very rarely spotted. Flowering time is from late spring until summer, and the flowers are long-lasting when picked. It can be easily grown from sections of rhizome. Seed can be sown outside into finely tilled loamy soil, and the seedlings will take up to 18 months or more before flowering.

Z. rehmannii is a small species with 30–45 cm tall flower-stems carrying slender flowers. These are about 10–12 cm long in shades from soft to deep pink. It flowers in summer and is useful for picking.

Numerous crosses between the summer-flowering species have been made over a long period of time. This has resulted in a vast array of colour forms, and many cultivars have been selected which must be propagated by division or by tissue culture. The production and export of both cut flowers and rhizomes is now a thriving industry. Most of the modern hybrids have been bred in New Zealand, where the plants grow particularly well; in other parts of the world they are often more difficult to grow. Well-drained loamy and sandy soils are most suitable for modern hybrids. These can be easily worked in late winter or early spring to prepare them for planting. The rhizomes should be lifted in early winter, dried and then stored in trays in a cool shed. They can be dusted with fungicide to prevent disease developing. Rhizomes should be planted in early spring and will flower by mid-summer. At planting time tubers can be dipped into gibberellic acid, which will increase the number of flowers produced per bulb. The rhizomes should be planted 10–15 cm deep.

As with most crops grown in large numbers, pests and diseases are a problem. The main insect pest is usually thrips, and soft rot (*Erwinia* sp.) can cause severe losses, especially during warm wet seasons.

ZEPHYRANTHES
Amaryllidaceae

This is a genus of about 30 species from the Americas. They flower after rain, mainly in spring or summer, and are best grown in full sun in well-drained soil which is moist during their growing period. Most are dwarf plants suitable for rock gardens and containers. They are best left undisturbed in the ground once established. White is the predominant flower colour, often flushed with pink, but yellow forms also occur. They are closely related to *Habranthus* and have similar requirements.

Z. citrina is a good subject for warm climates but not hardy where winters are severe. The flowers are bright lemon with greenish tubes. They appear after rain in late summer and early autumn, on short stems up to 25 cm long. The leaves emerge with the flowers and grow through the winter. It is ideal for rock gardens and pots.

Z. candida is sometimes listed as *Argyropsis candida*. White crocus-like cups with lilac tips appear on short stems in late summer after rainfall. Often several flushes occur until late autumn. The narrow erect grassy foliage is evergreen. It is best grown in a sunny position in well-drained soil, which should be kept moist during summer. It is easily grown and multiplies rapidly, forming small dense clumps, and is an ideal rock garden plant. When established it is best left undisturbed.

Z. flavissima is an outstanding species from Brazil and Argentina, and it is regarded as the best of all species by many enthusiasts. It can flower for up to nine months of the year, peaking in late summer. The crocus-like blooms are brilliant golden yellow and nestle among the dark green foliage. It resembles *Z. candida* except in the colour

Opposite: *Zephyranthes macrosiphon*

Zephyranthes candida

of its flowers. It requires moist soil and does well in containers placed in a saucer of water. It is vigorous and multiplies freely, flowering a few days after each watering.

Z. *grandiflora* has large flat flowers of clear pink with prominent yellow stamens. These are carried on 20 cm stems, and the leaves are strap-shaped. It is good for naturalising in warm climates. It resembles *Habranthus robustus,* but often the pink colouring is less appealing.

Z: *macrosiphon* is a Mexican species with large flowers carried in summer on stems about 15 cm long. The flowers are usually rose with a greenish tube. A beautiful lemon-yellow form with golden anthers also occurs.

The plant that has been available variously as Z. *pedunculata, Hypoxis alba* and *Cooperia* sp. is correctly *Spiloxene alba.*

BIBLIOGRAPHY

Barnes, Don, *Daffodils for Home, Garden and Show*. Portland, Oregon, Timber Press, 1987.

Bird, Richard, *Lilies*. London, New Burlington Books, 1991.

Bond, Pauline and Goldblatt, Peter, *Plants of the Cape Flora: A Descriptive Catalogue*. Kirstenbosch National Botanic Gardens, 1984.

Bryan, John E., *Bulbs*. Portland, Oregon, Timber Press, 1989.

Cassidy, G. E. and Linnegar, S., *Growing Irises*. Portland, Oregon, Timber Press, 1982.

Davies, Dilys, *Alliums: The Ornamental Onions*. London, Batsford, 1992.

Duncan, G. D., *The Lachenalia Handbook*. Kirstenbosch National Botanic Gardens, 1988.

Du Pleissis, Neil and Duncan, Graham, *Bulbous Plants of Southern Africa*. Cape Town, Tafelberg, 1989.

Eliovson, Sima, *Wild Flowers of Southern Africa*. Seventh edition, Johannesburg, Macmillan, 1984.

Everett, Thomas, *The New York Botanical Garden Illustrated Encyclopaedia of Gardening*. New York, Garland, 1981.

Goldblatt, Peter, *The Genus Watsonia*. Kirstenbosch National Botanic Gardens, 1989.

_____*The Moraeas of Southern Africa*. Kirstenbosch National Botanic Gardens, 1986.

Grey-Wilson, Christopher and Mathew, Brian, *Bulbs: The Bulbous Plants of Europe and their Allies*. London, Collins, 1981.

Hammett, Keith, *The World of Dahlias*. Wellington, Reed, 1980.

Hilliard, O. M. and Burtt, B. L., *Dierama: The Hairbells of Africa*. Johannesburg, Acorn Books, 1991.

Hitchmough, James, *Garden Bulbs for Australia and New Zealand*. Melbourne, Viking O'Neil, 1989.

Innes, Clive, *The World of Iridaceae*, Ashington, Sussex, Holly Gate International Ltd, 1985.

Kohlein, Fritz, *Iris*. Portland, Oregon, Timber Press, 1987.

Mathew, B., *The Smaller Bulbs*. London, Batsford, 1987.

BIBLIOGRAPHY

Phillips, Roger and Rix, Martyn, *Bulbs*. London, Pan Books, 1989.

Redgrove, Hugh, *A New Zealand Handbook of Bulbs and Perennials*. Auckland, Godwit Press, 1991.

The New Royal Horticultural Society Dictionary of Gardening. London, The Macmillan Press Ltd, 1992.

SUPPLIERS OF BULBS AND SEEDS

NEW ZEALAND

Beautiful Begonias
Rocklands Road
Clifton, Takaka
via NELSON

Blue Mountain Gardens
Tapanui
WEST OTAGO

Daffodil Acre
PO Box 834
TAURANGA

Chris Duval-Smith
(Iridaceae specialist)
Kaiaua
via POKENO

Joy Plants
Runciman Road
RD 2
PUKEKOHE EAST

Kellydale Nursery
12 Kelly Road
Oratia
AUCKLAND

Kereru Nursery
Okuti Valley
Little River
CANTERBURY

Maple Glen Gardens
(not mail order)
RD 1
Wyndham
SOUTHLAND

Mara Nurseries
7 High Road
HAWERA

Parva Plants
PO Box 2503
TAURANGA

Robertson's Daffodils
Omaha Flats Road
RD 6
WARKWORTH

Van Eeden Tulips
Dept G
West Plains
RD 4
INVERCARGILL

Wairakei Garden Centre
270 Greens Road
CHRISTCHURCH

AUSTRALIA

The Botanist
16 Victor Close
GREEN POINT NSW 2251
PH: 043.67 7524

Country Garden Perennials
Wensley Farm
Laings Road
NAYOOK VIC 3821
PH: 056.28 4202

Diggers Garden Company
105 Latrobe Parade
DROMANA VIC 3936
PH: 059.87 1877

Drewitt & Sons
PO Box 202
WOORI YALLOCK VIC 3139
PH: 059.67 4037

Penny Dunn
'Mandalay'
MOUNT MACEDON VIC 3441
PH: 054.26 1735

Glenbrook Bulb Farm
28 Russell Rd
CLAREMONT TAS 7011

Island Bulbs
C/- Post Office
NUBEENA TAS 7187
PH: 002.50 3614

The Mail Box Gardener
PO Box 728
SEVEN HILLS NSW 2147

Pine Heights Nursery
Pepper St
EVERTON HILLS QLD 4053
PH: 07.353 2761

Laurie Smith
PO Box 428
MOUNT BARKER SA 5251

Bryan Tonkin
Olinda Creek Rd
KALORAMA VIC 3766
PH: 03.728 1295

Viburnum Gardens
8 Sunnyridge Rd
ARCADIA NSW 2159
PH: 02.653 2259

Woodbank Nursery
RMB 303
KINGSTON TAS 7150
PH: 002.39 6452

SOUTH AFRICA

The Botanical Society of South
Africa
Kirstenbosch
CLAREMONT 7735

Rust En Vrede
PO Box 231
CONSTANTIA 7848

Cape Seeds and Bulbs
PO Box 4063
Ida's Valley 7609
CAPE TOWN

Sunburst Bulbs
PO Box 183
Howard Place 7450
CAPE TOWN

Silverhill Seeds
18 Silverhill Crescent
KENNILWORTH 7700

GREAT BRITAIN

Chiltern Seeds
Bortree Stile
Ulverston
CUMBRIA LA12 7PB

R. Bowlby
Gatton
Reigate
SURREY RH2 OTA

Potterton & Martin
Cottage Nursery
Moortown Road
Nettleton
N. LINCS

Tile Barn Nursery
Standen Street
Idew Green
Benenden
KENT

UNITED STATES

Mad River Imports
PO Box 1685
Moretown
VERMONT 05660

Van Engelen, Inc.
313 Maple Street
Litchfield
CONNECTICUT 06759

John Scheepers, Inc.
PO Box 700
Bantam
CONNECTICUT 06750

Bundles of Bulbs
112 Green Springs Valley Road
Owings Mills
MARYLAND 21117

The Bulb Crate
2560 Deerfield Road
Riverwoods
ILLINOIS 60015

McClure & Zimmerman
PO Box 386
Friesland
WISCONSIN 53935

Skolaski's Glads & Field Flowers
4821 County Trunk Highway Q
Waunakee
WISCONSIN 53597

The Waushara Gardens
Route 2, Box 570
Plainfield
WISCONSIN 54966

Bio-Quest International
PO Box 5752
Santa Barbara
CALIFORNIA 93150-5752

Kelly's Plant World
10266 East Princeton
Sanger
CALIFORNIA 93657

Antonelli Brothers, Inc.
2545 Capitola Road
Santa Cruz
CALIFORNIA 95062

GreenLady Gardens
1415 Eucalyptus Drive
San Francisco
CALIFORNIA 94132

Robinett Bulb Farm
PO Box 1306
Sebastopol
CALIFORNIA 95473-1306

Fairyland Begonia Garden
1100 Griffith Road
McKinleyville
CALIFORNIA 95521

Dr. Joseph C. Halinar
2333 Crooked Finger Road
Scotts Mills
OREGON 97375

B & D Lilies
330 P Street
Port Townsend
WASHINGTON 98368

INDEX

Entries in bold type are illustrations.

189